IF I AM NOT FOR MYSELF

MIKE MARQUSEE was born in the United States and emigrated to Britain in 1971. He is a writer, political activist and the author of a number of ground-breaking books on politics and popular culture, including *Wicked Messenger: Bob Dylan and the 1960s*, *Redemption Song: Muhammad Ali and the Spirit of the Sixties*, *War Minus the Shooting* and *Anyone but England: An Outsider Looks at English Cricket*. He is a contributor to the *Guardian* and lives in London.

IF I AM NOT FOR MYSELF

Journey of an Anti-Zionist Jew

MIKE MARQUSEE

1953 −1/13/15

VERSO

London • New York

First published by Verso 2008
© Mike Marqusee 2008
This paperback edition published by Verso 2010
All rights reserved

The moral rights of the author and translator have been asserted

1 3 5 7 9 10 8 6 4 2

Verso
UK: 6 Meard Street, London W1F 0EG
US: 20 Jay Street, Suite 1010, Brooklyn, NY 11201
www.versobooks.com

Verso is the imprint of New Left Books

ISBN-13: 978-1-84467-435-0

British Library Cataloguing in Publication Data
A catalogue record for this book is available from the British Library

Library of Congress Cataloging-in-Publication Data
A catalog record for this book is available from the Library of Congress

Typeset by Hewer Text UK Ltd, Edinburgh
Printed in the US by Maple Vail

Contents

Preface

As long as there has been Zionism, there have been anti-Zionist Jews. Indeed, decades before it even came to the notice of non-Jews, anti-Zionism was a well-established Jewish ideology and until World War II commanded wide support in the diaspora. Today, as cracks show in the presumed monolith of Jewish backing for Israel, increasing numbers of Jews are interrogating and rejecting Zionism. Nonetheless, the existence of anti-Zionist Jews strikes many people—Jews and non-Jews—as an anomaly, a perversity, a violation of the first clause in Hillel's ethical aphorism: "If I am not for myself, who will be for me?"

Zionism is an ideology and a political movement. As such it is open to rational dispute, and on a variety of grounds. Jews, like others, might well view the Jewish claim to Palestine as irrational, anachronistic, and intrinsically unjust to other inhabitants. They might consider the Jewish state to be discriminatory or racist in theory and in practice or might object, on political, philosophical, or even specifically Jewish grounds, to any state based on the supremacy of a particular religious or ethnic group. As Jews, they might reject the idea that Jewish people constitute a "nation," or at least a "nation" of the type that can or should become a territorial nation-state. Or they might have concluded on the basis of an examination of Israel's treatment of the Palestinians that the underlying cause of the conflict was the ideology of the Israeli state.*

Any or all of the above should be sufficient to explain why some Jews would become anti-Zionists. But that doesn't stop critics from placing us firmly in the realm of the irredeemably neurotic. In their eyes, we remain walking self-contradictions, a menace to our fellow Jews.

Of course, being an anti-Zionist Jew is a negative identity. It's a disavowal of a politics commonly ascribed to Jews. And if one's anti-Zionism is made up exclusively of a rejection of Zionism, then it's not worth much. But for myself and for the anti-Zionist Jews I know, anti-Zionism is part and parcel of a larger opposition to racism and inequality, an expression of a positive solidarity with the Palestinians as victims of injustice and specifically of colonialism.

It should go without saying, but unfortunately cannot, that being an anti-Zionist by no means implies a desire to destroy the Jews who live in Palestine. On the contrary, anti-Zionism is founded on a refusal to countenance discrimination on racial or religious grounds. The Jews of Israel have every right to live safely, to follow (or not) their religious faith, to adhere (or not) to their cultural heritage, to speak Hebrew. What they do not have is the right to continue to dispossess and oppress another people.

Nonetheless, it is the anti-Zionists who are deemed to have transgressed an ethical boundary and thereby forfeited legitimacy. Like the Palestinians, we are doomed to fail the decisive test: recognition of Israel's right to exist.

It's extraordinary that a demand so often repeated is so rarely subjected to scrutiny. No one denies the fact of Israel's existence, and the realities that flow from that, but why should anyone

---

* There is a strand of Orthodox Jewry which rejects Zionism on theological and scriptural grounds: they believe Zionism has pre-empted God's prerogative. Their critique is at root anti-secular and anti-modern, and I feel little in common with it.

anywhere be compelled to recognize the "right to exist" of a particular state formation? What's being demanded here is ideological conformity: support for the right of the Jewish state to exist, in perpetuity, in Palestine, regardless of what that fact entails for others (or indeed for the welfare of Jews). Anti-Zionists are condemned because they refuse to certify as democratic a national project built on dispossession and ethnic supremacy. For a Jew to fail to subscribe to the unsustainable notion that the State of Israel can be both "Jewish" and "democratic" is a sure sign of self-hatred.

Whenever Jews speak out against Israel, they are met with *ad hominem* criticism. Their motives, their representativeness, their authenticity as Jews are questioned. There is often assumed to be a disjunction between what we say we believe and what we actually believe; implications are assigned to our words that reflect only the political prejudices of our critics. We are pathologized. For only a psychological aberration, a neurotic malaise, could account for our defection from Israel's cause, which is presumed to be—whether we like it or not—our own cause. So we are either bad Jews or Jews in bad faith. The self-appointed gatekeepers seem bent on measuring us all with their own personal Jewometers, in keeping with a Jewish tradition better honored in the breach. Their presumption that they can adjudicate on our Jewishness or lack thereof is as fatuous as the anti-semites' presumption that our Jewishness determines our character.

Anti-Zionist Jews are not and do not claim to be any more authentic or representative than any other Jews, nor is their protest against Israel any more valid than a non-Jew's. But "If I am not for myself," then the Zionists will claim to be for me, will usurp my voice and my Jewishness. Since each Israeli atrocity is justified by the exigencies of Jewish survival, each calls forth a particular witness from anti-Zionist Jews, whose very existence contradicts the Zionist claim to speak for all Jews everywhere.

But what makes me a Jew? I'm an atheist. I am unmoved by religious ritual. I think there is wisdom to be found within religious traditions, including Judaism, but I can't say I find more of it in Judaism than in other religions. Nonetheless, I've never had the slightest doubt that I am a Jew.

According to both anti-semites and Zionists, I am objectively a Jew and will be a Jew whatever I believe or practice. For this reason the Nazis would have marked me out for persecution and extermination, and Israel marks me out as a potential recipient of privileges, a rightful inheritor of others' land and resources. But as should become clear from what follows in this book, my Jewishness is far more than the sum of others' perceptions. It's a locale where the self intersects with history, past and present.

Every attempt to narrow down Jewishness has backfired, broken down or produced manifest absurdities. Even reducing it to "religion" fails to clarify its nature. Religion is itself a multifaceted package, incorporating ritual, observance, faith, theology, custom, inwardness and outwardness. There is no religious consensus about the precise boundaries between Jew and non-Jew. So if the Jews are not, or not only, a religious body, then what are they? Tribe, people, culture, "race," nation?

The words *goy* and *goyim* appear in the Hebrew Bible first in reference to the various peoples who descended from Noah and the flood survivors. The term is specifically applied to the Jews themselves in Genesis 12:2, when God promises Abraham that his descendants will form a *goy gadol* ("great nation"). In the world recalled in the Torah, a *goy* was an extended clan network claiming common ancestry and customs: the Hebrews were one among many. However, later biblical texts apply the term mainly to other peoples. Similarly, the word *ethnikos*, which the Greeks used to translate *goyim*, first denotes groups of people living together, and later becomes a synonym for "foreigner" or "barbarian." The translators of the King James Bible chose the word "nation." "Ethnic group" is probably the closest we'd come in today's usage, but it is infinitely less resonant and wouldn't really resolve any of the ambiguities.

Being a category blurred at the edges and internally inconsistent does not make Jewishness any less of a category, any less a human, historical reality. Nor is this indeterminateness unique to Jews. There's always something arbitrary in the way we break up the multidimensional spectrum of human diversity. Groups overlap and mutate, expand and contract, and Jewishness is no exception. Its indeterminateness cannot be overcome, nor can I see why it should be overcome. It's not a problem except in so far as it is denied—and, along with it, much of Jewish history. That indeterminateness is part of the story of Jewish survival through successive social orders and eras. Anti-semites and Zionists alike freeze the Jewish identity and fix it in relation to other identities. Both prize an unambiguous demarcation between the Jew and the non-Jew. In contrast, the very negativity of anti-Zionism—the constrictions it denies—opens one to the multiplicity of Jewish reality.

Hence this particular anti-Zionist Jew's particular journey, through past and present, stretches across both sides of the Atlantic, and of necessity beyond, through the evolving relations between Jews and the left, and the shifting place of Palestine in that axis. It straddles my upbringing in New York (and early immersion in the US left) and my adulthood in Britain (and involvement in the anti-war and pro-Palestine movements). In tracing the role Jewishness has played in my own life and the world I've lived in, I've also traveled the backward path of family history, which in modern Jewish experience is always penetrated by—and serves to illuminate—larger histories. In particular, I've burrowed deep into an old leather case stuffed with yellowing newspaper clippings and brittle typescripts, the literary remains of a grandfather whose life on the American left, whose approach to Jewishness, to the enemies of the Jews and to his fellow Jews, posed unexpectedly pertinent questions and at times disturbing lessons. In trying to decipher his legacy, I've been compelled to investigate circumstances, movements, individuals. I've discovered affinities (not all of them reassuring) and unbridgeable gulfs.

My itinerary is unapologetically diasporic, but its compass is set in Palestine, in the realities of conquest, subjugation and suffering. In navigating this course, I have tried to follow the advice of the Andalusian Hebrew politician and poet-warrior Shmu'el HaNagid:

> You who'd be wise
> should inquire
> into the nature of
> justice and evil
> from your teachers,
> seekers like yourself,
> and the students
> who question your answers.[1]

Part One

1

Names and Faces

Like many American Jews of his era, my grandfather Ed changed his name. Unlike most, he changed it to something that would sound more, not less, Jewish. His parents were both immigrants to New York, his mother a Jew from eastern Europe and his father a Catholic from Ireland. Since his father died before his first birthday, he was brought up entirely by his Jewish mother, in a Jewish milieu, but he was stuck with the Irish name Moran, and struggled with the consequences for many years. In 1932, at the age of thirty-two, he went to court to have it changed—from Moran to Morand. According to an FBI report compiled years later, he gave the following reasons for wanting to add that *d*: "He had always been associated with the Jewish people and the name Moran caused most of the people with whom he was associated to think him to be of Irish extract. In many instances he had been deprived of joining certain Jewish clubs, lodges, etc. and he desired always to be associated with the Jewish people."

It's strange that all he did was add the *d*. His daughter, my mother, was never convinced it really made a difference. "When I stayed home from school on a Jewish holiday," she recalled in a memoir she wrote in 1999, two years before her death, "the teachers always questioned my right to stay at home with a name like Morand, and I would point out that it had a 'd' on it. How I wished it had been changed to Goldberg."

Through most of my childhood, Ed was an absent figure. In 1950 he left my grandmother Olga after twenty-five years of marriage, and he was not invited to my parents' wedding two years later or to subsequent family gatherings, including my bar mitzvah, though we all continued to live in the New York area. Once a year or so, he would pay us a visit with his second wife, Mabel. They quarreled incessantly. I remember him as gruff and distant, a pale, portly, stubby man who wore wide ties. He never spoke to just one person, but always addressed everyone in earshot, and truculent sarcasm was his habitual mode.

I knew Olga much better. She was part of our life, if not always a happy part. Yet Ed was a legend. My mother told us often about his achievements. He'd had a radio show and a newspaper column; he was a lawyer who fought for equal rights, civil liberties, and progressive causes; and once he had run for Congress. Years later, after I departed for Britain, I came to know him better and we formed a bond. The legend fell away and for a few years, until his death in 1976, I acquired a flesh-and-blood grandfather, whose cantankerousness was a constant irritation to my mother but a source of amusement for me. So, when my mother died in New York, in October 2001 and I inherited a battered, boxlike leather case stuffed with Ed's papers, I was curious to delve into them, to find out more about the man. That was only weeks after 9/11. It's taken me some time to explore, and even longer to understand, the contents of the case.

The earliest document is a passport on which he traveled, with his mother, to Russia in 1903, the latest an article in *The American Hebrew* from 1953. There are several thick scrapbooks bulging with newsprint: numerous columns and articles he wrote in the thirties and forties. There are speeches, neatly typed. There are diaries or, really, fragments of diaries. Poems as well as notes for and passages from uncompleted novels. Job applications. Election campaign literature, leaflets, meeting notices. And letters—only a few written to Ed, most written by him. From an early age he kept carbon copies of the letters he sent to others, including the intimate ones, a reflection of his sense of destiny, his self-importance and his acute self-consciousness, which he buried under the barbed exterior.

Altogether it's the paper trail of a man at war with the world and with himself, hectically engaged with the events and debates of his time. As I've read and reread this documentary legacy, events unfolding in the outside world have infused it with a pertinence and piquancy I never suspected. In Ed's papers I've explored a world where being a Jew with an Irish name had disturbing ramifications, where fascists and anti-semites openly paraded in the streets of New York, protected by a sympathetic police force, where figures like Fiorello La Guardia, Sidney Hillman, Ed Flynn, Mike Quill, Vito Marcantonio were household names. Where the slogan "Free Palestine!" meant support for a Jewish state and a "Palestinian" was a Jewish settler. Where the Zionist anthem "Ha Tikva" took its place with "The Internationale" and the Red Army marching song. Where Jews argued ceaselessly with Jews, not least about whether there should or should not be a "Jewish vote" and how that vote should be cast. A world where New York Jewry—today a global synonym for diasporic Jewishness—was very much in formation, riven by cultural and political divisions, its fate unsettled, its power and prominence yet to be established.

He was Eddie to old cronies and to his first wife, Ed to more distant acquaintances and to grandchildren, Edward V. Morand in public print. The V. was for Vivien, which he detested and never used, though he was punctilious about the middle initial. In his notes and briefer articles, he's EVM, which is how my uncle says he thinks of him and how I have also come to think of him. Lawyer, poet, columnist, radio show host, political activist, militant Jew, congressional candidate, anti-fascist and anti-racist. Champion of civil liberties, free speech, world peace, and in 1948 of the new state of Israel. EVM is a revealing witness to his times, even, or especially, when he's wrong, where the craziness that made him unique and the context he shared with others, that wider world he was always addressing or assaulting, seem inextricable.

My mother remembered a grandmother who was "gypsylike," dressed in bright colors with long red hair—which, as she was then in her seventies, must have been dyed. My uncle recalled how she used to visit with hard candy and the comics from the *Daily News*, which Ed had otherwise banned from the household as a "fascist rag."

Dora was born in 1859 in Kovno (modern-day Kaunas), the second city of Lithuania, on the western fringe of the Russian empire. The first twenty-two years of her life were lived under the relatively liberal rule of Czar Alexander II. In the 1860s, Jews who had previously been confined to the old ghetto in Slobodka crossed the river and settled in the centre of Kovno, which at this time underwent rapid economic growth. A railway was established to the German border, raising property prices and lowering export costs, while the czar surrounded the city with great military fortresses in which, eighty years later, the Nazis were to torture and execute Jews by the hundreds.[1]

During the years of Dora's youth, Jews made up some 30 percent of Kovno's population. New Jewish cemeteries and hospitals were established. Synagogues, Talmud Torahs and yeshivas abounded. Kovno became one of the Russian empire's major centers of Jewish thought—and inevitably Jewish argument. Chasids were small in number; their base lay further south. For thirty years, the community was led by the renowned Rabbi Yitzhak Elhanan Spektor, who acquired a reputation throughout Russia as a religious authority. Though Orthodox, he was not a fundamentalist, and he was responsive to some of the educational and social proposals of the Haskalah, the Jewish movement for rationalist enlightenment. However, his associate, Reb Jacov Livschitz, became famous as an opponent of secular remedies for the problems of the Jews and leader of what his freethinking enemies dubbed the "black party." Kovno was known as a stronghold of the Musar movement, a hybrid alternative to both Chasidism and Haskalah. The Musar stressed the need for Talmudic study, and the centrality within that of the ethical tradition, of service to humankind (*tikun olam*), and of the need for inner piety, cultivated through meditation and prayer. In addition, there was a small Karaite community which had settled in Lithuania in the seventeenth century.[2]

It was also in Kovno, in the early 1860s, that Judah Leib Gordon, then working as a teacher in a government school for Jews, wrote the Hebrew poems that established his European reputation. Gordon believed that Russian Jews should study Russian and Hebrew (not Yiddish) and redefine themselves as modern Russian citizens. The rabbis "have taught you to deny real life / to shut yourself behind fences within fences / to be dead to the world, to seek pie in the sky . . . you've been filled with petty laws and decrees." In 1863, he composed what was to become his most famous poem, the signature of his worldview. It begins: "Awake, my people! How long will you sleep? . . . Remarkable changes have taken place / A different world engulfs us today." Jews, he wrote, should no longer see themselves as transient, unwelcome guests in their host country: "This land of Eden is now open to you / Its sons now call you brothers." In the tradition of the Haskalah, he argued: "Be a man in the street and a Jew at home" or, more literally, "Be a man on your going out and a Jew in your tents."[3]

In addition to the rabbis, teachers and intellectuals, the Jewish middle class was made up of merchants, lawyers, engineers and physicians. The bulk of the Jewish population, however, worked in small workshops: tailors, seamstresses, cobblers, cigarette makers, butchers, fishmongers, bakers, bookbinders, blacksmiths, barbers, oven makers; there were also Jewish gardeners and laborers.

In notes for a very thinly veiled autobiographical novel

(written in the 1920s), EVM reconstructs Dora's early life. His mother as a child was of a "very light-hearted, generous disposition, not over intellectual, not at all inclined to be studious, not beautiful but exceptionally attractive and of a very vivid personality." But she was oppressed by her father, "the usual type of Jewish talmudic student who because of his Orthodox training had been given the respectful title of 'Reb'." For all his "good-hearted generosity," he was "tyrannical and fanatical." Dora's mother, in contrast, was "a business type, very shrewd and very wise. The dominant figure in the family."

> Whatever laughter and dancing even in its remote manner Chasidic Jews might enjoy was forbidden to her people. Mishnagadim they were. Protestant Jews, ever protesting against beauty in any shape, against poetry of rhyme or of the soul. Awaiting with docility a messiah who never would come.

Nonetheless, from the first, it seems, Dora's was "a nature of rebellion." She possessed "a beauty of body and face and a healthy vivacious disposition." But in EVM's notes, tragedy awaits. At the age of fifteen, in 1874, she was married off to a rabbi some ten years her senior, a "weak, serious-minded divinity student." The climax of EVM's narrative is the shearing of his newly married mother's beautiful long red hair. She resists, and when told the act is demanded by the law, she cries, "God is cruel. It is unbearable." This trauma, "the cutting of the scissors," EVM says, becomes the root of "the final estrangement between the husband and the wife and later the entire family." Her life after marriage is a dreary one. "The barriers of race and creed, social ostracism from the finer and more cultured traits of life and above all else a weary monopoly of ritual in the home and taboos and superstitions everywhere. As disagreeable as it was to man, it was ever more so for woman."

Following the assassination of Alexander II in 1881, Jewish

communities across southern Russia were assailed by anti-semitic mobs. (Reports of these events in Western newspapers introduced the Russian word "pogrom"—attack—into English.) The new czar, the reactionary Alexander III—champion of "Autocracy, Orthodoxy and Nationalism"—introduced what came to be known as the May Laws. These established a new pale within the Pale, prohibiting Jews from living outside designated towns and cities. Jewish farms were expropriated. Jewish entry to schools and universities was restricted. More pogroms followed, many clearly initiated with state support, and in 1886 an edict of expulsion was issued against the Jews of Kiev.

In this context, liberal faith in Jewish absorption into Russia wavered. Zionists made their first appearance on the Russian scene, arguing that only in Palestine was there a future for the Jews. They were opposed by Judah Leib Gordon, who acknowledged the grimness of the times but argued that if Jews were to leave Russia, then "It is preferable to direct Jews to America or other enlightened lands, for there they will learn how to be free men, liberated from both sorts of exile"—spiritual and political.[4] In the forty years following the pogroms of 1881, some 2 million Jews left the Russian empire—1,700,000 traveling to the USA, and 45,000 to Palestine.

Among the immigrants to the USA were five of my great-grandparents, including Dora. Somehow, she had procured a divorce (a *get*), a remarkable feat for a woman married to a rabbi in Jewish Kovno and powerful testimony to a determined and independent spirit. In 1888, she left for the United States with her young daughter, Rebecca. How she fared in those early years in New York is unknown, but in 1898, at the age of thirty-nine, she married an Irish immigrant, John Moran, who managed a bar on 52nd Street. (Dora took Ed there when he was fifteen, by which time it had become "a high-class Rathskellar.") The next year, my grandfather was born in an apartment on East 41st Street. EVM liked to claim he was a twin but "the good one died at birth." In a note from the 1920s, he imagined his own *briss* (circumcision), at which his father arrived "as if he was on his way to the guillotine."

> In spite of his independence of thought and action and his dislike of all matters concerning the church, [he] still has in his blood the tinge of fear and superstition . . . one of his sisters is at the moment lighting candles and having a mass said for the repose of his soul.

John Moran lived only another six months. Dora was left on her own, a forty-year-old immigrant woman with an infant child and teenage daughter. Somehow, she survived and prospered. She opened a hairdressing salon and moved the family into an apartment on West 92nd Street, not far from Central Park. And in October 1904 she did something almost unheard of among her generation of immigrants: she made a trip back to Kovno, accompanied by her four-year-old American son. (According to her passport, Dora was five feet two inches tall, with light gray eyes, small face, a medium nose, short chin, light brown hair, and fair complexion.) They went by ship to Hamburg, then by train to Berlin, and from there across what was still the Russian border.

In the Kovno Dora returned to, there were more Jews and different Jews. Poor Jews crowding into the city from the shtetls joined Jewish craftsmen as employees in capitalist industries, mostly small factories and workshops, in which—for the first time in history—Jews faced, *en masse*, the brutal vicissitudes of modern industrial life. Their response was the "General Jewish Labor Union of Lithuania, Poland and Russia," known as the Bund. Founded in 1897 at a clandestine conference in Vilna, the Bund developed rapidly from a federation of Jewish unions into a wider political and social movement.

From the outset the organization combined a revolutionary Marxist ideology with a practical, intimate link with daily Jewish working-class life. It organized strikes (mainly against Jewish employers, since these were the main employers of Jewish workers), massive leafleting campaigns (more than half a million pieces of literature in the year 1904, when Dora and Ed visited), and a wealth of educational and cultural activities, conducted, crucially, in Yiddish. Where the Haskalah and the Zionists favored Hebrew and frowned on Yiddish as a debased jargon, the Bundists embraced Yiddish as the language of the Jewish masses of eastern Europe.*

In 1898, the Bund helped create the Russian Social Democratic Workers' Party (RSDWP), forerunner of what became the Communist Party of the Soviet Union. Though rooted in the Jewish working class of the Pale, the Bundists defined themselves first and foremost as internationalists and sought, with Lenin, Martov and others gathered around the magazine *Iskra*, to unite the Russian empire's dispersed "social democrats" (that is, Marxists). In the following years the terms of that unity were to be fiercely contested, and never fully resolved.

At its 1901 Congress, the Bund declared that the Jewish proletariat had "national aspirations based on characteristics dear and peculiar to it—language, customs, ways of life, culture in general—which ought to have full freedom of development." What the Bund sought was not Jewish territorial jurisdiction but "national autonomy" within a larger democratic state. In the debate, concerns were expressed about the potential dilution of working-class consciousness by the embrace of "national autonomy," but delegates stressed the distinction between being "national" and being "nationalist." At this congress, the Bund also debated the challenge from Zionism, which it condemned as a nationalist, utopian and bourgeois response to anti-semitism.[5]

---

* Ahad Ha'am, founder spirit of the Lovers of Zion, told a meeting in Russia in 1902 that "there is now among us a party [i.e the Bund] which would raise this jargon [Yiddish] to the dignity of a national language" when it could never be but "an external and temporary medium of discourse."

In the following years, the Bund emerged as a mass workers' party the likes of which existed nowhere else in Russia. It commanded the loyalties and energies of thousands of workers, artisans, intellectuals and students who shouldered the workload of building a mass base capable of collective action in conditions of state repression. They also faced increasingly violent anti-semitism. In response, in 1902 the Bund declared: "We must handle ourselves like people with human dignity. Violence, no matter from where it stems, must not be glossed over. When we are attacked, it would be criminal on our part to bear it without resistance."[6]

The Kishinev pogrom (in today's Moldova) of February 1903 took some fifty Jewish lives and hundreds of Jewish properties and spread alarm among Jews across the Russian empire. "It burst upon the Jewish proletariat like a clap of thunder," a Bundist writer reported, "and left no doubt in any heart." Two months after Kishinev, the Bund began organizing self-defense programs in Jewish communities, including in Kovno. At the same time, it insisted: "Only the common struggle of the proletariat of all nationalities will destroy at the root those conditions that give rise to such events as Kishinev."

For the Zionists, Kishinev was further proof that there was no future for the Jews in Russia. Theodor Herzl, the founder of modern political Zionism, visited Russia to meet with Von Plehve, the Interior Minister widely believed to have had a hand in the Kishinev events. "I have an absolute binding promise from him that he will procure a charter for Palestine for us in 15 years at the outside," reported Herzl. "There is one condition however: the revolutionaries must stop their struggle against the Russian government."[7] They did not. In 1903, the Bund established street fighting credentials—against anti-semites, strikebreakers, police and employers. Between June 1903 and July 1904, 4,467 Bundists were arrested.[8]

The Bund clashed with Lenin and the RSDWP leadership at a

crucial congress held in Brussels in July 1903. The Bund had demanded autonomy within the party, the right to elect its own central committee, to form policy on Jewish issues, and to be recognized as sole representative of the RSDWP among Jewish workers. To the previously agreed demands for equal rights, they added a demand for Jewish "cultural autonomy," including education in Yiddish.

The *Iskra* leadership—soon to split bitterly into Bolsheviks and Mensheviks—stood united against the Bund's proposals. Interestingly, *Iskra*'s side of the debate was presented exclusively by Jews—so this was not an argument between Jews and Russians, but at least in part among Jews. *Iskra*'s rebuttal was led by the future Menshevik leader Julius Martov, whose exile to Vilna in the 1890s had helped inspire the formation of the Bund. Martov warned that "to squeeze the Jewish workers' movement into a narrow channel of nationalism" would weaken its ties with the general workers' movement. "Federation" as conceived by the Bund would obstruct the development of the stronger party organization that was the very purpose of the RSDWP and would be an obstacle to the rapprochement of Jewish and non-Jewish workers.

Trotsky then rose to inform the Congress that twelve Jewish delegates, members of the RSDWP, had signed Martov's anti-Bund resolution—"and still considered themselves representatives of the Jewish proletariat." This assertion was angrily challenged by Bundists who asked how Trotsky and his comrades could represent people "among whom they have never worked."[9] Trotsky hit back by charging that in resisting Zionism, the Bund had absorbed some of its nationalism.[10]

Despite the charges and countercharges of separatism and assimilationism, the opposition between Bund and Iskraites was not as clear-cut at the time as it may seem in retrospect. Both sides agreed that there was a distinctive Jewish culture and workers' movement, and, vitally, that its ultimate fate rested on the advance of the larger social democratic movement. What they could not agree about was the framework for that interaction. And that was partly because both sides were burdened with an intellectual apparatus of "nationality" which could not accommodate the indeterminacy of Jewishness, and the multidimensionality of Jewish relationships with non-Jews.

Even after the Bund withdrawal, Jews continued to join the RSDWP in disproportionate numbers, and there remained a substantial number of Jews among especially Mensheviks but also Bolsheviks (famously Zinoviev and Kamenev).* Yet the Bund continued to outstrip the RSDWP as a force on the ground. In the summer of 1904, it claimed 23,000 members, three times the Russian party's membership.[11]

Kovno was a Bund stronghold. On May Day, 1904, months before Dora and Ed arrived for their visit, it had dared to mount a massive public demonstration through the city's streets. One of the leaders that day was a seventeen-year-old Bund agitator named Simcha Hillman. As a prodigal Talmudist from a remote village, he'd been sent to Kovno's famous Musar yeshiva but had soon drifted into secular studies, becoming a full-time clandestine operative for the Bund in 1903. Repeatedly imprisoned, he left Russia for the USA in 1907, and in 1910 played a leading role in the Chicago garment workers' strike that gave birth to the Amalgamated Clothing Workers Union of America which, as Sidney Hillman, he was to lead for more than thirty years. Hillman became one of the most influential American trade unionists of any era, a close confidant of Roosevelt, and one of the masterminds of US involvement in World War II. He was also to play a significant role, from a distance, in the lives of EVM and his future family.[12]

---

* In 1917 Jews thronged to the Bolsheviks and were numerous in the Cheka and its successors. Anti-Bolshevism leaned heavily on anti-semitism, as did Stalin's anti-Trotskyism. In the Great Purge of 1937–38, most of the Jewish Bolsheviks and the remaining Bundists were wiped out.

Three months after Dora and Ed returned from their trans-atlantic journey, Russia was gripped by the revolution of 1905. In the northwest of the empire the Bund spearheaded the rolling series of strikes, demonstrations and meetings. They battled the government, the employers and the anti-semitic gangs of the Black Hundreds, sometimes with revolvers and bombs. At the high point of the agitation, in October, 82.1 percent of workers in the province of Kovno joined the strikes.

In later years, EVM recalled nothing of his trip to Kovno except long days of ocean voyaging. But the debates between and within the Bund and the RSDWP were to echo through his political life as a Jew on the American left. In my own activist career, I've experienced the debate re-created and re-worked (never merely repeated) in the relations between black people and the left, and between feminists and the left, in both the USA and Britain; in regard to caste struggles in India; and, most recently, to Muslims and the left in Britain post-9/11. It's never merely a theoretical argument about "race" and "class"; it's about individuals and communities—historical agents—shaped and driven by an inescapable intersection of the two.

Growing up in New York in the years before World War I, the young Ed was doted on by his mother and sister, but not, it appears, by his sister's husband, who also lived with the family and who ultimately became a successful stockbroker. "When I was a kid my brother-in-law used to hit me," he confided in a letter to a friend. "Always in the face. To this day, I fear a blow in the face." He refers elsewhere to "my youth of blows" as the source of his desire to "escape punishment." Although he made innumerable acquaintances and acquired many cronies in the course of his life, Ed never seems to have forged a lasting, intimate bond with a male friend, and in later years he observed that he had always felt more comfortable around women—whom he nonetheless felt compelled to belittle.

Later, in a talk he wrote in 1940 entitled "This Assimilation Business," he looked back at the Upper West Side neighborhood of his youth. "There was to be found a distinct middle-class type of Jew, one who hovered between allegiance to Reform and Conservative Judaism." A few of "the grandpas and grandmas" displayed more Orthodox inclinations. There were also the wealthy Jews on Riverside Drive whose "kids were fortunate enough to go to summer camp and partake of many luxuries which were denied me." He attended a Reform congregation where, he says, he "absorbed all the information possible about Jews and things Jewish." (In those years, prior to World War I fewer than one quarter of Jewish children in New York received any kind of Jewish education.) While there might be occasional shouts of "sheenie" or "kike" in the streets, "in truth our surroundings were tranquil." Yet peppering his recollections of his childhood and youth are repeated laments over what he calls his "adverse parentage," "mixed heredity," and "the discomforts of half-caste social ostracism." His problem stemmed from "the fact that I looked particularly Jewish and bore a name that was anything but Jewish." As a result of "this incongruous situation," he suffered "hours of torment." He feared that people would think he was "seeking a refuge, a passport" out of the ghetto. "Teachers conversed about me behind books raised to their lips."

From an early age he conceived of himself as "a devotee of tolerance," champion of "a new brotherhood of man," even as "the Disciple of this new understanding and the Bearer of this new Tolerance." Intermarriage was to be embraced; in racial science tomes he discovered theories about "cross-breeding" and the development of "a race of hybrids." Perhaps, in his case, the fusion of "the Nordic" with the "semitic" had produced "not someone who should be a subject of derision" but a new and better strain.

If out of all this assimilation business a more perfect product should appear, the loss of any one nationalistic characteristic in this melting pot would be more than compensated by the pure gold that must result from this spiritual alchemy.

At DeWitt Clinton High School, EVM entered "a new world" of intellectual and political challenge. The school, then located in central Manhattan, attracted academically inclined boys from across the city. The faculty was largely gentile, but the students were increasingly Jewish. "I saw the youth of the East Side," EVM recalled, "more ambitious than I was, even lower in the financial scale than poor me, coming joyously to study, seemingly marvelously equipped to absorb, digest and retain." Most had to work after school but despite their hardships, they seemed contented. "There was no difficulty in their minds concerning their birthright, nor how they stood in relation to the world at large." He envied them their "nonchalance."

Politics at DeWitt Clinton was "overrun by Jewish students" who "grasped every office and gained every honor hungrily, scrambling for more." It was here that EVM says he first heard the word *goy* used derisively; he berated the classmates who used it for their intolerance and "lack of Americanism." He decided to act on his "assimilationist" views. In his first year, he backed the Protestant candidate for class president, in the interest of "forgetting petty nationalistic impulses and being thoroughly Americanized." The election resulted in a tie, whereupon EVM's candidate gracefully declined in favor of the Jewish candidate. Not for the last time in his political career, EVM found himself hoist with his own petard.

In his second year, he decided to attend school on Rosh Hashanah because, given his lack of religious convictions, "it would be hypocritical of me not to." Strangely, however, he felt uncomfortable, the object of others' "silent disdain." When Yom Kippur came around, he stayed at home. Reporting to class the following day, he was reprimanded by his teacher: "My name required that I be present, and either her near-sightedness or her general stupidity did not prove to her my right to stay at home." When EVM informed her he was Jewish, she told him he was lying and sent him to the principal, a man named Dr Francis Paul who did more than any other to shape the school's reputation (Paul Avenue in the Bronx, where the school is currently located, is named after him). When the fifteen-year-old EVM—in high dudgeon—explained the teacher's error, Dr Paul was amused. The episode proved "the foundation for a long and intimate acquaintanceship." Paul himself had chosen to leave the Catholic school system out of a commitment to secular education. He encouraged EVM to pursue his radical ideas—although he himself strongly disagreed with them.

In 1916, EVM attended a pro-Irish street rally in Manhattan: years later he recalled "thousands of people of all nationalities, addressed by Irish men and women . . . the speeches were for liberty—for tolerance—for an Irish homeland!" A year later the US entered World War I—simultaneously with the launch of the country's first anti-red scare. "In 1917 many of my best teachers were subjected to a red-baiting investigation," EVM later re-called, "all the result of war hysteria." At DeWitt Clinton, EVM would have been exposed to arguments among pacifists, patriots, pro- and anti-German and pro- and anti-British voices. When the US entered the war, EVM took the lead in raising the funds to purchase a DeWitt Clinton High School ambulance to send to the front in Europe. He then enlisted, determined to drive the ambulance himself, though at the time he was still some months short of his eighteenth birthday, and under the minimum legal age for service.

In later years EVM proudly declared himself—especially on his campaign literature—a "veteran of World War One" and always boasted of his membership in the Jewish War Veterans, though he never spared its leadership the benefits of his criticism. The story we heard was that when his concealment of his real age (an expression of his patriotic zeal) was discovered, he was sent home, but immediately re-enlisted (legally) and was about to be shipped off to France when the war ended. "The Kaiser heard I was coming so he surrendered," he used to tell my mother.

But the papers in the leather case hint at a more complicated, enigmatic tale. In "This Assimilation Business" EVM explains that when he first enlisted in the ambulance corps he found himself the only Jew in the outfit. "It would take volumes to cover my two months' experience in this company," he writes. "Let it suffice to say that I arranged for a transfer because of anti-semitic feeling." When he re-enlisted—in the signal corps—he was posted to a battalion of six hundred, of whom twelve were Jews.

> I had a dispute with the top sergeant and managed to get him alone in the barracks. I voiced my disapproval of the manner in which the Jewish boys were treated, especially concerning holiday leaves. He was very frank about the situation. He said to me that he was a member of the United Christian Brethren. That he honestly and firmly believed that the only salvation that existed was that every man in his outfit, should he unfortunately be killed, would at least, as he put it, "die a Good Christian." I retorted very bluntly that the only thing I was certain about in this war was that the twelve Jews in this outfit would die as Jews.

On his discharge from the army in January 1919, EVM was required to return to DeWitt Clinton for a full year to complete the studies he had abandoned when he enlisted. Finally, in 1920, he received his diploma from Dr Paul, to whom he then wrote a lengthy, pained and accusatory letter in which his military experiences appear in a more candid—and confused—light. Clearly, there had been an angry rupture between the principal and the headstrong pupil, and it had something to do with the war. "Whatever there is that we could actually hold each other accountable for, at least I owe you my sincere thanks for your kindness in giving me my diploma," he writes, then adds bitterly that he did resent "sitting idly in class a full year just to make up time." Even as he offers the hand of reconciliation, he insists, "My views have not changed . . . I believed in independence of thought and action. Every concession that I have made, every new angle of thought, was of my own desire. I never could be browbeat into accepting dogma or creeds." There follows what is probably the most candid account of his time in the army and his attempt to escape from it:

> I won't attempt to justify my war record. Let it suffice that after making a mistake of judgement and not conscience I re-enlisted, not that my ideas had changed but I felt that I owed it to my future to go through with the thing according to schedule. That was a hard thing to do. I had no love for the army, in fact I detested it. The army is a man's game, and I was a boy . . . My ambulance company was anti-semitic, so much so that I sacrificed my reputation, your friendship and a whole lot besides to get out. To stay in meant a living hell. Once out, I appreciated my situation. Who in the frenzy of war hysteria would have believed my story? So I went back . . . There is much that has not been told. Some day, God granting, I shall try and tell it . . . Remember, petted and pampered as I was, a leader in my school, it was hard to be yelled at and to clean pots. Of course there were a million others like myself . . . Your opinions are your own, so shall mine ever be. Really, should I have suffered for mine? I said I would not talk war, but I have.

Did EVM use his under-age enlistment to get himself out of the army after those two bitter weeks in the ambulance corps? Initially, he was not given an honorable discharge; only in 1925 did Congress pass an act granting honorable discharges to those who'd concealed their minority status at enlistment, thus enabling EVM to boast later that he was "the proud possessor of two honorable discharges from the same war." What seems clear is that his precipitate return to New York—along with the bitter opinions about the war and the army he seems to have expressed at the time—profoundly displeased Dr Paul (who for his part must have known of EVM's under-age enlistment from the start). "I prided myself on your friendship. There is much I resent . . . some of the things you stand for and some of your views are still unalterably not to my liking. I admit my radical tendencies have become less red. I still maintain my right to be called a real American." He ends the letter expressing confidence that he is now on "firmer ground" and that the future holds much for him.

> I intend to go into politics. I want to try and shape the destiny of this land as much as any one man can, and I hope to succeed. I want a place in the sun. You see, I have not changed, I still have the ego. But that is a necessity if one is to be a politician. I learned that lesson in the General Organization.

In a letter to a friend written some years later he says: "I wouldn't join the infantry because the thought of plunging a bayonet into somebody chilled me. I was willing to string wires and run a wireless and take chances. [They] never came." What did come, though EVM never wrote a word about it, was a military experience of a different kind, in its own way as gruesome as the carnage at the front.

According to the record, EVM was stationed at Camp Devens, a complex of barracks and warehouses outside Boston, from August 1918 to January 1919. At this time the camp was home to 50,000 men, twice the number it was built for. Some were undergoing training in anticipation of being shipped out to the front, and some were on their way back from it. The first influenza cases were reported in early September. The onset of symptoms was abrupt:

headache, sore throat, runny nose, fever. Even more abrupt was the deterioration into pneumonia and death, sometimes within forty-eight hours of the first sniffle. Reddish-brown spots would appear on the cheekbones of the doomed, then spread across the face until, a young doctor observed, "it was hard to tell a colored man from a white one." By the end of September, the epidemic had brought military life in the camp to a standstill. The hospital built to hold 2,000 patients was now crammed with four times that number. While influenza generally preys on the old or the very young, the strain of 1918 seemed to target those in the prime of life. "This infection," wrote Dr Victor Vaughan, an epidemiologist sent to Devens, "like war, kills the young, vigorous, robust adults." Coffins ran short and bodies piled up in the makeshift morgue. "It beats any sight they ever had in France after a battle," another doctor noted. In the midst of all this, a US district court judge arrived in camp to administer the oath of citizenship to more than 2,000 soldiers, new immigrants recruited off the streets of New York and Boston.

At Camp Devens, Victor Vaughan was disturbed by his calculations. "If the epidemic continues its mathematical rate of acceleration," he wrote, "civilization could easily disappear from the face of the earth." But within a month, the epidemic began to recede. In the end, its disappearance was as stealthy and inexplicable as its onset. And though it had taken 20 million lives worldwide, as it receded it was crowded out of the popular memory.[13] The disease did not fit the prevailing paradigms of war and heroism, and so, like other historical realities that undermine the stories we tell about ourselves, it was erased.

EVM was at Camp Devens when Victor Vaughan was making his apocalyptic calculations. I've searched his papers for some reference to the flu epidemic but could find none. "There is much that has not been told," he wrote to Dr Paul. "Some day, God willing, I shall tell it." As far as I can see, he never did, though he had more to say about Camp Devens.

2

The War Against Analogy

> *An' here I sit so patiently*
> *Waiting to find out what price*
> *You have to pay to get out of*
> *Going through all these things twice.*
> Bob Dylan, "Stuck Inside
> of Mobile with the
> Memphis Blues Again"

"One should never judge a book by its cover, but in the case of former President Jimmy Carter's latest work, *Palestine: Peace Not Apartheid*, we should make an exception," declared Anti-Defamation League national director Abraham Foxman in 2006. "All one really needs to know about this biased account is found in the title."[1]

As Carter discovered, coupling the word "apartheid" with Israel is a quick route to getting branded an anti-semite. The campaign of vilification mounted against Carter—familiar to supporters of Palestinian rights but extraordinary in that its target was a Nobel Peace Prize winner and former President—confirmed how determined the Israel lobby is to rule this analogy out of bounds. The Central Conference of American Rabbis, the largest organization of rabbis in the US, declared that "use of the term 'apartheid' to describe conditions in the West Bank serves only to demonize and de-legitimize Israel in the eyes of the world." (For good measure it also accused Carter of "attempted

rehabilitation of such terrorist groups as Hezbollah and Hamas.")[2]
Eager to distance the Democrats from Carter's critique of Israel,
House Speaker Nancy Pelosi announced: "It is wrong to suggest
that the Jewish people would support a government in Israel or
anywhere else that institutionalizes ethnically based oppression."
Pelosi seems to believe not only that all Jews support Israel but
that Jews by nature are always politically correct, uniquely
shielded from the fractures and vagaries of history. If the generalization she had made had been a negative one, the racist nature of
her logic would have been obvious and would have been
condemned. But since she flattered the Jews, and backed Israel,
the Anti-Defamation League wasn't interested.

The more I travel and read, the more analogies I discover, and
at the same time the warier I become of all analogies. For an
analogy to do its job, there have to be clear distinctions between
those features that are and those that are not analogous. One has
to examine context and proportion. History does not repeat itself
exactly, but it is full of echoes, some revealing, some misleading.

Attacks on what has been dubbed "the new anti-semitism" (an
anti-semitism associated with the European left in particular) have
focused on the use of what are deemed to be inappropriate
analogies, which are interpreted as inherently anti-semitic. Curiously, this argument is usually linked to the further charge that
critics of Israel reveal their true, anti-semitic bias when they
"single out" Israel.

The European Union Monitoring Committee on Racism
and Xenophobia has published a "working definition" of anti-
semitism which declares that "anti-semitism manifests itself" in
"drawing comparisons of contemporary Israeli policy to that of
the Nazis" as well as "denying the Jewish people their right to
self-determination, e.g., by claiming that the existence of a State
of Israel is a racist endeavour."[3] Former Israeli minister Natan
Sharansky defined "the new anti-semitism" by applying what he
calls the "3D test": "demonization" (comparing Israelis to Nazis),

"double standards" (measuring Israel by different yardsticks than are applied to other countries), and "delegitimization" (denying the Jewish right to a state). Berlin Technical University's Center for Research on Anti-semitism characterized the new anti-semitism as a critique of Israel in which the Jewish state is "negatively distinct" from all others. Irwin Cotler, the Canadian Justice Minister, claimed that acceptable criticism of Israel ends and anti-semitism begins when critics deny the Jewish people's right to self-determination, when they "Nazify" Israel, or when they "single out Israel for discriminatory treatment in the international arena."

To single something out unfairly is to deny its analogous status: for example, Israel's crimes in relation to crimes committed by other regimes. This "double standard" is said to be a telltale sign of anti-semitism or, in the case of Jews, self-hatred.

Now I strongly agree that there must be a single standard when it comes to human rights and dignity, crimes of war, violence, occupation, and discrimination. Here I'm with the Prophet Amos, to whom the Lord showed "the plumb line" against which all, including Israel, were to be measured. However, in working out where the plumb line falls, determining that single standard of human justice, it is necessary to engage in the process of analogy. And on this the Zionists place *a priori* restrictions.

Israel demands exemptions: on refugees' right to return or compensation, on seizure and settlement of land acquired by military conquest, on torture and assassinations, on the indiscriminate use of violence in densely populated areas, on nuclear proliferation. These exemptions are embodied in hundreds of US vetoes on Israel's behalf at the Security Council. So who is really doing the "singling out"?

Of course, Israel is not the only offender in today's world. The US and Britain are both guilty of unspeakable crimes in Iraq; Burma, Sudan, Zimbabwe, and far too many other states are committing crimes that need "singling out." But if no protest against a particular crime is to be admitted unless all crimes are equally and presumably simultaneously protested against, then there will be no protest at all, against any crimes. This is an acute form of moral relativism masquerading as its opposite. The upshot is to minimize or relativize Israel's crimes and to attempt to delegitimize those who would judge Israel by universal standards of human decency.

Anti-Zionists, of course, do reject the idea that there should be a Jewish state in Palestine. In doing so it's said that we are "singling out" Jews by denying their right to the statehood that others enjoy. Here the Zionists move from objecting to inappropriate analogies to insisting on analogous status with other national groups. A rejection of that particular analogy, and the preference for other analogies—other readings of history—is ruled anti-semitic, either in motive or effect.

"Why should Jews be the only people denied the right to national self-determination?" The historical selectivity lies with the accusers. There can be no doubt that very large numbers of Tibetans, Western Saharans, Kurds, Kashmiris, Chechens, Tamils in Sri Lanka, Mizos, Nagas and Assamese in India, Aceh in Indonesia, Pushtoon, Baloch, and Sindhis in Pakistan, Ibo people in Nigeria, not to mention Palestinians, believe their right to self-determination is being actively denied, not merely in theory but in practice.

By all the usually accepted definitions—language, culture, territorial contiguity and widespread national consciousness—the Kurds have long qualified as a nation, but none of the great powers has ever recognized Kurdish national aspirations. As a key backer of Turkey, the US helped suppress Kurdish revolt, and only discovered the cruelties inflicted by Saddam on the Kurds of Iraq when it became useful to do so. The subsequent suborning of the Kurdish leaders in Iraq by the occupation has, in turn, made it clear that even in such a relatively clear case, national self-determination throws up awkward questions, not least in regard to cities with mixed populations, like Kirkuk. Even just claims for national self-determination can be turned into pretexts for ethnic cleansing. At the moment, Kurdish politics is marked by cavernous divides, and a free and independent Kurdistan seems to be on no one's agenda. Are those Kurds who support the pursuit of autonomy, not nationhood, within a larger national framework, those who consider themselves Iraqi nationalists and support resistance to occupation, "self-hating Kurds"?

In Sri Lanka, there has been a long and violent struggle for an independent Tamil homeland, but that demand is not supported by all Tamils, and many democratically minded people do not see it as a wise, just or feasible solution to the island's ethnic conflict. Does that make them anti-Tamil racists? The Liberation Tigers of Tamil Eelam think so, and seek to eliminate, physically, those "self-hating" Tamils who advocate another path. Like Zionism, the Tamil Tigers' brand of Tamil nationalism secures vital support from a diaspora imbued with a memory of racism, in this case the institutional and sometimes violent racism of the Sri Lankan state.

Were those who opposed national self-determination for Afrikaaners and Zulus in post-apartheid South Africa "singling out" these ethnic groups by denying them this universal right? Both groups could boast their own language and culture, and the Afrikaaners could boast a distinctive religion. Yet their claims were universally rejected by liberal and left opinion. They were recognized as undemocratic, exclusivist nationalisms, either preserving or seeking to establish ethnic privileges. In the end, the bulk of the South African population decided that only majority rule across the country, not separatism, could guarantee minority rights. World opinion was in complete accord, yet to advocate that self-same solution for Palestine is deemed—officially—antisemitic.

None of these examples, it will be argued, compare precisely with the Jews. After all, Catholics, Protestants, Muslims, Hindus all have their own countries, why not the Jews? But what about the Sikhs? There are 23 million Sikhs globally, of whom 15 million live in the Indian state of Punjab. In the 1980s, Sikh militants seeking to convert Punjab into a separate Sikh homeland, Khalistan, fought a war with the Indian state (one of whose casualties was Indira Gandhi and the thousands of Sikhs murdered in Delhi in revenge for her death in 1984). Although the Khalistan movement received support from the Sikh diaspora, the demand divided Sikhs in the Punjab itself, and no longer enjoys widespread support. No one seriously claims that to oppose Khalistan—and wish to remain within a secular India—is tantamount to being anti-Sikh.

There are currently no Protestant or Catholic or Hindu or even Muslim states that legally privilege members of those religions in the way that the state of Israel privileges Jews. There are Muslim states that give privileges to Islam and to Muslim citizens, but there is no Muslim state that offers all Muslims worldwide a homeland, or that endows foreigners with full (indeed privileged) citizenship, simply because they are Muslims. While religion may affect citizenship rights, it is not the determinant—which is birth or long residence within the borders of the state. Paradoxically, although the Jewish state is said to belong to Jews everywhere, it does not define Jewishness by religious observance. It claims to be a secular state, unlike those Muslim states that require public observance of specific forms of Islam.

The founder of Pakistan, Muhammed Ali Jinnah, envisaged his Muslim homeland as a secular state; he was not personally devout and his contempt for mullahs was very much in keeping with the Labor Zionists' contempt for rabbis. His Two Nations Theory defined Muslims in the subcontinent as a separate nation with the right to a separate state in a defined territory where they would comprise the majority. Was it Islamophobic to oppose the Two Nations Theory? That would make Islamophobes of the Congress, Gandhi, Nehru, the entire Indian left, not to mention the majority of Indian Muslims, who chose not to emigrate. Jinnah's secular promise was not borne out by history. The birth of the state was accompanied by murderous ethnic cleansing (on both sides of the border). Over the following decades, minorities were persecuted and mullah-ism of the sort Jinnah disdained ran rampant; like a number of Israel's founders, he would be appalled at the role clerical obscurantism plays in his country today. The marriage of the secular and confessional under the banner of "nationhood" is invariably uneasy, and in this sense Israeli experience is not unique.

Nations, nationalism, and national self-determination are the building blocks of the modern world, powerful social realities, but they remain analytically elusive. Nationalisms run the gamut from exclusive to inclusive, from territorial, transparent and democratic to transcendental, opaque and authoritarian. There are racial, linguistic, cultural, and religious nationalisms, often in combination. There's Nazi blood-and-soil nationalism; there's French Revolutionary nationalism; there's an internationalist nationalism—preached by Garibaldi or Castro or Hugo Chávez or an earlier generation of Palestinian and Arab leaders. Where does Zionism sit in this constellation? The measurement must be—as for all other nationalisms—the democratic content of the national demand and the national identity in question. (When the Nazis annexed Sudetenland, Hitler cited in his defense the German-speaking Czechs' right to national self-determination.) In many situations it is unclear where the balance lies. But in the case of Zionism the verdict is dramatically stark: Zionism involves, unavoidably, a denial to others of democratic and equal rights. It is an obscurantist claim dressed in the garb of secular modernity, underpinned from the beginning by naked power.

If there were as many states as there are ethnic identities, or even putative nationalities, the UN would have to be enlarged several times over. Crucially, even in the most clear-cut claims for national self-determination, there is no right to build a state on land already inhabited by others, or to sustain an ethnic majority in a state through the dispossession of others. It is here that Zionists make for Israel an exceptional claim among the nations. Their case cannot be sustained by analogy, so they delegitimize the process of analogy.

However, there is, even here, one analogy they do claim: that between Americanism and Zionism. Like Palestine, North America was a land without people for people without land. Both Americanism and Zionism are settler-colonial ideologies infused with utopianism—and racism. Both the Israeli and the US state are presented as embodying extra-territorial ideas. The "city on the hill" is an outpost, and in latter days an embodiment, of white European civilization. American exceptionalism and Israeli exceptionalism are mirrors and partners. Like the Zionists who founded Israel, the Protestant settlers who founded the USA were fleeing from and supported by an empire. They dispossessed the indigenous people while declaring them the beneficiaries of their good intentions. Among the charges the Declaration of Independence makes against King George III is that he has blocked "new appropriation of lands," failed to encourage migration from Europe, and sided with the "merciless Indian savages" against the "inhabitants of our frontiers," namely, the white settlers seeking to expand the colonial domain. The American Revolution, like the Zionist struggle against the British mandate in 1945–47, was partly a response by settler-colonialists to imperial restrictions on their right to dispossess natives.

I've heard this analogy used to justify the Nakba, the Palestinian "catastrophe" of 1948: terrible things happened to the Native Americans but these are the casualties of progress, and cannot be undone. Every people acquires its land, at one point or another, by conquest, so why should the Jews be any different?

But that raises the less comfortable case of another settler-colonialism, white South Africa. When it comes to the apartheid analogy, what's decisive is not Carter's legitimizing of it but the fact that it arises, spontaneously and irresistibly, to the lips of black South Africans visiting the Occupied Territories. What they see there—the Jews-only roads, the confinement of Palestinians in camps and villages, the checkpoints, the harassment, the second-class citizenship based on ethnicity—reminds them graphically of the system they suffered under and struggled against. The Afrikaaners were immigrants from Europe with a religious-nationalist consciousness whose racist assumptions about their right to the land were underpinned by superior European technology and weaponry. White settlers acquired control of the state thanks ultimately to British imperial power, with which, like the Zionists, they were often nonetheless in conflict.

There is at least one major difference between Israel and white South Africa, though it's not one that favors the former. Under apartheid, the dominant whites used the black population as a source of cheap labor. In contrast, Zionism has aimed to remove the Palestinian population, to replace Palestinians with Jews. And this has been evident from what Zionists called "the conquest of labor" in the 1920s (when Jewish settlers campaigned for the non-employment of Palestinians), to the Nakba of 1948 and its aftermath, to the current calls within Israel for "transfer," the final expulsion of the bulk of the Palestinian population.

As for the Nazi analogy, it is indeed indiscriminately used, as is the word "fascist," applied too readily to anyone who is authoritarian and racist. This is name-calling and it's no substitute for analysis. The prime culprit here, however, is not the left. In my lifetime, every US military action, from Vietnam to Iraq (and now the threat against Iran), has been justified with analogies drawn from World War II. Every enemy is a new Hitler (Qadaffi, Noriega, Milošević, Saddam Hussein, Mugabe, Ahmadinejad), every call for peace is Munich-style appeasement, and every challenge to Israel is an existential threat akin to that posed by the Nazis—from the days of Nasser down to Hamas and Hezbollah.

Of course, the Nazis and the holocaust represent an acme of inhumanity, an evil so enormous that any comparison seems dubious. Yet if we remove them from history and treat them as *sui generis*, we debar ourselves from learning and applying the broader lessons. When the world discovered the extent of Nazi barbarism in the wake of World War II, the cry was "Never again!" We cannot turn that cry into a reality, we cannot ensure that nothing even remotely like this happens again, unless we are permitted to draw appropriate analogies from the experience. Where there is Nazi-like behavior, a Nazi-like idea or a Nazi-like threat, then it is right that the comparison is noted. Is it permitted, however, to compare anything to the holocaust? Its industrial and ideological nature and scale seem to make it unlike anything in the annals of genocide. But even these salient features occur only within the broader phenomenon of Nazi imperialism, and Nazi imperialism has to be placed within the still broader phenomena of imperialism, racism and colonialism. That's where the story of the extermination of European Jewry belongs and it does not in the least belittle or relativize the magnitude of its horror to say so.

League tables of atrocities serve no purpose, or, rather, the only purpose they serve is to allow scope for the apologists for atrocities. The holocaust, the enslavement of Africans, the genocide of Native Americans and Australians, the centuries of "untouchability" in South Asia, the Belgian Congo (where, according to Adam Hochschild's revelatory book *King Leopold's Ghost*, some 10 million Africans may have perished in little more than a decade), Stalin's Gulag. All these are distinct historical phenomena, but share in common an institutionalized inhumanity on a mass scale. All are unspeakably, irredeemably horrific; they exemplify that which every human being has an absolute obligation to resist and not to aid, in any way, even by omission.

For many anti-Zionist Jews, one of the key analogies is between Jewish and Palestinian experience—exile, persecution, racism. "We travel like everyone else, but we return to nothing," writes the Palestinian poet Mahmoud Darwish. How can anyone study Jewish history and not draw the larger analogies with all those oppressed or displaced by empires, great and small? Palestinians themselves are alert to these analogies. They speak of the Palestinian "diaspora." The separation wall is daubed with the words "ghetto" and "concentration camp."

In the late forties, EVM started but never finished a memoir he titled "So You Want to Be a Politician?," the fruit of his years pursuing the ambition articulated at the end of his letter to Dr Paul. He recalled:

> I broke in in '21. The local Democratic Tammany machine had sold a bill of goods to Nathan Straus Jr to run for state senator. The district was so solidly Democratic that Hiawatha could have won. Straus was the antithesis of what a politician should be— aloof, too rich and too sensitive a stomach. He served one term and obligingly folded his tent.

Straus was the Princeton-educated scion of the German Jewish family that owned Macy's department store and the jeans manufacturer Levi Strauss. One uncle had been a congressman and another an ambassador. Unusually for wealthy American Jews of the period, they were Democrats and Zionists. To EVM, Straus was a "boob," one of that breed of charitable reformer who dabbled in politics but failed to engage with the nuts and bolts of political organizing.

Why did the professed idealist choose to join up with Tammany Hall, the New York Democratic Party machine notorious for patronage and municipal plunder? Partly it was a strong attraction to hands-on politics, and a belief that he could succeed at them, and make something of himself through them. Ed's brother-in-law was a Republican, as were many Jewish business-

men and professionals at the time, whereas most working-class
Jews in New York—strongly influenced by the Bund—voted
Socialist (the Lower East Side had sent a Socialist to Congress in
1914), and the Jewish-dominated unions were Socialist-orientated.
A solidly Democratic Jewish vote in New York was in those days
unimaginable. The Democratic Party was the creature of Tam-
many, and Tammany was still, certainly in the eyes of many Jews,
Irish-dominated. It was, in EVM's phrase, "the *ahrganization*."
But here he believed his name and his "hybridity" could be turned
to advantage. He could stake out a position for himself as a liaison
between Tammany and the Jews. It never worked out that way.
At one point he resorted to forming—and having himself elected
chairman of—a kind of front group called the John E. McCarthy
Association, for which John E., an elderly Tammany time-server,
provided merely a name. Later, EVM recalled his years as a
Tammany foot soldier:

> A saga of doorbell ringing, writing envelopes—speaking on street
> corners—making the club so the leader would see you. Watching
> the *Law Journal* to see if the Judge you broke your fool neck for in
> November remembers your name in July for a bit of patronage
> . . . law committees, publicity work, ghosting speeches.

The Tammany EVM joined was a well-oiled machine, but it
was also a machine nourished by countless concrete links to the
city's working-class communities, and under the leadership of
Alfred E. Smith it was turning to the left. Smith was the son of
Irish immigrants, a boy from a poor family who started off in
politics running errands for the Tammany District leader. EVM
campaigned for him for Governor in 1922. In a precursor of the
New Deal, Smith introduced labor laws, safety regulations,
workers' compensation, and rent control. He also stood up against
the renascent Ku Klux Klan and spoke out against the 1924
Quotas Act, which blocked immigration from eastern and south-

ern Europe (admitting only 124 people a year from Lithuania, but 28,000 from Ireland). The Democratic Convention of 1924 was held on Tammany's home turf, at Madison Square Garden, and Smith was the organization's candidate for the presidential nomination. While the urban ethnics backed Smith, the Protestants from around the country despised him (some turned up in white hoods and sheets). The convention was deadlocked for 99 ballots before Smith and his opponent, three-time presidential candidate William Jennings Bryan, withdrew and the nomination was handed to a nonentity named Davis. For Tammany this was a bitter blow, especially for young Smith men like EVM. That November, Davis duly lost the state to Coolidge while Smith was easily re-elected Governor.

The EVM who plunged into Tammany politics in the early twenties is hardly visible at all in the diaries and private letters of the period. Here he appears a romantic introvert, quoting Omar Khayyam and Romain Rolland's Jean-Christophe: dreaming, posturing, hungering, spewing out overwrought prose about dawn and death and love and the stars, self-pitying but at times delirious with the excitement of an unknown future. In 1922, he puts what he calls an "epilogue" on the first page of a new diary: "The Dreamer wants to put at the end of his story the beginning. The Dreamer still hopes. The epilogue of shattered romance is really the prologue of a new desire." In a long entry bemoaning his special fate—"burdened with a dual ancestry" in "a world of hate"—he muses:

> There doesn't seem much contentment in having a strict individuality. I have always gloried in being different, each and every mood of mine that partook of eccentricity was sponsored to become a habit by the thought that in it lay inanimate some future potentiality that made for success. I still sense the wall, feel the sting of the word "different" and loathe those people who hate their memories of a ghetto and yet place others in a prison of

mental abhoration . . . One cannot be both Jew and Christian. One can't forget the Inquisition by remembering that Christ was born a Jew. It is possible at times to feel relieved and read scientific treatises on the similarity between the races, but it is but flattering for the moment.

In a primeval wilderness, he suspects, a man and a woman could meet and love each other without regard to heritage, "But God, they tag you here from birth!" To Jews, he belongs "out there"— in the non-Jewish world—but to gentiles he belongs "back in the ghetto." "Not only am I a member of an outcast race, but an outcast in the race." Those he resents most "have put a sign on their door: 'thou mayest eat and drink with us, but marry into our lives, never.'" And here he seems to be referring to Jews, not gentiles: "I can't blame them though. Perhaps if I saw a troop of Black Hundred kill my relations, that barrier of blood would antagonize me even if it reached but an infinitesimal quantity." Yet, typically, he finishes this entry on a note of defiance: "Israel has lived and been revitalized because of being pressed almost to extermination. I glory in your hatred. I mock your fooling childish fancies. I am nearer God than you. I am of more strains of life."

There's something of the same oscillation in his jottings on sex, love and marriage. "I have not been a victim of sex," he boasts. "That one big bogey has no terrors for me. The so-called wild woman hasn't a chance." Yet he fears "the mistake of falling in love before being loved." He pursues the object of his desire but meets only frustration: "Month after month to look forward to the ultimate consummation of one's desires—and then to lose the prize!" But when he does succeed in the chase, his reactions prove ambivalent: "It was wonderful the sensation of having someone say, I love you. It was wonderful to hold someone in your arms— and defy the world to take you from her side. But it's not always the bolting of doors that keeps the thief away." Reflecting on the lesson of this failed relationship, he vows never to lose respect for his future wife, whoever she may be: "intimacy should not breed contempt."

He seems to have met Olga and begun courting her in 1923. They married in 1925. Between these two dates EVM wrote a series of letters to other women friends (Lilla, Mutchie, Mamie, and Mollie); the letters are flirtatious, hinting at past intimacies, or his own desire for intimacy. Sometimes the tone is pontificating: "Too often among the Jewish race the old talmudic and rabbinical idea exists that a woman is man's inferior and just a breeder of children." Sometimes it is whimsical: "I am in love, kid, and really so and methinks that my chase is over. I am wondering if I shall enjoy a domestic existence and shall forget the wanderlust. It is amusing how quickly I change, and yet don't you think me adaptable?" He feels the hand of destiny—"an unknown publisher of works is giving me material to live that perhaps may be good copy some day to write"—but rues his foibles and continuing frustrations:

> I have tried to analyze myself and discover why I should detest to do things that ordinarily I should do, work for instance. I think were I never to have been pampered from the beginning I might now have succeeded in making my brain accomplish something. But ceaseless nagging and having people tell me that my views were all wrong changed my decision. My Jewish ancestry betokens work, success, brains . . . which parent can I attribute my idealism to, which my impracticality? Both equally and neither.

Writing to a fraternity brother he protests bitterly at having been mocked after showing friends something he had written in his diary. "Don't you see that there are two races in me? Two widely diversified strains. Were I a boob I wouldn't think about these things and all would be well."

Finally, there are two letters from Ed to Olga, in both of which he analyzes in some detail the reasons why they were not meant for each other. The first appears to be written immediately after a break in their courtship:

> I am sorry that we could not have found a more congenial way in which to end our friendship. I almost said love but love typifies immortality, and as this ends it cannot be love. I appreciate your frankness. It repays me for my own to you . . . I feared this ending and I shall tell you why. I recall first kissing you. You said you had never kissed in return before. That was enough to thrill even so experienced and so youthful a man as myself. Then I remember your face, it appeared as though you were conscience-stricken. I never had seen anything so ghastly.

The decision to end the relationship seems to have been Olga's, and she seems to have told him that she could see "no future" in him. "Perhaps you are right," he muses, then springs to his own defense:

> I never have felt the need of practicality. Is a man a man who would refuse a loan without interest to a friend? That is your practicality . . . I am not of the multitude . . . more's the pity. Yet were I of the multitude I could forget the taste of your lips, your arms about me . . . This then is the end. Please do not feel hurt, and as I told you, have no tears, for tears have air waves, and my heart is a radio. I may be of a most diversified inheritance, but I have always believed in God, who, what or why, unlike you mortals that are sure, I am not sure.

But this was not goodbye. They renewed their relationship, and after some months of indeterminate courtship, EVM wrote again: "The distinct and different point of view that you hold towards life in general makes it utterly impossible to even have a starting point, where at least there might exist a common ground to reason upon." That might sound conclusive, but it's only the beginning of the letter. He reflects on his past:

> I never seemed to be right. Maybe I never shall be right, but here is where our paths separate. My family never thought well of me, I was different. My mother alone has faith, and when you coldly tell me you think I am doomed to failure you belong to that pack that has ever snarled at me and whom I hate since I can first remember.

Olga complains that in over a year of promises he has shown her "nothing material"—presumably in the way of making a living and supporting a family. "Can't you fathom my soul that maybe never will see anything material on this earth?" he replies, then rues the absence of "a counterpart of femininity that could mate with my own temperament and see the sky when I see the sky." The ostensible purpose of the letter is to assuage Olga, to repair a breach between them, but its main thrust is self-justification. EVM mingles promises and threats, emollience and defiance.

> I was and still am willing to drop my cloak of poetic aspirations towards that which may be aesthetic and non-productive and turn down your path. Don't you see that sacrifice I was willing to make for you? And yet you call me selfish . . . Olga don't you realize that you and I have not lost each other because there is no money but because we can't agree? A saint couldn't stand the constant bickering I have had to and the Lord knows I am no saint! I undertook law as a profession and I think I will do well in it, supplemented by such writing as I shall begin when I am better equipped. I cannot work for another. Nothing can make me . . . Other people! Other people be damned. Life is but a spark that blows out when least we expect it to. Life must be enjoyed. Not that I crave social activity, merely freedom of thought. This is my ultimatum.

The two of them ignored their better instincts and in January 1925, at the West End Synagogue in Manhattan, they solemnized "in conformity with the laws of the State of New York and the rites of the Jewish faith" what my mother described as "a marriage made in hell." Is it really that hard to reconcile the streetwise Tammany hotshot with the moody aspirant poet? They were both graspings at something EVM wanted to be, needed to be, could not be, at least not completely. Likewise his marriage to Olga. What drove him to ignore all the obvious objections, the predetermined failure of the enterprise, was his need for what she represented: normalcy, convention, a firmer place in New York's ethnic mosaic. Olga was a respectable young woman from a respectable and unmistakably Jewish family. In marriage to her, EVM sought release from that sense of never fitting in that had haunted his youth.

Soon after their marriage EVM, now twenty-five years old, began his long and singularly unsuccessful career in private legal practice. The young couple moved to the Bronx, where EVM joined the local Democratic Party, which was run then— as it was for another twenty-five years—by Ed Flynn, the Boss of the Bronx, who became the national chairman of the Democratic Party and a confidant of Roosevelt. For EVM, Flynn became a byword for the hypocrisy of organized politics, but also an alter ego, one of those larger-than-life public figures against whom EVM compulsively measured himself. In the Bronx, he later recalled, "Everybody and his cousin gets a letter. They usually read like . . . 'Dear Vince: Bearer is an extremely intelligent, etc. see what you can do for him.' Signed 'Ed Flynn' . . . But there is a code in the initials which means 'be nice—but no job' or 'this guy has something on us—put him to work.'"

The only note pertaining to his life in the second half of the twenties is a typewritten jotting made years later, referring to a particular night in August 1927:

I remember walking up the Grand Concourse. I was on my way to a well-known social-political clubhouse. When I arrived the place was crowded, especially the bar . . . Well, you know the spirit of camaraderie that makes for good bar fellows. There he was leaning against the bar, slightly tipsy.

"C'mon fellers," he bellows. "Have a drink on me—in five minutes they'll blast those lousy wop bastards' souls to hell!"

Factually he was partly right. At precisely eleven that night, Sacco and Vanzetti were due to go to the chair.*

That's why I had been walking around. That's how I came to be at the club—couldn't sleep . . . I refused to drink with him. He became abusive. I told him off—and plenty. Everybody was in on it. I sobered that barfly up that night. I guess I was pretty well labelled, socially and politically, thereafter.

But it took him another ten years to make his formal break with the Democratic Party.

---

* Nicola Sacco and Bartolomeo Vanzetti were Italian-born American anarchists convicted and sentenced to death for murder in 1920. The trial was conducted amid anti-radical and anti-immigrant hysteria, and was widely considered a miscarriage of justice. An international campaign in their defense, including the high-profile advocacy of future Supreme Court Justice Felix Frankfurter, failed to halt their execution.

3

An Intimate Accusation

The first person to call me a self-hating Jew was my father. It was in the autumn of 1967. Dad was thirty-nine, a successful business-man who was also, along with my mother, active in the civil rights and anti-war movements. I was the oldest of his five children and had already, at age fourteen, intoxicated by the ideals of justice and equality, begun my career as a foot soldier of the left. It was not only the first time I had been called a self-hating Jew, it was the first time the phrase, the idea, entered my consciousness, and it was a shock.

As a young man, against the family grain, my father had taken an interest in social and especially racial justice, and at college he was drawn to the Communist Party, which is how John Marqusee ended up with Janet Morand, Ed and Olga's daughter, the product of a very different strand of the New York Jewish tapestry. This was in the heyday of anti-Communist hysteria, of which my parents were first victims, then accomplices. After giving a speech against the Korean War at a student conference in Prague in 1950, dad was denounced as a traitor. His passport was seized. His father told the press that if his son had said such things, he was no son of his. It was in this period, I think, that he came to rely implicitly on my mother, the girlfriend who had stood stubbornly by his side when his life seemed most precarious.

They were married in 1952 and a year later I was born. Shortly after that, the FBI came knocking on the door. After months of pressure, from his own family as much as from the repressive organs of the state, my father, with my mother by his side, just as before, reached a deal and agreed to name names. "To this day we regret the mutual decision we made," my mother wrote. "It has been a source of incredible pain and shame." When my father, forty-five years after the event, lay dying, sapped by chronic pain and humiliating dependence, he went over it yet again, as he had with me many times. "I fucked it up," he moaned. The note of helplessness went right through me. There was no absolution anyone could give him. All the other contributions he'd made seemed outweighed by this ineradicable betrayal.

In the early 1960s, somehow having a wife and five kids, a big suburban home, a blossoming career as a real estate developer, was not enough, and he and my mother both threw themselves into the struggle in the American South, raising money, organizing meetings, sheltering young activists, supporting boycotts and pickets. In 1964 my dad went to Mississippi to deliver supplies to the beleaguered grassroots movement. It was a frightening time: they were now killing whites as well as blacks. Years later I learned that my mother was furious with my father over this adventure. She told him he was trying to compensate for his earlier sin, that he had no right to put his life at risk, to put this need for redemption above his obligation to his children. But in my eyes, the Mississippi visit, followed up by his participation in the Selma march a year later, made my father a hero, along with the other heroes of the movement, who for me in those days included everyone from Martin Luther King to Stokely Carmichael.

All of which partly—but only partly—explains why, when he lowered the boom on me in the autumn of 1967 by suggesting I was a self-hating Jew, it came as an uncushioned blow, an attack out of nowhere, or out of a place of which I was previously unaware. For my parents, as for others of their generation, the post-World War II realization of the scale and nature of the holocaust had prompted a return to organized Judaism. They felt a duty to respect and preserve this entity that had come so close to extinction, a need to embrace Judaism more explicitly, more positively, coupled with shame at the very idea of trying to escape one's Jewishness—when the Nazis had shown that it was inescapable. It was decided that I would be sent to Sunday school and receive the kind of Jewish education of which my parents themselves had no experience. Like others of my generation, I was expected to pay the price for their renewed sense of Jewishness. As a result of this, I quickly came to know more about Judaism than they did.

The first step for a young couple newly resident in the suburbs (we lived in Westchester County, twenty miles north of New York City) was joining a temple. Interestingly, my parents' first choice was a Reconstructionist congregation. This fourth major branch of organized American Jewry, the only one born and bred entirely in the USA, defined Judaism as an evolving religious civilization, left ultimate beliefs about the deity up to the individual, and stressed Jewish "peoplehood" and the centrality of building Israel. Crucially for my parents, it also embraced an ethic of social responsibility.

Reconstructionism was then in its infancy, and the congregation we joined was a small one, housed in an old mansion in a neglected neighborhood. I remember it as dark and cavernous, with creaking wooden floors and classes held in rooms without blackboards. The guiding spirit here was the rabbi, portly and smiling but nonetheless in deadly and perpetual earnest. I knew my parents respected him as a man of ideals and integrity. I was enrolled not only in Sunday school, where we learned Torah stories, but also in Hebrew classes. These were taught by an Israeli woman with a heavy accent and a heavier hand. I suspect we were even more incomprehensible to her than she was to us. When one of my classmates just couldn't fathom the difference between *ch* as in *church* and *ch* as in *chutzpah*, she berated him and he broke down in tears. I remember feeling profoundly relieved that I had been able to master this alien sound and had escaped, for the moment, the verbal lash.

In contrast to my own weekly routine, the only synagogue activities my parents took part in were the High Holidays, Passover (Reconstructionism favored a communal seder) and occasional meetings with our Sunday school teachers. It must have been in the course of one of these that complaints about the Israeli teacher's methods were voiced, and subsequently we had a visit from the jolly rabbi, who tried to explain to us that different cultures had different expectations of behavior. The teacher had been spoken to, but the students also had to do their part.

Sometime after this, my parents decided to leave the Reconstructionists and join the local Reform temple, the most popular in the area and the one whose approach to religion was least likely to disturb our family priorities. ("It was also all tied to being a giver to the Federation of Jewish Philanthropies and the United Jewish Appeal," my mother wrote.) The Reconstructionist rabbi asked for a chance to talk my parents out of the switch, and they must have felt they owed him at least a meeting. He came to our house with his usual smile, shook my hand, and joked with dad. Then I was sent upstairs to my room while the adults met downstairs in private. I was aware that for my parents this was an unpleasant task. And I felt complicit: in some way this was being done for my sake, to give me an easier life, because I'd chafed under the Israeli Hebrew teacher. But years later, I learned that I had nothing to do with it. "The rabbi decided that John should be bar mitzvahed," my mother recalled. "He was then in his mid-thirties and the idea intrigued him, mostly because he would enjoy being a novelty, but you couldn't get away with this unless you actually studied, and John was not ready for that kind of discipline."

Initially, I was anxious about going to a new synagogue, partly because it was new, and partly because it was a synagogue and my only experience of one had been weirdly disturbing. But as soon as our car turned into the blacktop driveway, I sensed this would be an entirely different proposition. The building was purpose-built and sleekly modern. The parking lot was crammed with station wagons. Dad escorted me to my classroom, where at once I felt relief. The room was filled with kids I knew from school. There was the one who played quarterback, the one who made funny noises, the one who had all the Batman comic books. So they were Jewish too. I hadn't known that. There was a map of Israel alongside a map of the USA, but apart from that it looked like the classrooms I knew from school, with colorful posters and a big blackboard.

I felt at home. We all did. We were the most comfortable Jews that had ever walked the planet. Not for us the longing of exile, the pain of dispersal. We were Americans in America. And we were, in particular, suburban American Jewish kids in the early 1960s, blithely self-confident about our privileges and our position in the world. Sublimely safe. That was the beginning of my eight years of Reform Jewish education, which sputtered to an end when I was fifteen and declared, in my confirmation speech, that God was dead and man was condemned to be free.

For the most part, I enjoyed Sunday school. It combined history, literature, philosophy, and politics, the subjects that excited me even before I knew their names, a world of abstract ideas and compelling narratives in which I revelled. I rarely studied but excelled at the exams. Once I was accused of cheating, or rather helping a friend to cheat. He sat next to me, and, without thinking much about it, I had allowed him to copy the answers from my test sheet. The two of us were hauled before the rabbi, who pointed out that we had given identical answers to all the questions. I insisted, and actually believed, that I hadn't cheated, since I hadn't benefited, and was astonished when the rabbi refused to swallow this and held me equally guilty of the crime.

Ritual, even in its diluted Reform version, always left me cold. It was something to be squirmed through. (The boy who made funny noises imitated the cantor's nasal tenor.) But the stories intrigued me, those weird Old Testament tales of sons cheating fathers, brothers selling brothers, spurned wives and martyred daughters, heroic figures who were also incongruous and flawed. Moses was forever irritated with both his people and his God. David and Jacob were deceitful men. Abraham was near murderer of his own son, Isaac. The lessons embedded in these tales were often hard to unravel, but I liked the sweep of them: the history of a whole people and its vexed but special relationship with God. We Jews kept getting it wrong and had to be corrected, and the voices of correction came either as destruction from without or dissent from within. Usually, it was the refusal to heed the latter that led to the former. The prophets warned and were ignored, but in the end they turned out to be right. Somehow all this perversity—on both sides—was for a purpose, testing and shaping us. From Ur to Canaan to Egypt to Canaan to Babylon to Canaan. From Europe to the USA. And back to Canaan. Dispersal and return. Suffering and redemption. We were taught to see this cycle of persecution and survival as more than a tale out of the Bible. The drama of Exodus had been re-enacted in modern times, with the holocaust and the state of Israel, and an end of Jewish history in the twin Zions of America and Israel.

We should have distrusted it from the beginning. It was too rounded.

We learned about the holocaust, the monstrous climax of a centuries-long saga of intolerance. We read *The Diary of Anne Frank*. We were shown a documentary: trenches in the death camps filled with naked emaciated bodies, piles of gold teeth, skull-faced survivors. "Arbeit Macht Frei." Even the kids who never paid attention, the kids who couldn't resist a wisecrack or a giggle, were rapt, solemn. When the film ended there was silence. The teacher then explained in a quiet voice that the lesson of all this horror was that "never again" should such a thing be allowed to happen. When I heard this, I assented with my whole being. It seemed the most undoubtedly truthful big truth I had ever heard, or maybe it was just the first one I had really grasped. Back then I thought it meant "never again" to anyone, anywhere, not just never again to the Jews.

Only twenty years separated us from the events in the film, yet they seemed to have taken place in a remote past. The victims, we were told, were people like us, but we could not imagine ourselves in their place. How could we? We were the most comfortable Jews the world had ever known. We knew Jews as powerful, as achievers in every imaginable field, as world leaders, as inventors and reformers, as leaders in business and champions of democracy and tolerance and the higher civic virtues. The notion that we were or could ever be taken for anything other than bona fide Americans never occurred to us. It never occurred to us that there might be any reason to deny you were a Jew. We were senators and governors and Nobel Prize winning scientists and novelists and movie stars and even baseball players. (Sandy Koufax wouldn't pitch on the Sabbath.) It was, self-evidently, a good thing to be a Jew—a blessing, an advantage, especially as it seemed you could be a Jew without actually having to follow many prescriptions or proscriptions. The Catholic kids had a much tougher regime.

The goods of the world were accessible to us as to none of our forebears. The dominant culture was our culture. The synagogue molded itself to this world, blending with the suburban landscape, streamlined with its sloping roof and giant windows. Poor Jews were a memory, a postcard image from a Hollywood past. We were taken on a Sunday school outing to the Lower East Side, the land of our forefathers. The Jews in the street didn't look like us. We were taken to Katz's delicatessen. We ate and ate. Jewishness, as much as anything, was food—tastes of pastrami, pickles, rye bread, gefilte fish, chopped liver, smoked fish. Our view of the shtetl was Chagall-tinted. The modernist Jewish folklorist with a passion for Jesus was a strange transmission belt for the only certified Jewish imagery we knew. (It was not until many years later, when I saw Chagall's earlier, hard-edged fantasies, that I came to savor his mordant poetry.)

Then there was *Fiddler.* A number of the kids had already seen it, it had been plugged in Sunday school, and I was charged up with anticipation as I arrived with my dad at the theater, only to discover that the star of the hit show, Zero Mostel, was indisposed for the evening. That meant more to my dad than to me: he was fully aware that the role of Tevye had completed Mostel's public rehabilitation after he had languished on the McCarthyite blacklist for more than a decade.* Even without Mostel, I was entranced. The book and the presentation had a clarity and gentle humor that made the plot and its social implications easy to follow, even for an eleven-year-old. The sets themselves were apparently evocative to older members of the audience, who sighed in recognition at the customs depicted on stage. "Tea in a glass!" a woman sitting near me intoned, an observation that returned to me many years later, when I traveled in Morocco, Turkey, and Afghanistan.

Fiddler on the Roof was an origin story for American Jews, a recollection of the world left behind in eastern Europe, an account of the upheavals that had brought us to where we were and made us who we were. Anti-semitism (depicted in a highly sanitized pogrom) was the context, but the real drama derived from the incursions of modernity and secularism into shtetl provincialism. As Tevye's pragmatic-fatalistic faith is tested by his daughter's marriages—to a poor tailor, a socialist agitator and finally, unthinkably, a gentile—his adaptability reaches its limits. *Fiddler* was easily digestible *yiddishkeit* for the 1960s, but I suspect if it were written today, its approach would be different. The threats of Bolshevism and rationalism, of intermarriage and women's freedom, might not be depicted with such equanimity, and the

---

* The leftist Mostel had been named as a Communist to the House Un-American Activities Committee in 1952 and appeared before the committee in 1955. He refused to name names or to answer questions about his political activities.

near-complete absence of any references to Palestine or Israel would surely be remedied.

From an early age I conceived of myself as a rationalist and though I made spasmodic efforts at belief, I never felt a divine presence. During "prayer," I was acutely aware of the gap between what I was supposed to be thinking and what was actually going through my head. But in the end what alienated me from the synagogue was not the make-believe of the after-life or the all-seeing omnipotence of an invisible God. Not in this synagogue. Here the absolutes were kept in the background. God was there, mentioned in the prayers, but he had been discreetly updated and denatured. No one seemed over-concerned about his judgement.

So what was the creed we were taught in Sunday school? It was not about God. It was about the Jews. A singular people who had given wonderful gifts to the world and whom the world had treated cruelly. A people who were persecuted. A people who survived. A people who triumphed. Despite the holocaust, we were not a nation of losers, of victims. There was a redemptive denouement. There was Israel, a modern Jewish homeland, a beacon to the world. A shiny new state with a squeaky clean people. Up-to-date, Coke-drinking people like us. Liberals, like us. Bearers of democracy and civilization, making the desert bloom. A little America in the Middle East.

Our Jewish history was full of heroes who stood up for the truth, who defied the powerful. The civil rights movement in the South was our cause, not only because the Negroes were the latter-day Jews, slaves in Egypt land, but also because so many Jews were involved in the movement. The synagogue raised funds for voter registration projects in Mississippi. The rabbi excoriated the Southern bigots. "Justice, justice shall you pursue," he quoted from Deuteronomy. On the wall of the temple's multipurpose room the words of Isaiah were inscribed: "They shall beat their swords into ploughshares, and their spears into pruning hooks. Nation shall not lift up sword against nation, neither shall they learn war any more." This was a Jewish teaching but we knew it had now become a world teaching, a watchword for the United Nations. This was further confirmation that we were a people of enlightened progress.

For the over-subscribed High Holidays our temple rented the multi-seated White Plains County Center arena (later I saw the Harlem Globetrotters and the Lovin' Spoonful play there). In 1964, with the presidential election weeks away, the rabbi used his Rosh Hashanah sermon to attack the Republican candidate, Barry Goldwater, and inveigh against the threat from the right wing— the eternal seedbed of anti-semitism. What was remarkable was that only one out of the many thousands in attendance walked out. In the election, the Texas Baptist Lyndon Johnson received some 90 percent of the Jewish vote (though Goldwater's paternal grandfather was a Jew from Poland). Two years later, LBJ became the first US president to sell warplanes to the Israelis.*

Israel was both our own cause, a Jewish cause, and a moral cause, a universal cause. Like America. A land without people for a people without land. Like America. That was the gift we received in Sunday school—an extra country. For us there were two nations and best of all we didn't have to choose between them. As Jews and Americans we enjoyed a double birthright and a double privilege.

"And I will make of thee a great nation," the Lord promised Abraham, "And I will bless them that bless thee and curse them that curse thee." The coming home of the Jews to the land of our forefathers completed the epic saga stretching back to Genesis and

---

* But it was under his successor, Richard Nixon, that US military support for Israel really expanded, from $76.8 million in 1968 to more than $600 million in 1971. As the Watergate tapes revealed, Nixon regarded Jews with paranoid hostility, and a substantial majority of Jewish voters backed his opponents in both 1968 and 1972. Nixon acted as he did not because of pressure from the Israel lobby but because of his vision of US strategic interests.

ensured it ended with a huge upswing in mood: from near-annihilation in the holocaust to the pride of statehood in a few short years. We took this outcome less as a sign of the divine inspiration of the ancient prophets than as another manifestation of the order and justice that generally prevailed in our world. It was a testament to progress and the Jewish mastery of progress. Thanks to America and Israel, the Jews were safe at last. Thanks to America and Israel, we all had two homelands. We could visit Israel and work on a kibbutz, which was like a grown-up summer camp. We were taught to revere Ben Gurion and his heir, the Jewish-American farm girl Golda Meir. In our Sunday school textbooks the Israelis looked like us: white, youthful, healthy—American teenagers with Hebrew names. And the country they were building looked familiar, with modern buildings and girls in jeans. These were Jews who read books but also drove tractors and tanks.

As always, the Jews had enemies. Israel was menaced by "Arabs" (not "Palestinians," a word never uttered in our synagogue). They were exotically attired bedouin—people who did not have or want a home. In our Sunday school texts, they appeared swarthy, coarse, ignorant, duplicitous. These descendants of Pharaoh and the Philistines seemed curiously ungrateful and irrational. For no reason at all they hated us. We watched the movie *Exodus*, with Paul Newman as Palmach commando Ari Ben Canaan. It was the story of Chanukkah all over again: the Maccabees defying the ruthless might of the Syrians.

I was intrigued by the holidays. Simchas Torah, a year marked out in chapters of a book. Succoth, the Jewish Thanksgiving, was a harvest festival, a deeply exotic idea to kids who knew food only from supermarkets. Purim commemorated the revenge of integrity. Yom Kippur disturbed me (I knew I should atone for something but wasn't sure what), but Pesach was special: the food (Olga visited with matzoh balls and latkes), the slouching at the table, the search for the afikomen, Elijah's cup. Most of all, it was the story that pulled me in: that epic of liberation, with the oppressed triumphing over their oppressors, right over might. It was an intoxicating narrative, as exciting and satisfying as the food. People should be careful when they teach this stuff to kids. It sinks in deeper than they realize. It can even turn someone against the land promised them in the Pesach story.

One day Dad took me for an outing in Manhattan. As I had become a keen camper, we made a pilgrimage to Abercrombie and Fitch to buy a hunting knife which I had seen in a catalogue and on which I had set my heart. Afterwards, we went for a meal at Ratners, the legendary Jewish restaurant in the Lower East Side. The hunting knife in its leather sheath sat on the table, much to the dismay of the elderly Jewish waiter. "For cutting the leaves of a book a Jewish boy uses a knife . . ." he said. My dad was delighted by the episode, but I felt tongue-tied and ashamed.

In the summer of 1965, I persuaded my parents to send me, along with two others from our neighborhood, to a Boy Scout camp. We slept in saggy, gray-green tents pitched in a small clearing in a forest in the Catskills. The tents provided minimal protection from the wind and rain and even less from the mosquitoes, which feasted on our tender twelve-year-old flesh. We were soon covered in bites, which we scratched, and which turned to scabs. After a while, we gave up battling the mosquitoes and took to watching them land on our bare arms or legs, insert their needles into our skin, then fill their tiny bulbous bodies with our red blood.

The food was terrible and there wasn't much of it. When we were taken on a hike to a mountaintop with a long-range view, we failed to carry enough water with us, and at the summit we found ourselves utterly parched. Desperate for moisture, we scoured the brush for blueberries, stuffing any we could find in our dry mouths. It became a kind of delirium, with all of us giggling and showing each other our blue-stained teeth.

Like nearly all the members of our local Scout troop, the three of us were Jews. However, it didn't even dawn on me for several days that we were the only ones in the camp, until a kid named Jimmy, a lanky kid with stooped shoulders and a loud voice, walked up to me, looked into my face with a broad grin, and said: "Hey, you're a kike, aren't you?"

"I'm Jewish."

"Yeah, you know how I could tell?"

I stared back at him blankly, my mind frozen.

" 'Cause your shoe's untied!"

Without thinking, I looked down. It was true. My shoe was untied. Again, without thinking, I bent down to tie it. The laughter erupted and I felt something deeply unpleasant rush through me, which later I came to understand as the blood of shame and embarrassment and impotence. The other kids at the camp were mostly Catholic, Irish and Italian, and though they read the same comic books as us, they all seemed tougher, more streetwise, more adept at sarcasm and insult. I had been intimidated by them even before they began the Jew-baiting.

When one of us stumbled or dropped something or made any kind of clumsy error we were met by howls of "Being Jewish again?" or "That's a Jew thing to do" or "What a Jew!" or "Now I know you're a real Jew." Then there were the jokes. "Hey, Mike, you know why Jews have big noses?" ('cause the air is free) or "What's the difference between a pizza and a Jew?" (a pizza doesn't scream when you put it in the oven).

We already knew that anti-semitism existed, but that knowledge had come from lessons, from books, from stories told of a distant world. We knew anti-semitism as something that had been triumphed over. But now, like EVM in the army, we discovered that there was a world out there where Jews were not the norm, where some people hated us for no reason at all. I was confident that the repartee of my fellow Scouts was ignorant and idiotic, that I was superior to them for not thinking or talking the way they did. Yet I also felt inferior for not being able to stop the abuse, for not being able to stand up for myself in terms they would understand. There was no doubt in my mind that people who judged others by their race or religion were plain wrong, and especially wrong about the Jews. My fear was that they might be right about me: that I was a klutz, that I was impractical, that I was clumsy, weak, and hesitant. Though I never for a moment accepted that Jews were worthy objects of derision, I certainly felt that I was.

It was worse for the one black kid in the camp. Mornings often began with the cry, "What's for breakfast? Fried nigger on toast!" met with hilarity on the part of some and uneasy silence among others. I desperately wanted to be accepted by these kids but I also wanted to leave, to walk away from the whole dismaying experience. There was a stream near the camp. I caught a tiny fish and cooked it for myself, feeling pleased with the whole process until Jimmy spotted me and said, "Hey, that's not kosher, you're not supposed to eat that." For a moment I feared that he might be right, but I wolfed down the fish defiantly.

Looking back, I wonder how much of the Jew-baiting was just Jimmy, who had probably picked up the habit from his family and wanted to show off with it. I wonder how much the others just followed his lead, how much they had already been exposed to, how much they really embraced. I think most joined in for the obvious reason: Jews were being picked on and it was a relief to them that they weren't Jews.

Mostly we suffered in what we hoped was a dignified and superior silence. Sometimes we answered haughtily, "You sound just like Hitler," or "That's what Hitler said," certain that the Nazi reference would trump them. Sometimes we tried another tack. "Jonas Salk was a Jew, he cured polio." "Yeah, and Einstein . . . Jerry Lewis . . . Tony Curtis . . ." We threw the names back at them, maintaining a tone of reason, while grizzling under their utter and seemingly undentable unreasonableness.

In any case we were outnumbered. And they also enjoyed the significant advantage of being familiar with a greater variety of obscenities and sexual references than we were. Our resort to rational argument only made them more scornful of us. Nonetheless, we still joined with them in the daily activities, worked on projects and played games together, and for a time we really would be just a bunch of boys interacting without distinction. Until the Jew-baiting started again, leaving the three of us sulky and isolated.

I don't know at what point I resolved to appeal to a superior authority. The name-calling seemed to have been going on for an eternity (it couldn't have been more than two weeks). The scoutmaster was himself no more than twenty. He supervised us with good humor and with a light touch goaded us into doing things we didn't want to do. He often asked me about the books I was reading, and it was during one of these chats that I told him some of the other boys were criticizing us for being Jews and it wasn't fair.

I remember the sudden change in his expression. His neck went rigid and there was a grave look in his eyes. "We'll see about that," he muttered. We watched as he took Jimmy and some of the others aside and gave them a stern lecture. Somehow, I knew he was telling them about the Jews, about the holocaust. The boys looked somber, discomfited. After that, the teasing stopped. But the mosquitoes didn't. My parents were appalled at the state they found me in when they came to visit, and with my ready assent, they took me home, though the camp season had several more weeks to run.

For several years I took twice-weekly Hebrew lessons in preparation for my bar mitzvah. Then came a year of lavish celebrations, services, dinners, dances in marquees on suburban lawns and ballrooms in midtown hotels. Mountains of gifts. Checks or bonds or little stakes in IBM or ITT. Compared to some, my own bar mitzvah was a low-key affair; my mother disapproved of the conspicuous display made by some of our neighbors. I got the checks, I got a set of left-handed golf clubs, but better yet I got elegant illustrated editions of Thomas Paine's *Rights of Man* and Thoreau's *Walden* from a couple who were close friends of my parents from their left-wing student days. There seemed nothing in the least incongruous about offering such secular testaments as bar mitzvah gifts. I still read today the inscription the couple added to the astutely chosen texts: "These two books provide the always exhilarating blend of the search for individual freedom and oneness with nature, with the struggle for political freedom and social responsibility." Thus my reaching out to non-Jewish sources began within my Jewish milieu. Thoreau and Paine were not Jews but they were very much part of my liberal democratic American-Jewish legacy.

Within weeks of my bar mitzvah, every word of Hebrew vanished from my head. The language had been learned solely in order to complete a public performance, a rite, that had little meaning for me. I certainly did not feel that I had become a man, an adult, a member of a congregation, that I was enfranchised. Instead, I began to look for and find some of that sense of growth, of emergence as an autonomous human being, in politics, in the world of the left, in battles against racism and for civil liberties. Soon I just could not stop talking about the Vietnam War and how it was wrong on every count. This, in 1966, did not make me popular. So why was I so determined to pursue the course? Did I like being different? Was I showing off, calling attention to myself? Yes, I was. But there were other ways to do that and I did not choose them.

Like EVM, I enjoyed the idea of being part of a vanguard of truth-seekers and rebels. I was sustained in opposing the Vietnam War, supporting the Black Panthers and the Yippies by the proud tradition of dissent I'd imbibed as a package that combined Americanism, Jewishness, Thoreau, Galileo, and a gallery of figures of conscience. My Jewish role models shifted: Lenny Bruce, Paul Krassner, Dylan, Ginsberg, Abbie Hoffman, Norman Mailer, Andrew Goodman and Michael Schwerner.

For years it was a family tradition to buy sandwiches once a week from our neighborhood deli. Here I acquired a lifelong taste for pastrami, corn beef with the works, fresh rye and new pickles. One morning in mid-1967, aged fourteen, I went off on the familiar errand with my dad. The old man who owned the deli—his thick glasses held together by Scotch tape—seemed genuinely distressed by the long, unkempt hair I'd grown since he'd last seen me. "Mike, you used to be the all-American boy."

"He still is," my dad chirped in my defense. But in fact I knew I was mutating into something other than that all-American boy.

In Sunday school, Israel's victory in the Six Day War was a great moment of Jewish pride. I don't remember much thanking of God, and no mourning for the victims on either side, just a sustained note of elated triumph. To cap all our other Jewish achievements, to confirm our eminence, we had now proved ourselves masters in war. It had taken us just six days to defeat Arab armies attacking from all sides, to sweep across the Sinai, unite Jerusalem, drive the enemy back across the Jordan. No one spoke then, not in my hearing, of the beginning of an occupation. We had redrawn the lines on the map. That was our prerogative. That was justice. We were unbeatable and we were righteous. Israel married moral virtue and military strength—another sign that we lived in an age of order and progress, that all we wished for would be ours. When a friend who liked to tease me about my anti-Vietnam War views suggested I might not support Israel against the Arabs, I was outraged and offended.

I'm not sure exactly when or how I began to doubt. But I remember what happened the first time I expressed that doubt. It was a few months after the June war. A special visitor came to our Sunday school class. He was in his early twenties, with thick fair hair falling over his forehead, a snappy sports jacket and polished loafers. Some of the girls whispered that he was cute. He had an accent but it was nothing like our grandparents' accents. He looked and dressed like us but he had been a soldier in a war, and that made him an alien being. Smiling, he perched himself casually on the front of the teacher's desk and told us about the remarkable achievements of the Israeli army. He told us that the Arabs had planned a sneak attack but had met with more than they bargained for. They were bad fighters, undisciplined soldiers. And they were better off now, under Israeli rule. "You have to understand these are ignorant people. They go to the toilet in the street."

Now something akin to this I had heard before. I had heard it from the white Southerners I'd been taught to look down upon. I had heard it from people my parents and my teachers described as prejudiced and bigoted. So I raised my hand and when called upon I expressed my opinion, as I'd been taught to do. It seemed to me that what our visitor had said was, well, racist.

I felt the eyes of the teacher and the other kids turn on me. They were used to my spouting radical opinions, but this time I had gone too far. Angrily, the teacher told me I didn't have any idea what I was saying and that there would be no discourtesy to guests in his classroom. The young Israeli ranted bitterly about Arab propaganda and how the Israelis treated the Arabs better than any of the Arab rulers did.

I can't remember how long it was after that that I decided to share this experience and my thoughts on it with my family. This was something I was usually encouraged to do and for which I usually received approbation. We were sitting around the dinner table—all seven of us—so it must have been a weekend, because during the week my father rarely made it home from the city in time to eat with us. I launched into my story about the Israeli in Sunday school and how what he said was racist. I had been thinking about the matter and now added, for my family's benefit, a further opinion. It was wrong for one country to take over another, or part of another, by military force. If the US was wrong in Vietnam—and that was a given around our dinner table—then Israel was wrong in taking over all that Arab land. I was reasoning by analogy, and nobody had yet told me that some analogies were off-limits.

For some time I remained unaware that my father was listening to me not with approval but with rising fury. When he barked, "Enough already!" the shift was disturbingly abrupt. Like my Sunday school teacher, he made me feel that I'd said something obscene. Then he drew a breath, turned to me and seemed to soften. "I think you need to look at why you're saying what you're saying," he said, and then the softness vanished. "There's some Jewish self-hatred there."

I felt then, and still feel now, when I look back on it, deeply and frustratingly misunderstood. My motives had nothing to do with self-hatred or any feeling about being Jewish. Nor did they have anything to do with compassion for a people—the Palestinians—about whom I knew nothing. I was merely following, as best I could, and in typical fourteen-year-old fashion, what seemed to be the dictates of logic. If in following them, the results appeared to defy assumptions, then that just made them more curious and compelling. Judging people by their color or religion was wrong. Racism, making a generalization about a whole people, stereotyping a whole people, was wrong. Taking over other countries was wrong, even if they attacked you (it was years before I learned that it was Israel that had launched this war, justified at the time by Abba Eban, American liberal Jewry's favorite Israeli, as a "pre-emptive" strike). Among the shibboleths I was brought up on was the belief that "my country right or wrong" was wrong. No one liked to insist more than my dad that if you really loved your country you criticized its flaws. Surely that also applied to religion, and "my religion right or wrong" must also be wrong. I was only trying to apply general principles to a particular case. It was an exercise in logic, an exercise in teenage stubbornness. I was unprepared for the response, with its implication that I did not know myself, coming from my father's lips. An attack on my selfhood.

I was startled and bewildered by the phrase "Jewish self-hatred." I didn't know what it meant. I hadn't imagined that Jews would hate themselves, or that anyone would think that I hated myself. The charge seemed so farfetched, yet so personal. And so bitterly unfair. Burning from head to toe, I threw down knife and fork and left the table in a huff, pounding up the stairs to my room, where I hurled myself on my bed and wrestled with my frustration.

Some might by now have concluded that the roots of my anti-Zionism lie in Oedipal trauma. For sure, this was a deeply distressing incident. Later, I looked back on it as my first political disagreement with my father, later still as one of a number of raw episodes in our relationship, most of which had nothing to do with politics. Now, looking again at the history behind the incident, I see more clearly why the opinions I was expressing would have infuriated nearly everyone in my father's milieu in those days. To me, they were a logical development from the agreed shared ground of democratic liberalism, but to liberals of my father's generation they were an insolent abrogation of that shared ground. Israel was a just cause and a Jewish cause, those who opposed Israel were anti-semites, and the only Jew who could fail to recognize these truths was a self-hating Jew. Without in the least intending to, I had breached a taboo.

4

The Emancipation of the Jews

What is the great task of our age? It is emancipation. Not only that of the Irish, the Greeks, the Frankfurt Jews, the blacks in the West Indies and such oppressed peoples; it is the emancipation of the whole world, especially of Europe, which has come of age and is now tearing itself free from the iron leading-strings of the privileged class, the aristocracy.

Heinrich Heine, *Pictures of Travel*[1]

In Sunday school, we learned about Spinoza and Moses Mendelssohn, two in a long series of Jewish geniuses, and about Napoleon tearing down the ghetto walls. But overall the story of Jewish emancipation in Europe was sadly neglected. Compared to the saga of Israel or the memory of the shtetl or the progress of the Jews in the USA, not to mention the chronicles of the Bible, it was a footnote. More time was spent on Chasidism than Haskalah. Yet here we were, the beneficiaries of emancipation, Western Jews sitting in a Reform synagogue whose history was inseparable from that development.

In popular Jewish consciousness, Jewish emancipation has steadily lost ground. There are a number of reasons for this. It's a protracted, fragmented process, beginning in the mid-eighteenth century, and for the next 150 years moving in small eddies back and forth across the European continent. There is no emancipation proclamation, no moment of freedom at midnight, no May 15, 1948. Though individual Jews and Jewish groups played a significant role in shaping it, there was no mass Jewish agitation for emancipation until the Bund. The deliverers of Jewish emancipation were wars and revolutions, crises and upheavals in which, for the most part, the Jews themselves played only a marginal role.

The awkward fact about emancipation is that it was always in part a struggle within Jewry, a struggle against Jewish authority, against rabbis, who even in our Reform milieu were treated with a deference that rarely appears in the literature of the Haskalah. Most significantly, emancipation has become tainted by association with "assimilation" and "self-hatred." The story is not only one of the emancipation of Jews from the legal restraints imposed on them for centuries, but emancipation of Jews from the rule of other Jews, and even sometimes from the constraints of Judaism or Jewishness.

In 1655, even before he'd published a word, Spinoza was accused of heresy (materialism and "contempt for the Torah"), and at the age of twenty-four he was excommunicated from the Amsterdam Synagogue. Spinoza was the son of Portuguese Jews, a lens grinder who wrote in Latin and spoke Dutch, Hebrew and Ladino, and his view of Jewishness was of a piece with his broader rationalism, with his insistence that "no one is bound to live as another pleases, but is the guardian of his own liberty." In 1660 the synagogue petitioned the municipal authorities to declare Spinoza a "menace to all piety and morals." In his *Tractatus Theologico-Politicus*, denounced by the Calvinist Church Council as a "work forged in Hell by a renegade Jew and the Devil," he argues:

> As men's habits of mind differ, so that some more readily embrace one form of faith, some another, for what moves one to pray may move another only to scoff, I conclude . . . that everyone should be free to choose for himself the foundations of his creed, and that

faith should be judged only by its fruits; each would then obey
God freely with his whole heart, while nothing would be publicly
honoured save justice and charity.[2]

Spinoza was one of the first modern critics of scripture, subjecting
the Hebrew text to the kind of analysis previously reserved for
secular works. "I learnt that the the law revealed by God to Moses
was merely the law of the individual Hebrew state, therefore it
was binding on none but the Hebrews, and not even on Hebrews
after the downfall of their nation." He was also a pioneering, pre-
Freudian student of the emotions, which he identified as the
source of human conduct. Above all, he was a stubborn prophet of
intellectual freedom. "Religious and political prejudices are the
cause of all tyranny," he wrote. "As a negation of reasonable
thoughts, the fruit of a terrible fear, prejudice obliges the people to
believe blindly in the tyrant, to adore him as a god." His studies
led him to conclude that "in regard to intellect and true virtue,
every nation is on a par with the rest, and God has not in these
respects chosen one people rather than another." As for the Jews,
"their continuance so long after dispersion . . . [has] nothing
marvellous in it." They "have been preserved in great measure by
Gentile hatred."

Moses Mendelssohn was dubbed a "second Spinoza," but his
impact on Jewish—and European—life was much greater. A
rabbinical scholar from a humble Yiddish-speaking home in
Dessau, he made his way to Berlin and taught himself European
culture, mastering German, French, English, Greek and Latin.
Under Frederick the Great, Prussia was emerging as an economic,
military and intellectual powerhouse, and with the support of elite
Christians, Mendelssohn established himself as a renowned es-
sayist and a major theoretician of the German Enlightenment.

Like other advocates of Jewish equality at the time, Mendelssohn saw legal emancipation as going hand in hand with internal
reform. He called upon Jews to renounce those customs—notably

usury—that gave them a bad name. He belittled Yiddish as a "jargon" that "has contributed more than a little to the uncivilized bearing of the common man,"[3] and he urged Jews to speak German, embrace German culture and German patriotism. At the same time he called for and encouraged a revival of classical Hebrew. His German translation of the Hebrew Bible was banned by the rabbis, who also resisted his attempts to reform Jewish education. He argued for an end to the communal and commercial licenses enjoyed by a minority of Jews, but for which the majority took the blame.

Mendelssohn blended caution and boldness. "I am a member of an oppressed people that finds itself compelled to appeal to the good will of the authorities for protection and shelter," he reminded readers. In 1763 the king granted Mendelssohn, then aged thirty-five, the status of Protected Jew (*Schutz-Jude*)—under which he was permitted to continue to live and work in Berlin. His discretion and reluctance to engage in full-tilt public combat over the Jews now make him seem, to some, an Uncle Tom, overeager to make concessions to the enemy. But for Mendelssohn, Jewish emancipation—and his own intellectual freedom—required a change in the place of religion in general in society. "I hate all religious disputes, especially those conducted before the eyes of the public," he explained. "Experience teaches that they are useless. They produce hatred rather than clarification."[4]

In 1769 he was called upon to defend and define himself by the Protestant cleric-scientist Johann Kasper Lavater, who challenged Mendelssohn either to refute what Lavater considered the rationalist arguments for Christianity or to convert. Mendelssohn was affronted by Lavater's demand: "Among all the heretics known to him personally, I cannot be said to be his one and only friend." He acknowledged that Judaism like Christianity and other religions was swathed in a "pestilential vapor of hypocrisy and superstition." In particular, he sought to rid rabbinism of the tradition of disputatious "pilpul," which he regarded as a "a sterile sort of acumen." He could see little benefit in extending its competitive spirit into Christian–Jewish relations. As for himself, he intended to "change the world's despicable image of the Jew not by writing disputatious essays but by living an exemplary life."[5]

In *Jerusalem, or On Religious Power and Judaism*, published in 1783, three years before his death, Mendelssohn subjects clericalism (of whatever denomination) to corrosive scrutiny, while at the same time arguing that Judaism has a place in the modern world. He reminds the reader how shocking is "that inadmissible idea of the eternality of punishment in hell—an idea the abuse of which has made not many fewer men truly miserable in this life than it renders, in theory, unhappy in the next."[6] Conflict between state and religion gives rise to "immeasurable evils," but worse comes when the two are in agreement: "for they seldom agree but for the purpose of banishing a third moral entity, liberty of conscience, which knows how to derive some advantage from their disunity."[7] Both religions and states should be stripped of coercive, punitive powers over citizens' minds. If beliefs, or rituals, are forced on individuals, they cease to be truly religious:

> Reader! To whatever visible church, synagogue or mosque you may belong! See if you do not find more true religion among the host of those excommunicated than among the far greater host of those who excommunicated them.[8]

As someone who believed that "not a single point in the entire sum of human knowledge . . . is to be placed beyond question,"[9] Mendelssohn asked of Judaism the same question he asked of Christianity. He argued that Judaism was based on laws, rules of life, not a revealed theology, and to that extent was in conformity with reason and had a right to be considered a distinct faith with its own merits. He believed the Hebrew Bible was "an inexhaustible treasure of rational truths," but that with the destruction of the temple, and the end of the ancient Judaean state, many of its prescriptions no longer pertained. "The civil bonds of the nation were dissolved" and as a result Judaism "as religion, knows no punishment, no other penalty than the one the remorseful sinner imposes on himself." As for "the Mosaic constitution" adumbrated in the Torah, "it has disappeared, and only the Omniscient knows among what people and in what century something similar may be seen." Mendelssohn kept the sabbath, observed kashrut (Jewish dietary laws) and attended synagogue, but dispensed with customs he considered relevant only to the Hebrews' ancient experience as a nation-state. "Adapt yourselves to the morals and constitution of the land to which you have been removed," he advised his fellow sons of Jacob, "but hold fast to the religion of your fathers, too."[10]

Mendelssohn's life overlaps by thirty years that of the Baal Shem Tov, the founder of Chasidism. Both were products of the intersection of Jewish life with the larger historical forces of migration and modernity (and the very different ways these were experienced in Germany and in eastern Europe). Yet where the Baal Shem Tov is considered a touchstone of Jewish folk authenticity, entirely intrinsic to Jewry, Mendelssohn is tainted with cosmopolitan inauthenticity, seen as extrinsic to Jewishness (after all, his grandchildren converted to Christianity). The Baal Shem Tov, whatever his merits as a storyteller and dispenser of proverbial wisdom, and his significance as the progenitor of an enduring religious movement, never once raised his voice for the freedom of Jewry from legal oppression, a public cause to which Mendelssohn was unwaveringly steadfast.

In Sunday school we certainly never learned the name Zalkind Hourwitz, though we should have. Born in 1751 in a Polish village, he somehow made his way to Paris and in 1774 was living in a hovel on the Rue St Denis, one of a small, impoverished community of about 1,000 Parisian Jews—all present in the city on sufferance, since the fourteenth-century edict of expulsion had never been overturned. Later, Hourwitz recalled that he learned his ABCs from a Hebrew—German dictionary, and that at the age of twenty-two he was unfamiliar with the use of a fork. He makes his first appearance in print in 1783, responding to criticisms of the alleged ill-behavior of Polish Jews: "The Polish, French, English, Irish and Portuguese, are they all responsible for the massacres and regicides committed by some scoundrels of their nation? . . . Why not permit the same equity to the Jews?"[11] What's bracing even now in Hourwitz's advocacy for the Jews was his insistence that Jews have as much right to be rogues and fools as members of any other group. In the context of a debate in which it was widely assumed that Jews collectively required either vindication or reform, his unapologetic and realistic response to criticisms of Jews (and ethnic or national groups in general) was a liberating step forward, one that many in Europe and North America have yet to take.

In 1787, the Royal Society of Arts and Sciences in Metz posed a question for a public essay competition: "Are there means for making the Jews happier and more useful in France?" Hourwitz's entry, his *Apologie des Juifs*, was ultimately one of three joint prize winners published in 1789. What's stunning about Hourwitz's essay is his critique of the assumptions buried in the question:

> Are so many verbiages and citations necessary to prove that a Jew is a man, and that it is unjust to punish him from his birth onward for real or supposed vices that one reproaches in other men with whom he has nothing in common but religious belief? And what would the French say if the Academy of Stockholm had proposed, twelve years ago, the following question: "Are there means for making Catholics more useful and happier in Sweden?"

Hourwitz went so far as to mock the would-be reformers. "After having oppressed them for many centuries, without even knowing why, one takes it into one's head finally to discuss seriously not if it is necessary to absolve them honorably and pay them damages and interest for their long oppression, but if it is necessary to continue to oppress them."[12] His answer to the essay question was brisk and precise:

> The means of making the Jews happy and useful? This is it: stop making them unhappy and useless. Give them, or rather return to them the right of citizens, which you've denied them against all divine and human laws.[13]

Hourwitz argued that Jews should enjoy the right to reside where they liked, to acquire land, to practise all professions and trades. In keeping with the Haskalah, he called on Jews to reform themselves. The use of Hebrew or Yiddish should be forbidden in account books. Usury should be banned. Jews should attend public schools, study secular subjects, and learn French. Above all, there had to be an end to the "despotism" of the rabbis.

> Rabbis and leaders must be severely forbidden from claiming the least authority over their co-religionists outside of the synagogue, from prohibiting entry and honors to those who cut their beards, who curl their hair, who dress like Christians, who go to the theater, or who fail to observe some other custom that is irrelevant to their religion and only introduced by superstition in order to distinguish the Jews from other peoples.

Hourwitz defended the Jews' right to observe kosher laws, to marry their own kind and to preserve their faith and rituals. He noted that the claim to chosenness, so resented by Christians, was in fact shared by a wide variety of Christian sects. Internal reform was necessary, but it should not be a precondition of legal emancipation. Hourwitz refused to blame the victim. "The Jews are foreigners neither by nature nor by their religion but only as a result of the injustice of regarding them as such."[14] He always refused to accept that Jews had to cease to be Jews as a price of citizenship or that they should have to show that they were worthy of citizenship as a corporate body. He had no truck with the popular notion of Jewish regeneration because "it is not the Jews but the Christians whom one should regenerate."

In dismissing the idea of collective guilt, Hourwitz is in advance of even the more radical of the *philosophes*. Reading Voltaire and Rousseau had transformed Hourwitz. They were the rocks on which he built the edifice of his own thought. But Voltaire and Rousseau calumnied the Jews. "True, some celebrated writers, modern apostles of tolerance, are also intolerant towards Jews," Hourwitz observed, "but a celebrated writer, like all others, is susceptible to error and passion."[15] Considering the specific case of Voltaire, he argued that the Jews should issue him a pardon, weighing "all the bad he has said of them" against "the good he has done for them albeit without wishing it." If Jews "have enjoyed a little rest during these last years, it is due to the progress of enlightenment to which Voltaire in his numerous works against fanaticism has surely contributed more than any other writer."[16]

In 1789, 40,000 Jews lived in France. The two major Jewish communities—the Ashkenazim in the eastern provinces of Alsace and Lorraine (with their capital in the Jewish quarter in Metz) and the Sephardim in the south and west (Avignon and Bordeaux)—were considered in effect two separate nations within France. The less numerous but more prosperous Sephardim enjoyed nearly full civic rights and took part in the election to the Estates General in 1789. In contrast, the 30,000 Jews of eastern France had no civil rights, except the right to be judged by their own courts.

The Declaration of the Rights of Man and the Citizen seemed to imply Jewish emancipation, along with the abolition of slavery, but the process of applying the grand new principles to a living society with varied vested interests proved contentious. On the very day of the declaration, August 26, 1789, an ad hoc group of

"Jews of Paris" published an address to the National Assembly in which, under the terms of the declaration, they claimed the title of citizens. "In order that there is no ambiguity, that the long oppression of which we have been victim does not become in the eyes of some individuals a pretext to oppress us again," they argued, the Assembly should "make particular mention of the Jewish nation and thus consecrate our title and our rights as citizens." At the same time, the signatories renounced Jewish courts and constables and asked that Jews join the citizenry as a whole in "a uniform plan of police and jurisprudence."[17]

The Metz leadership greeted the revolution more hesitantly. Their representatives in Paris welcomed citizenship but wanted to keep juridical autonomy, restrict freedom of movement to the wealthy, and retain the old Jewish quarters. Hourwitz was outraged that these syndics should be received as the authentic representatives of their people. "They will sacrifice the well-being of their brothers to their superstitions and their private interests."[18] The Metz leadership feared that their authority among Jews would be undermined by greater intercourse with the wider populace; they also owned property in the Jewish quarters where restrictions on movement kept rents artificially high. Hourwitz wrote to the Assembly:

> I have just learned with surprise that you have authorised my co-religionists of Metz to plead their cause before the National Assembly. If everything I have told you and written you is insufficient to convince you of the injustice of their pretensions, let me know. I flatter myself that I can satisfy you entirely and prove to you that the devout of my nation can practise their religion and pay their debts without tyrannising the conscience of their fellow Jews with a rabbinical inquisition and without living in a cesspool.[19]

In December 1789, the Assembly debated the eligibility of non-Catholics for full citizenship. The anti-Jewish delegates were quick to seize on the Metz leadership's equivocations. "They demand to be Frenchmen, but still wish to preserve Jewish administration, Jewish judges, Jewish notaries" as well as "their particular laws on heritage, marriage, tutelage, majority," noted Jean-François Reubell, a Jacobin delegate from Colmar (and later President to the Directoire). The Bishop of Nancy objected on the grounds that Jewry's "eyes turn incessantly toward a homeland which will one day reunite all its dispersed members" and "perforce cannot commit itself to the land in which it dwells."

In reply, Clermont-Tonnerre (guillotined in 1794) decreed that in the spirit of emancipation "everything must be refused to the Jews as a nation and everything granted to them as individuals." In the end, while granting full citizenship to non-Catholic Christians, the Assembly postponed any decision on the status of the Jews. For the Sephardim, it seemed that their already existing rights were threatened by the more difficult questions posed by the Jews of the east. They lobbied successfully for a specific resolution confirming their own rights, which the Assembly passed in January 1790 by a vote of 374 to 244.[20]

Hourwitz joined the National Guard in the summer of 1789, one of perhaps 800 to 1000 Parisian Jews, mostly young and poor, who shouldered musket and saber for the revolution in its imperiled infancy. In October, he publicly pledged one quarter of his net salary to the revolution (he worked, for a low wage, curating "eastern" (that is, Hebrew) manuscripts at the Bibliothèque Royale). In June 1790, he was received by the Assembly as a member of an international brigade of revolutionary "foreigners" led by the Prussian nobleman Anacharsis Cloots: as "ambassadors of the human race," they declared that the Declaration of the Rights of Man and the Citizen should be applied everywhere, regardless of borders.

The National Assembly returned repeatedly to the matter of the Jews but, under pressure from the anti-semitic delegates from Alsace and Lorraine, made little headway. In contrast, the agitation for Jewish emancipation was taken up with zeal by the Paris Commune, as Hourwitz galvanized neighborhood committees with his speeches. "Behold the men whom one seeks to deprive of the rights of man. And why? Because, having been burdened by taxes and deprived of the freedom to exercise most legitimate professions, they are bound to include in their number some individuals who prefer to devote themselves to usury rather than to become highway thieves." In February 1790, the Paris Commune unanimously petitioned the National Assembly to acknowledge all Jews as citizens.

On several occasions, Hourwitz linked the fate of the Jews and the blacks in France and noted that both were now victims of government foot-dragging. "It is astonishing that the National Assembly has adjourned the business of Jews of all colours and men of color of all religions." It seemed that "to be a citizen and even a legislator in this country of equality and liberty, it suffices to be the owner of a white foreskin and to have just enough honesty to avoid being hanged."[21] For Hourwitz, the freedom granted the Sephardim made the remaining anomalies even more unacceptable:

> I have the honor, Monsieur, of being your relative although a distant one, since I too am directly descended from Adam. In spite of the relationship, I have not, as you, the right of citizenship: the reason for this is that the man and woman who produced me (without consulting me) prayed to the Supreme Being in Hebrew and lived in Poland, that is, beyond the frontiers of Bordeaux and Avignon.[22]

On September 27, 1791, after twenty-five months of pleading, debate and adjournment, the National Assembly at last annulled "all adjournments, restrictions and exceptions contained in the preceding decrees affecting individual Jews who will take the civil oath." The next day, in response to an appeal by Reubell, the legislators added the stipulation that in taking the oath Jews would be considered to have renounced "all privileges and exceptions introduced previously in their favor."

For many, the legislative emancipation of the Jews—the first explicit eradication of legal distinctions between Jews and non-Jews—came as an anti-climax; the vote was seen more as an ironing out of inconsistencies than the emancipation of a long-oppressed people. Yet that takes nothing away from its epochal significance. It was an inextricable part of the progress of the Revolution, embodied in a series of landmark votes in the National Assembly: from the Declaration of the Rights of Man and the Citizen, through the nationalization of church property, the abolition of hereditary titles and feudal guilds, and the suppression of monastic orders. The day after the decision on Jewish emancipation, in one of its last acts the Assembly voted to free blacks and mulattos living in France (slavery overseas was outlawed three years later).

Hourwitz was forty when the Jews of France were finally welcomed into citizenship. After that, he largely disappears from recorded history, though it can be presumed he continued to live in poverty. In 1793, he opposed the execution of the king, but escaped the purges that followed. During the anti-clerical phase of the Jacobin regime, all religions were suppressed; a national deistic cult was instituted, synagogues along with churches were closed, and circumcision was banned. In 1794, Hourwitz reacted angrily to a decree forbidding foreigners from residing in Paris or in ports and had the boldness publicly to rebuke Saint-Just at the height of his powers. He seems to have dedicated the remainder of his life (he died in 1811) to perfecting his *polygraphie* and *tacographie*—universal systems for transcribing languages. To the aristocrat Malesherbes he once wrote, "I am well instructed in the Talmud, without being its dupe, and I speak less as a Jew than as a man." Sadly, such a statement is enough these days to write this true hero of emancipation out of our collective history altogether, even to qualify him as a self-hater.

The French Revolution brought down ghetto walls and emancipated Jews, if only temporarily, in northern Italy, Holland and Germany. Nonetheless, everywhere the march of emancipation divided Jewish opinion. Some joined the dance around the liberty tree; others appealed to the old powers for protection. Followers of the Haskalah in central and eastern Europe initially supported the French Revolution, but later in Prussia and Russia they resisted Napoleon with nationalistic fervor. In Livorno, the Jews lost citizen status when the French troops left; soon after, local Jewish leaders joined with the bishop in suppressing the work of Aron Fernando, a Jewish revolutionary who had called for the abolition of some of the Commandments and a reform of the Jewish rite in line with deistic rationalism.

Napoleon's initial philo-semitism turned gradually into its opposite. Peasant grievances against Jewish creditors in Alsace led in 1805 to an outbreak of anti-Jewish violence. As Napoleon and his ministers were aware, the real problem facing peasants was the shortage of rural credit, something that was not the fault of the Jews. Nonetheless, they declared a moratorium on repayment of debts owed to Jews in eastern France and began a reconsideration of the Jews' place in the empire. In 1807, Napoleon convoked a "Grand Sanhedrin," named after the Jewish ruling body in Roman Palestine and designated by the Emperor as Jewry's official voice. Its seventy members (mostly rabbis and all chosen by the Emperor himself) sat in ceremonial state, dressed in the black silk coats and three-cornered hats prescribed by a newly devised, Orientalist-tinged court protocol. Not surprisingly, the Grand Sanhedrin ruled that the Torah taught obedience to the laws of the empire. Nonetheless, in March 1808, Napoleon issued his "infamous decree," which reintroduced restrictions on Jewish rights of residence and trade (though the Jews of the south and west were exempted).[23]

The subsequent history of Jewish emancipation was chequered, reflecting the fortunes of the wider movement for civil and national rights. A number of Jews played prominent roles in the revolutions of 1848 but full emancipation had to wait for German and Italian unification, and in the case of Russia the revolution of 1917.

But even before the process was complete, emancipated Jews came to be seen as the sufferers of a new malaise: creatures cut off from their roots, condemned to an uncertainty identified by some as a specifically Jewish neurosis, by some as a type of modern life, and by others as a combination of the two. With the rise in the second half of the nineteenth century of a new anti-semitism drawing on pseudo-scientific racial theory, the forward march of emancipation seemed bogged down in an unforeseen crisis. This became the seedbed of Zionism, which promised not only safety and security, but a healing of the Jewish "neurosis."

After World War II it became hard to argue that Judaism was a religious or personal choice and nothing else. Assimilation was painted as futile—because the anti-semite will always sniff out the Jew—and a betrayal of Jewishness, a concession to anti-semitism, an expression of self-hatred. And thus, post-holocaust, nearly every figure in the story of Jewish emancipation has been pathologized. Any note of ambivalence about Jewish identity, any criticism of Jews, any reluctance to make Jewishness a public statement, is seen as a neurotic evasion of the burden of Jewishness. Here a selective hindsight has diminished and simplified a rich saga: the members of a long-oppressed minority group staking their epochal claim to equality, to freedom, both as Jews and as individuals who were more than the sum of their Jewishness. Spinoza, Mendelssohn, Hourwitz, Heine, Marx put their souls into the battle to live as free individuals, accountable to their own higher ethics, in a society that cast them as Jews and therefore suspect or inferior. They waged this fight within the context of their times and were unable to transcend entirely the current ideas about Jewishness, diversity and the culture of universal rationality. These are confusions we still have not outgrown: witness the muddle between the national, the universal and the culturally particular in the French ban on the hijab. (And what would Zalkind Hourwitz have had to say about that?)

The hostility to Yiddish is held against the Haskalah as a sign of self-rejection. And yes, the protagonists of emancipation were guilty (along with nearly all Enlightenment rationalists) of a blind spot when it came to linguistic diversity and linguistic hierarchies. In disdaining Yiddish they placed a barrier between themselves and the Jewish majority. But nor were they slaves of the Romantic cult of rootedness. The Yiddish spoken across central and eastern Europe was variable (in some areas closer to the local language than in others), changeable (infused with loan words), and at that time lacked a significant written tradition. Spelled with letters of the Hebrew (or, more precisely, Aramaic) alphabet, it was a language regarded by outsiders as suspicious and by internal reformers as provincial and underdeveloped, holding back the Jewish people from a full engagement with modern European culture and science. The great flowering of Yiddish literature occurs only in the late nineteenth century. Then, in the hands of writers fuelled by both the Haskalah and Chasidism, Yiddish becomes, briefly, one of the central languages of literary modernity. There should be no surprise that Mendelssohn or Heine failed to foresee these developments. The only surprise is that this short-sightedness about Yiddish (shared with Zionists and just about everybody else until the advent of the Bund) should be added against their names as one more telltale sign of the self-hatred that is, we are told, the inescapable fate of the assimilationist.

To the Zionists and other guardians of Jewish identity, to assimilate is to hide. But the likes of Spinoza, Mendelssohn, Hourwitz, Heine and Marx can hardly be accused of seeking a safe anonymity. All were touched by, and passed on to others, the

Promethean fire that makes the Enlightenment, at its best, irreplaceable and ever-inspiring (because its tasks are unfinished). Ah, that great wind of liberation, the Shelleyan vision of human beings "sceptreless, free, uncircumscribed," when you breathe it, pristine, in its major testaments—in Paine's *Age of Reason*, the autobiographies of Olaudah Equiano and Frederick Douglass, the anti-caste manifestos of Jyotirao Phule and B. R. Ambedkar, or Mendelssohn's *Jerusalem* and Hourwitz's *Apologie des Juifs*—it still makes your scalp tingle, still makes you want to rush out and brave bishops, priests, rabbis, mullahs, media pundits and politicians, and insist, despite the odds, that, in Mendelssohn's words, "no deception against reason goes unavenged."

The invigorating challenge of the emancipatory spirit of the eighteenth century is notably absent from the ruminations of many of today's self-proclaimed champions of Enlightenment values. In place of the spirit of fearless inquiry, the willingness to turn cultural assumptions upside down, the scepticism about state power, these apologists for US, British and Israeli foreign policy display a very different side of the same movement and moment that gave us the French Revolution: Western supremacy and Western assumptions, a proprietary technical mastery of nature used to subordinate those human beings unfortunate enough to be born outside the circle of European enlightenment. This "universalism" is actually a parochialism, and unlike the ever-widening embrace of the universalism of a Paine or a Hourwitz, it actually narrows the field of application of Enlightenment values, and even goes so far as to conflate them with the Green Zone in Baghdad, the prison in Guantanamo Bay and the settlements on the West Bank.

Assimilation has also been undermined by the evolution of multiculturalism—as a social reality as well as a theory—and a less absolutist reading of religious and ethnic categories. That's one reason why many of the phrases used about Jews not only by Haskalah writers but also by EVM and Jews of his era now make us uncomfortable (the same discomfort we feel in response to some statements by African-American thinkers before the civil rights era). Bigotry had been rejected, but not the framework of racism; it remained in place as a largely unexamined habit of thinking about human diversity, subdivisions taken for granted. The premise of assimilation was too often that the majority or dominant society was what ought to be assimilated into, no questions asked. The norm to which oppressed minorities should aspire was the norm set by power, its language, culture and politics. Nor is this a confusion merely of the past. Today young Muslims are often being asked to choose between Britishness and Muslimness—including by some of the same people who lament or at least seek to limit assimilation among Jews, as well as by Zionists who are always outraged at the suggestion that loyalty to Israel makes any British Jew any less British.

The Haskalah and the Enlightenment were infused with presumptions about the progressiveness of Western society, presumptions enhanced by technological and military power. Universal claims and national, cultural or linguistic norms were superimposed on each other. The emancipators—fired as they were by a drive to express their own distinctiveness as human beings—nonetheless tended to see universality as colorless, without ethnic specificity of any kind (in practice, white). Along with that they adopted a functional view of culture and personal expressiveness that generated a mighty backlash: in the case of British and German Romanticism, from within the Enlightenment itself; and among the Jews, from the pietistic mysticism of the Chasidim.

The desire to assimilate (in the sense of absorb or embrace) that which is life-enhancing, scientifically verifiable or demonstrably for the common good is not a symptom of self-rejection, and it's part of today's Jewish malaise that so many seem to think of it that way, however they may actually lead their lives. The desire to assimilate in order merely to conform, to benefit from power, is

altogether less admirable and undoubtedly a real factor throughout Jewish history, as it has been in African-American or British
Muslim history.

As an anti-Zionist Jew, I want to see the dominant society not
emulated but transformed. Here Zalkind Hourwitz is the true
prophet, his radical anti-racism, his refusal to apologize for being
oppressed, makes him a forerunner of Fanon and Malcolm X and
B.R. Ambedkar. And, at his best, EVM.

Reform Judaism, born out of the Haskalah and the teaching of
Mendelssohn, scored a series of successes in German rabbinical
conferences in the 1840s. The real significance of these, however,
turned out to be as a stimulus to the development of Orthodoxy as
a self-conscious, irreplaceable alternative to Reform. In Europe,
Orthodoxy could appeal to the state to uphold its traditional
authority. After 1848, would-be Reform Jews, along with many
other Germans, joined the migration to the USA, where Reform
would blossom, becoming and remaining the single biggest
Jewish denomination in the country.

Emancipation was a given in the USA, built into the foundation
of the state. What's more, rabbis and traditional communal leaders
held little sway and no residual powers. Tellingly, the first episode
in the march of North American Reform predates the arrival of
the German émigrés. In 1824, forty-seven Charleston Jews
petitioned for changes in their local synagogue service. They
were Sephardim, as were most American Jews at the time. The
dissidents wanted shorter services, English translations to accom-
pany Hebrew prayers, and a sermon by the rabbi in English. They
wished to worship no longer as "slaves of bigotry and witchcraft"
but as part of the "enlightened world." When the petition was
turned down, they set up their own Reformed Society of Israelites
for Promoting True Principles of Judaism According to its Purity
and Spirit. They introduced choral singing, dispensed with head
coverings and issued their own prayerbook. The congregation

disappeared within a decade, but when a fire destroyed the mainstream Charleston synagogue in 1838, the reformers won a battle to install an organ in the new building—the first synagogue in the USA to do so. Confirmation classes were introduced for boys and girls, and seating at services was by family instead of gender. All this owed more to Thomas Jefferson than to Moses Mendelssohn.[24]

By 1880, more than 90 percent of US synagogues were Reform, and the movement coalesced in 1885 when it endorsed the Pittsburgh Platform. Today, this founding statement of American Reform Judaism would be regarded as heresy by most of those who call themselves Reform Jews. It dismisses "such Mosaic and rabbinical laws as regulate diet, priestly purity and dress" as anachronisms. "Today we accept as binding only its moral laws, and maintain only such ceremonies as elevate and sanctify our lives, but reject all such as are not adapted to the views and habits of modern civilization." The messianic mission of Judaism, to be a light unto the nations, was retained but secularized:

> We recognize in Judaism a progressive religion, ever striving to be in accord with the postulates of reason . . . We acknowledge that the spirit of broad humanity of our age is our ally in the fulfilment of our mission . . . We deem it our duty to participate in the great task of modern times, to solve, on the basis of justice and righteousness, the problems presented by the contrasts and evils of the present organization of society.

Reform did not lament the diaspora fate. It was, unequivocally at this juncture, anti-Zionist:

> We consider ourselves no longer a nation, but a religious community, and therefore expect neither a return to Palestine, nor a sacrificial worship under the sons of Aaron, nor the restoration of any of the laws concerning the Jewish state.[25]

Among the great influx of eastern European Jewry in the years following the Pittsburgh Platform, a large number had no interest in synagogues of any type, and lent their energies to the labor movement. A minority set up Orthodox shuls; some joined existing Conservative (Masorti) and Reform congregations. It's often said that these newer immigrants had a conservative impact on Reform in America, but I think that's only part of the picture of what happened to Reform Judaism in the USA.

Initially, Reform stressed that Judaism was a religion and nothing else. But it found itself doing this during a period in which the allure of the purely religious was decreasing, in which secular choices were becoming more real and diverse. Reform thus came under pressure to offer religion *plus*. In 1909, the Central Conference of American Rabbis (CCAR), Reform's rabbinical assembly, formally declared its opposition to intermarriage (which early Reform congregations blessed). Although decried as "archaic" and "barbarian," circumcision remained near universal. Gradually, Hebrew was added back into the service. And leading Reform rabbis spoke out as Zionists, notably Stephen Wise, for decades the most well known, most widely admired (including by EVM) rabbi in the country, a staunch liberal and Democrat. The Columbus Platform of 1937, the first major revision of the movement's charter since Pittsburgh, saw discarded practices reincorporated into the Reform canon and a major formal shift on Zionism:

> In the rehabilitation of Palestine, the land hallowed by memories and hopes, we behold the promise of renewed life for many of our brethren. We affirm the obligation of all Jewry to aid in its upbuilding as a Jewish homeland by endeavoring to make it not only a haven of refuge for the oppressed but also a center of Jewish culture and spiritual life.[26]

Given the irresolution of Reform's revised approach to Jewish religion, the specificity and urgency of the political program of

Zionism were bound to become salient. By the time I attended Reform Sunday school in the 1960s, Zionism had become the underpinning feature of Jewishness, and certainly an intrusion in every reading of the Hebrew Bible. We knew that when it came to observance, we Reform Jews had it easy compared to the Conservative and Orthodox. Despite the fact that I enjoyed some of the classes, found the material of study intriguing, was curious to know more about my Jewish identity, I was left uninspired. The message of Reform seemed to be that Jews (or at least American and Israeli Jews) should continue doing what they were doing: being successful and admired. So Reform ended up watering down the saga of emancipation—its own origin story— as it had earlier watered down rabbinism. Emancipatory rhetoric was certainly in the air in the 1960s, and young Jews were more than eager to listen and respond, but they heard it coming from other quarters, from other peoples. What I found nowhere in my experience at synagogue or Sunday school was any sense of that package of emotions we dub the spiritual. This I sought and sometimes found elsewhere, in music, literature, movies, politics, drugs, friendships, travel.

Since those days, Reform has labored mightily to retrieve its "spirituality," to compete in a market where rootsiness and mystery count. In 1999, meeting once again at Pittsburgh, the CCAR issued a new declaration of principles, embodied in a language that the framers of the original Pittsburgh Platform would have regarded as embarrassingly obscurantist.

> We are Israel, a people aspiring to holiness, singled out through our ancient covenant and our unique history among the nations to be witnesses to God's presence. We are linked by that covenant and that history to all Jews in every age and place. We are committed to Medinat Yisrael, the State of Israel, and rejoice in its accomplishments. We affirm the unique qualities of living in Eretz Yisrael, the land of Israel, and encourage aliyah, immigration to Israel.[27]

It's not that the old Reform impulse has been abandoned altogether. In 1983 the CCAR ruled that Jewish identity can be passed down through either the mother or the father—a view unacceptable to Orthodoxy and, more important, to the rabbinate in Israel. Reform has championed lesbian and gay rights and (after a struggle) women rabbis. In 1999 the CCAR issued *Gates of Prayer: A Gender Sensitive Prayerbook*. But here there was an overlap between the old reform impulse—in this case for gender equality—and a newer preoccupation with religiosity in tone and form. The new prayerbook, like the service it prescribes, is longer than the old one, includes more Hebrew, and reintroduces numerous prayers and psalms from the traditional (but not traditional Reform) liturgy.

In recent years "spirituality" has become a lodestar among Reform rabbis. The classic Reform doctrine of *Judische Wissenschaft*—rational Judaism—takes a distant second place to gestures that blend the ethnic and the transcendental. Ceremonies are reintroduced not because of any newly found commitment to the niceties of the Law, but because of their mystique. Rabbis sport yarmulkes outside the synagogue. Kashrut are making a comeback as is kabbalah, whose theosophy and mysticism would have given the original Reformers nightmares.

Yet all of this also reflects Reform's continuing adaptation to prevailing American culture, not least a hunger for ethnic particularity shared with many non-Jews; it's one form of the consumerized revivalism found in Christian and Muslim groups worldwide. What makes it distinct is the role of Zionism. The irony is that for all its zeal for "Medinat Yisrael," Reform finds itself under attack by the Orthodox rabbinate in Israel, its Jewish credentials unacceptable in the land it has declared its homeland.

Part Two

5

The Prophet Armed

Shortly before my mother's birth in December 1931, three months before his change of name and six years into his marriage to Olga, EVM began but never completed a short story about one "Isaac Baron," a self-centered man-about-town with a pregnant wife whose face "showed a lifetime of suffering," and whose eyes "seemed to hold some somber meaning." EVM depicts his protagonist as torn between emotions:

> At heart he was not inhuman and her suffering touched him deeply. But he could not admit it to the world, to his wife and least of all to himself . . . As he looked into this woman's eyes he knew that any attempt to appear considerate would be mistaken. His conscience told him that his long neglect was responsible. He wasn't brave enough to break down the very wall he himself had built.

A year later, in the wake of FDR's first presidential victory, EVM was the subject of a glowing profile in a Bronx newspaper. Here he is hailed as "one of the better known lawyers in the borough, who played an important part in bringing about the large Democratic plurality in the Bronx in the last presidential elections." He is also, the reporter notes, "one of the few men who has two honorable discharges from the same war. And with such a record, he claims to be a pacifist."

He loves politics, though he is not a politician. It is in his make-up to always fight for the downtrodden, ever since his school political days . . . his political activities take up most of his time. During elections, Eddie Morand is one of the fiery speakers on the Democratic Speakers Bureau.

This EVM is a family man, happily married with a four-year-old son and infant daughter. In addition to being "one of the best all around attorneys in the Bronx," he clearly entertains literary ambitions. "Having been born and brought up in New York, he feels that the life of a typical New York boy has not yet been transmitted to the written page. Although denying that he is working on the great American novel, there are many neatly written chapters in one of his drawers which do not in the least resemble briefs." In sum, EVM—"versatile in his talents, with a keen interest not only in his immediate surroundings but the world at large"—embodies "the modern, well-educated citizen."

The purposeful man with a promising future portrayed in the newspaper is, however, nowhere to be found in the daily diary EVM started on January 2, 1934—and stopped on January 4. Instead, in these three days of intimate, if random, reflection, we get a glimpse of vast worlds of professional, personal and political frustration.

Of course business is so bad that it is depressing and yet things may change almost any minute. I suppose it would be a tragedy if I did not get an appointment [to a judgeship] and yet, what of it . . . Perhaps if I do not get a job and business gets so bad that I have to get out of this profession, as tragic as that may seem at the moment, it may be the very thing I need to make me follow some other pursuit that even though I am not better fitted for I might have some enjoyment out of.

In the meantime, he frets, "because of my present precarious financial position I am not getting the respect, attention and courtesy" of colleagues. After turning the matter over repeatedly he remains bemused—at his situation and at himself: "I wonder what will happen when I am definitely assured I am not getting anything . . . It is something tragic to think of but there is nothing that I can think of to do."

Bleak and profitless as professional life may have been, none-theless "when I come into the office, I step into another world, more nearly a creation of my own liking"—and clearly a relief from the stresses of home. Between 1933 and 1939 EVM and family were living in the Muriel Arms, a swanky ten-story Art Deco mansion on the Grand Concourse, the then fashionable boulevard running through the Bronx. It had a doorman, and it was expensive—$90 a month. Because the Depression had led to a dearth of rent-paying tenants, landlords were offering multi-month no-rent concessions and EVM, with his Micawber-like insistence that something would turn up, had struck a deal. In no time, however, and for the duration of their tenancy, they were behind on the rent. My uncle recalls:

> I would be instructed to respond to the evening door bell ringing and tell the rent collector that my father was not home. Whatever embarrassment this caused me it certainly was more humiliating for my father; he handled it by gruff anger at the rich capitalists. For my mother it was just one more bundle of straw on her bent back.

Though the family never went without food, clothing or medical care, "poverty" remained "the central fact" in my uncle's child-hood perceptions of his mother, with "her sense of the disgrace of not being comfortably middle class." At the Muriel Arms, "our kitchen window looked out on a shaft and at other apartments facing ours. Therefore, when she scrubbed the kitchen floor on hands and knees . . . she always pulled down the window shade. It was a 'shanda' [scandal] that she did not have a maid to do that for her."

With the onset of the Depression, many households had been forced to consolidate, and EVM now found himself titular head of a family unit of six: his wife Olga, her sister Gertie and her father Abe, and the two children, Martin and Janet. Grandpa Abe, who'd arrived from Lithuania in 1898 and had risen from a peddler with a sack on his back to the owner of a small dry goods store, doted on my mother. She remembered him as her "idea of a Jew" because of his accent, his eating flanken (a cut of beef from the ribs, stewed and eaten with horseradish) and drinking tea in a glass—though my uncle remembers him as a skeptic who approached a synagogue with great reluctance. When my mother was six years old she ate bacon at a friend's home and on her return home announced that she liked it so much that she'd rather be a Christian. *"Far a shtick bacon a kid dof velen zein a goy?"* was Grandpa's response ("For a piece of bacon a child wants to become a Christian?"). "Give her bacon." And out he went to buy bacon, though he was careful to tell the butcher it was for a neighbor.

In a poem called "Father's Day Reflections," written in 1933, EVM describes my uncle, then five years old: "He's a pal of mine these days/sharing all our joys, speaking/of wars and toys /—but forgetting the Depression." Though this pal "has placed you on a pedestal, he is still your severest critic." EVM vows to "try to become / worthy of the little man." His young son made EVM (who had grown up without a father) self-conscious, wary of the gap between the appearance and the reality of his life. When, two years later, "the little man" fell ill with scarlet fever, Ed was terror-stricken, and apparently even visited a synagogue to pray. After his son's recovery, he wrote another poem which begins: "My prayers are answered—my God is just / (Though superstition is a stumbling block)." In gratitude to "God or life or whatever there is that moves men's souls," he prays that the "respite" granted his son may be used "that he may lead a better / fuller life for all mankind." My uncle recalls this sardonically as the poem in which EVM "pledged MY life to mankind!"

EVM's income was fitful at best, and sometimes took unorthodox form. "One day he drove home with a huge tank for tropical fish" which a client had proffered in lieu of payment. In contrast, Aunt Gertie was a consistent breadwinner (she worked as a bookkeeper for an architects' firm) and that was one reason they heartily detested each other. Others included political disagreements and the fact that Aunt Gert was—probably even more so by the time I knew her—pompous, joyless and vindictive. For my mother, she was an ever-present reminder of the worst curse that could befall a woman: spinsterhood.

It was never a harmonious household, and the marriage at its core was already empty. In the diary, EVM confesses: "It does seem peculiar when one is married and has two children, who mean more than life itself, that one at thirty-four should be seeking romance. I certainly would like to fall in love again, even for the pleasure of being fooled. Of course the cynic might suggest that it would be a good start to 'go home and fall in love with your own wife' . . ." *That* he considers hopeless counsel. "It becomes essential to seek other avenues of escape, knowing all the while that there is no escape." Immediately, the potential avenue of escape is another woman, a refugee from eastern Europe who has come to him as a client. He confesses that one of her attractions is that she has already been married "and of course gone through everything, and that means sexually." In any case, "a normal sex life is essential. I still do not like prostitutes."

Politically, despite his role in the Democratic election effort, EVM felt more isolated than ever. Tammany itself was undergoing a crisis. The Seabury hearings of 1929–30 had exposed corruption on a monumental scale, and the once popular but now tainted Mayor Jimmy Walker was forced to resign and flee to Europe. He was followed by John O'Brien, a Tammany hack, who was elected for a one-year special term in 1932; the real news in the Bronx, however, was that the Socialist Morris Hilquit scooped 23 percent of the vote, pushing the Republican into third place. With the Bronx polity shifting, large numbers of votes were up for grabs. In the presidential elections of the same year, FDR scooped 73 percent of the Bronx vote, bringing into one tent for the first time a wide-ranging class and ethnic constituency. Ed Flynn, amazingly untainted by the Seabury revelations, engineered that local triumph. As one of FDR's key early backers for the presidential nomination, his authority over the Democratic Party was now unchallengeable, and that seems to have left EVM out in the cold, despite all the street-corner speeches he'd delivered.

The New Deal in New York could not be contained by Tammany, and was ultimately incarnated in the anti-Tammany mayoralty of Fiorello La Guardia, first elected in 1933 on a Republican–Fusion ticket. In the Bronx, La Guardia smashed the Tammany machine, replicating FDR's 73 percent of the vote. Two months later EVM reflected ruefully, "my first hunch to go with Fusion might have been good."

Fusion was the label for the loose coalition of reformers who had come together, in the wake of the Seabury hearings, to back La Guardia's challenge to Tammany. As a Republican congressman from the then Italian working-class district of East Harlem, La Guardia had sponsored labor legislation and attacked immigration quotas. He was the son of an Istrian Jewish mother and a Roman Catholic-turned-atheist father, and he spoke Italian, Yiddish and Spanish. For all these reasons he exercised a strong appeal to EVM, yet EVM balked at cutting his ties with the Democrats, only to find that Tammany had learned nothing in defeat. "It is almost impossible to break into the inner circle. The last contest merely solidified their position and made them adopt the attitude that even if they got licked they would not surrender any of their rights." All doors seemed closed.

Yet, like Tolstoy's Prince Andrei lying wounded after the

battle of Austerlitz, EVM at age thirty-four resolved that the world would yet hear of him. "Many of the things I held most sacred and wrote about years ago, while they have not been a part of my daily existence because of circumstances, still hold their allurement and if I have any regrets it is because I permitted things of the day to shunt away the ideals of my heart." In the years ahead, with the rise of the popular front—globally and in the Bronx—he found a vehicle for those ideas, and for his ambitions, and for a while, at least, a way out from his feelings of loneliness and uselessness.

The popular front was an international response to the international crises of economic depression and fascism. In 1935, the Stalinist Comintern had called on Communists to join socialist and democratic allies in a broad alliance against fascism and reaction. In Spain, in February 1936, a Popular Front government was elected, and in May a similar coalition triumphed in France. Franco began his fascist rebellion in July. The global struggle had been joined. In the US, the Communists re-entered mainstream trade unionism, endorsed the New Deal, and declared that "Communism Is Twentieth Century Americanism."

In this climate, EVM diversified his political activities. He joined the campaign for the Scottsboro Boys, nine black youths accused of raping two white women and sentenced to death by all-white juries in Alabama in 1931.* Here for the first time he worked side by side with Communist Party members, who were also activists in the Bronx Committee to Aid Spain, of which EVM became the first chairman. He was a founder member of the National Lawyers Guild, which was the embodiment of the popular front in the legal

---

* The evidence was weak (later, one of the alleged victims recanted her accusation) and the case became an international *cause célèbre*, especially after the Communist Party took over their defense (the NAACP dropped out) in 1932. The party arranged for New York attorney Sam Liebowitz to represent the defendants—a controversial move because the leftist Jew Liebowitz rapidly became a hate figure for the Southern press and Alabama judges and jurors.

profession. Presumably aided by the name change, he also commenced thirty years of active membership in the Free Sons of Israel. Founded in New York in 1849, the Free Sons was a mutual benefit society, with regalia, passwords and ritual, organized in local lodges which were often linked to political clubhouses, in EVM's case the Jackson Democratic Club in the Bronx.

From the beginning, EVM had his own pronounced and contentious ideas about the role of the lodge. In 1936, he assumed editorship of the *Bronx Flash*, the lodge's cyclostyled newsletter, and used it to broadcast his views about the crisis facing the Jews. In his first editorial, he asks: "Is there a Jewish question as distinguished from an American-Jewish one?" Adopting the editorial "we"—which in coming years was to become an addiction—he recalls "how violent an assimilationist we were, how we looked down on all things alien, how we had even come to look down on our own." But assimilation had not proved a defense against anti-semitism. Therefore "we must recognize the existence of a Jewish problem."

> The Jews of the United States, because of world events over which they have no control, must live, act and vote as a unit! Never before in the history of our people has this need for unity been so necessary.

EVM derides "our conservative Jews of prominence" who "still don't recognize that terror stalks the lands of Europe and unfortunately has more than a foothold here." He argues that "Jews should be Jewish conscious" but in the next breath insists—as he was always to do—that there should be no contradiction between this militant Jewish identity and a fully committed "Americanism." In the coming election, "every American Jew, for his own sake as an American, should vote for Franklin D. Roosevelt." Jews should align themselves firmly "on the side of liberalism . . . the real New Deal side for the underprivileged." They should not be fearful of the left: "In the time of peril who would we perforce turn to . . . and what group from experience would have helped us more . . . we turned rightly to the left!"

The Free Sons of Israel was avowedly a "non-partisan," apolitical order so EVM must have known he was treading on thin ice, especially when it came to the question of the boycott of Nazi Germany, a cause he embraced early and passionately, and which remained a touchstone for him. In the *Bronx Flash* he called for boycotts of all goods and services stemming from Nazi Germany, and specifically of the Berlin Olympics and of the first fight between Max Schmeling and Joe Louis (which Schmeling won, setting up the rematch in 1938, one of twentieth-century sport's great symbolic dramas).

The boycott campaign had been launched in March 1933 by the New York chapter of the Jewish War Veterans, of which EVM was a member. The JWV staged a huge protest parade, attended by La Guardia and other dignitaries, as well as by the Communists, who were forced by the organizers to take down their red banners.[1] As EVM frequently complained, the JWV was a timorous organization, and it certainly lacked the skills or the clout to organize an effective boycott. Nonetheless, support for the idea spread spontaneously across American Jewish society, and took organizational form in the Non-Sectarian Anti-Nazi League, of which EVM was a founder and long-time member.

The boycott was opposed by the American Jewish Committee (widely regarded as the arm of the Jewish American establishment, wealthy and politically conservative), B'nai B'rith, the Board of Deputies of British Jews, and the ultra-Orthodox Agudas Yisrael. The American Jewish Congress gave it nominal support, as did Stephen Wise, who wrote to a friend that he was having trouble containing the demands for action from the Jewish grassroots: "You cannot imagine what I am doing to resist the masses. They want tremendous street scenes."[2]

By far the most active opponent of the boycott was the World Zionist Organization, whose agents were at the time negotiating arrangements with the Nazi regime for the transfer of German Jewish money (and German Jews) to Palestine. The "Ha'avara" ("transfer") deal was unveiled by the Nazis in August 1933, on the day before the World Zionist Congress, meeting in Prague, was to debate a boycott resolution tabled by Ze'ev Jabotinsky, the right-wing Revisionist leader (whom EVM was later to meet and interview). The boycott proposal was rejected by a vote of 240 to 48. The Ha'avara itself was not put to the vote at the congress, but under the Zionist aegis—in the form of the Zionist Federation of Germany and the Anglo-Palestine Bank—it grew rapidly into a major banking and trading enterprise with offices in Jerusalem. Under the scheme, German Jews were permitted to remove some of their funds in the form of German-produced capital goods which were then sold in Palestine (as well as in the US and Britain). When the German émigrés arrived in Palestine, they could recoup a portion of their investment. The Nazis welcomed the export boost, but to them the principal advantage was the undermining of the boycott movement. For the Zionists, the Ha'avara worked: it accounted for some 60 percent of all capital invested in Palestine between August 1933 and September 1939, vital in sustaining the Yishuv (the Jewish settlement in Palestine) through global depression and Arab revolt. It also facilitated the emigration to Palestine of some 16,000 (relatively wealthy) German Jews.[3]

Nonetheless, the tie-up with the Nazis was a severe embarrassment to the Zionists. Hillel Silver, a leading Zionist Reform rabbi, declared: "The very idea of Palestine Jewry negotiating with Hitler about business instead of demanding justice for the persecuted Jews of Germany is unthinkable." Chaim Weizmann, presiding figurehead of the WZO and later Israel's first president, disagreed: "We, being a Zionist organisation, should concern ourselves with the constructive solution of the German question through the transfer of the Jewish youth from Germany to Palestine, rather than with the question of equal rights of Jews in Germany." Significantly, Weizmann's position was strongly backed by the labor Zionists, now the dominant force in the Yishuv: German capital was necessary to build Jewish socialism. Moshe Sharett, later Israel's foreign and prime minister, decried "protests and boycotts"; the only way to address the crisis of German Jewry, he insisted, was the "upbuilding of Eretz Israel."[4]

The Ha'avara was officially endorsed by the World Zionist Congress in Lucerne in 1935. In London, the *Jewish Chronicle* described the vote as "a spectacle . . . puzzling to the world . . . and disheartening to Jews for whom the boycott is one of the few weapons."[5] In the USA, Wise and Silver muted their criticism and stepped back from the boycott, which continued to be hampered by the absence of effective national organization and the reluctance of Jewish leaders to countenance picketing of stores selling Nazi goods.

Although EVM acknowledged that boycotts inevitably had an unfair effect on some people—why should anti-Nazi Germans suffer?—he remained convinced that "the boycott is our only weapon," perhaps a response to Wise's insistence that the boycott was only "*a* weapon," and not necessarily the best one. EVM had a liking for boycotts—a practical citizens' action, not just an opinion but a moral stand, one separating the sheep from the goats and, what's more, the only means by which an ordinary American could intervene in foreign affairs. "We have no desire to continue friendship," he declared, "with anyone who would make excuses for the participation in the Olympics in Berlin, the continual purchase of German goods, and a silent approval of Nazism with its attendant terrors."

EVM notes a report in the *New York Times* detailing the appalling conditions of Jews in Austria (two years before the Anschluss) and asks why Jews should be singled out for such suffering. It is, of course, absurd to hold Jews guilty of the killing of Jesus or to regard Jews as exploiters and parasites. Nonetheless, EVM avers, some fault must lie with the Jews themselves. "First and foremost in my opinion is the wrongful implication that Jews have concerning the phrase that they are God's chosen people. We may have been chosen as a race to give a new belief to the world, but we certainly were not put on this earth to be considered ipso facto the chosen among people."

He deplores Jews who harbor prejudices against other Jews. "If in our own society we discriminate between Litvaks and Gali-tizianer [Jews from Lithuania and Jews from Galicia in Poland], if the son of a *schneider* [tailor] is still considered a poor match for the daughter of a rabbi, what can we expect from the outside world?" Even more, he deplores Jews who discriminate against black people: "What can be thought of those Jews who have sat by complacently and agreed that the lily-white Southerner was right when he characterized all negroes as being potential rapists," especially in light of "the stigma now attached to Jews in Germany who for moral reasons are not permitted to employ female domestic help under the age of 45." In failing to challenge white racism against blacks, Jews are guilty of allowing "a perverted, general indictment to stand simply because it excluded our people."

Not surprisingly, EVM's comments attracted complaints, to which he responded robustly, lashing into unnamed lodge broth-ers who had been "critical of our frank and outspoken attitude for militant Judaism."

With Hitler in Germany, the appalling conditions in Poland, Roumania, Hungary and Austria, how long can any fraternal order of Jewish persuasion go blissfully unmindful that they tread on the edge of a world volcano! There lies more character in an active murderer than a Jew who would in these days remain indifferent.

To "our fervent Jews in the Lodge who have labelled as 'professional Judaism' every sincere attempt to make Bronx Lodge something more than a rendezvous of good fellowship," he commends a favorite passage from the *Inferno*, in which Dante observes the torments of the fence-sitters and the uncommitted, "the wretched souls of those who live without praise or blame." As for himself, he feels only that "it is a pity that when the putsch comes . . . those who warned will go down with the cabbage heads who never would listen or learn!"

The Popular Front took political form in New York in the summer of 1936, when Sidney Hillman, David Dubinsky (another Bund veteran) and Alex Rose, leaders of the Jewish-dominated garment workers' unions, announced the formation of the American Labor Party, "a new alignment" which they promised would become "the permanent political instrument of labor and progressive forces" in the city and state. While the ALP proved less than permanent, over the next decade it did become (and remains to this day) the most successful left-wing third party in American history since the demise of the pre-World War I Socialist Party. It also became the vehicle through which EVM mounted his most sustained and serious political engagement, into which he poured immense hopes, political and personal, and the source, in the end, of disappointment and bitterness.

The ALP was created by an intersection of national and local pressures. Hillman and the other ALP founders were enthusiastic supporters of FDR and the New Deal, and advocates of a more politically active unionism (partly a Bund legacy) but they were also determinedly anti-Tammany. La Guardia had already demonstrated that a progressive alliance could beat Tammany at the ballot box, and the aim of the ALP was to institutionalize that alliance.

In the short term, the immediate task of the ALP was to provide an independent, non-Democratic line on the ballot for

FDR in New York, not least so that the traditionally Socialist-voting members of the garment unions could back the President for re-election without strengthening Tammany. The Republicans tried to use the ALP to red-bait Roosevelt, as did Al Smith, who had turned against the New Deal, but La Guardia announced that he would be voting for FDR on the ALP line. In the end, the President won a landslide victory, nowhere more emphatic than in the Bronx, where he captured more than four-fifths of the votes. Significantly, 238,845 New York City voters backed FDR on the new ALP line, 12 percent of his total city vote.

On the same day they voted for Roosevelt, New Yorkers adopted a new city charter and—significantly for the ALP—opted for proportional representation in the election of a stream-lined city council. La Guardia, FDR and the unions strongly backed the reforms, as did Wall Street and the *New York Times*, all of them enemies of Tammany. Proportional representation promised to restrict Tammany's monopoly on elected office, but it coincidentally made running candidates under a third-party label a plausible strategy. The ALP could now stake a claim not just as an adjunct of the Democrats but as an independent electoral force.

It was at this point that EVM ended sixteen years' formal association with the Democratic Party. He cast his lot with the ALP, which promptly made him an "election liaison officer" in the Bronx. The municipal campaign of 1937 was a vigorous one, drawing on union resources and an army of leftist foot soldiers, many of them Communists. A climactic eve-of-poll rally at Madison Square Garden was described by the *New York Times* as the "liveliest political meeting" in the city's recent history. A "wildly enthusiastic" crowd of 18,000 cheered the union leaders and the ALP candidates, including Thomas E. Dewey, whom the ALP was backing, along with the Republicans, for district attorney. Dewey had achieved fame as a "racket-buster," and that night he duly laid into the links between Tammany and organized crime; despite being a Wall Street Republican, he was enthusiastically applauded. Such was the elasticity of the popular front. The loudest cheers of the night were reserved, however, for La Guardia himself, especially when he asked the crowd, "Are there any people here from the Bronx?" According to the *Times*, "When the response assured him that thousands from the Bronx were present, the Mayor denounced the Bronx Democratic organization, headed by Edward J. Flynn" and the "dirty, nasty, underhanded, unfair" campaign it was waging.[6] I can imagine EVM among the throng, and the vigorous assent he would have given to that part of the Mayor's speech.

The 1937 city elections were a triumph for the ALP and La Guardia, who took 60 percent of the vote in the Bronx, a humiliation for Flynn on his home turf. Of La Guardia's 272,000 votes in the borough, 138,000—60 percent—were cast for him on the ALP line. Across the city, the ALP took 20 percent of the vote and five of its candidates were elected to the council. The *New York Times* reported that the party "now holds the balance of power not only in the city but in the state."

For EVM, the great thrill of the 1937 elections must have been Mike Quill's victory in the Bronx. I remember Quill from the 1960s as a grand old man of militant bread-and-butter unionism, a loud-mouthed figure the New York papers loved to hate. In 1966 he led a twelve-day bus and subway strike that shut down the city, and at the age of sixty he was jailed for defying a court injunction. Legend had it that he had started his long political career as an IRA guerrilla. What's certain is that he arrived in New York in 1926, and like other refugees from the Irish Civil War found a job in the city transport system. Over a decade of often clandestine activity he built the Transport Workers Union with the aid of a Communist–Irish Republican alliance.

To many, including EVM, the election of this blazing Irish Bolshevik to a seat on the city council heralded an exciting expansion of political horizons. The new hopes were strengthened when, a year later, in November 1938, the ALP succeeded in electing its first congressman, Vito Marcantonio, a former Socialist and Republican who captured La Guardia's old East Harlem seat. Opportunities for the left were expanding, and along with them opportunities for EVM. He launched a career in radio with a weekly legal advice program called *Sue or Settle* on WBNX, a Bronx station that broadcast programs in Italian, Yiddish, Polish, and German as well as English. EVM explained "in laymen's terms" the intricacies of probate, mortgages, and injury compensation, as well as capital punishment (against) and the case for an anti-lynching bill. He also broadcast a single instalment of another series entitled *The Modern Diogenes* whose publicity described it as "a non-partisan, intimate narration concerning men and events of a political, civic and social nature in Bronx County." On the clipping announcing the show, EVM has scrawled: "The program was cancelled due to political interference."

He scored a brief success with a bilingual (English–Yiddish) program called *It's on the Tip of My Tongue*, described as a "dramatized quiz"—because EVM scripted both the host's questions and the guests' answers, ensuring that the latter were informative and witty. EVM was a radio nut, a fan of both Orson Welles and Jack Benny. He wrote a script for a Benny show in which Jack has to undergo a comically awkward initiation as a lone white man into Rochester's black fraternal order. He kept the rejection slip. Later he was to complain, "I feel that the entire radio executive field is peopled by guys who don't know a good thing when they hear it."

In August 1939, EVM began writing a weekly column for the *Jewish Review*, a weekly that dubbed itself "The Voice for New York Jewry," though its 60,000 subscribers lived mainly in the Bronx. EVM's column, like the "dramatized quiz," was dubbed "It's on the Tip of My Tongue." He greeted his new readers: "Sure I'm nervous, wouldn't you be?" But then, "writing a column is old stuff to me, dashing off a vitriolic editorial (ask my lodge brothers) as easy to me as a service ace to Don Budge."

Over the next eighteen months, he published tens of thousands of words in the *Jewish Review*, in the course of which he dropped hundreds of (mainly Jewish) names—of Bronx politicians, lawyers, judges, businessmen, activists in Jewish community affairs—adding a mix of naked plugs and obscure digs, and, in the case of women, courtly epithets ("charming," "delightful," "attractive"). He chronicled a whirlwind of meetings and social functions, reviewed books, movies, and plays. Most of all, he gave vent to opinions on issues global, national, and local.

In his first column EVM addressed the Jewish interest in the upcoming municipal elections. There is one question, he insists, all candidates must answer: "How do you stand on Father Coughlin's anti-semitism?" EVM was hardly alone in his concern about the growing popularity of Charles Coughlin, a Roman Catholic priest whose radio broadcasts reached millions. In 1932 Coughlin had been a Roosevelt champion, and always remained, in his own terms, anti-Wall Street, but thereafter he turned anti-New Deal, anti-Communist, and anti-Jewish. *Social Justice*, Coughlin's newspaper, reprinted "The Protocols of the Elders of Zion" and damned "Marxist atheism" as a "Jewish plot." By the summer of 1939, Coughlin's supporters, organized in the Christian Front, were staging aggressive demonstrations against Jews, replete with Nazi-like chanting and symbolism, on the streets of New York.

EVM's second column, published on August 17, 1939, was titled "They Shall Not Pass," after the Spanish anti-fascist motto. It begins ominously: "Violence has come to pass against the Jews in this cosmopolitan city of ours. Violence in the midst of a densely populated Jewish district." EVM describes himself as "an eye witness and participant" in a street-corner confrontation in which the Christian Fronters, "a group of nondescript, illiterate, bigoted people led by irresponsible leaders," found themselves under siege from a crowd of 1,500 protestors, of whom, EVM reports, "half were Jews." He jotted down the speakers' phrases: "We will drive the Jews out of business," "If anyone interferes with our plans, Jewish blood will run," "Let the hooked nose brethren beware," "Buy Christian," "Only the Jews have jobs." The police, EVM reports, did nothing to restrain the speakers but instead attacked the hecklers and arrested the protestors, principally Jews. The moment brings back an early memory: "I recalled seeing Cossacks on horseback flying down a street in Russia, spears carried at a most dangerous angle." Identifying himself as a legal observer, EVM pressed police officers (whose Irish brogues he notes) to intervene to stop the speakers and offered to swear out an on-the-spot formal complaint, but the cops weren't interested. A dialogue with one inspector "finally wound up in a private fight."

> Oh yes I believe in free speech. I have risen on occasions to oratorical heights quoting Voltaire . . . but there is no rule of law or reason, for me any more at least, which will permit beasts to stand on an American street corner and spout venom and lies!

He notes an encouraging sign: the number of non-Jews who joined the hecklers, but then wonders, "Will these non-Jews continue to be interested in our fight if we don't fight back ourselves?" EVM challenges, by name, B'nai B'rith, the Free Sons of Israel, the Jewish War Veterans, the American Jewish Congress, the American Jewish Committee, "and other kindred Jewish institutions": the time for a circumspect response to anti-semitism has passed, "the day of reckoning has sort of caught up with all of us."

EVM dedicates several columns to attacking Joe McWilliams, whose Christian Mobilizers—allies and rivals of the Christian Front—were active in the city. Observing McWilliams's smug performance in a magistrates' court, EVM welcomes the police testimony that ultimately convicted the Mobilizers of disorderly conduct. "Performance of one's duty becomes doubly hard when it means prosecution of people whose racial and religious ties are close to one. We don't always rush in to inflict a penalty upon our own landsmen!" For EVM, the clash with the fascists on the streets of New York was acquiring a disturbingly Jewish versus Irish cast.

> New York City is the last place to raise antagonism between the Irish and the Jew! In no other city has so cordial a relationship existed for so many years. As I read the Irish names of the leaders of this vicious movement, I cannot but recall some Irish names which have ever been an inspiration to me. I wonder what Parnell, AE, Sir Roger Casement, Collins, DeValera and hundreds of victims of the Black and Tans, people to whom the Easter Rebellion is as holy a cause as our own Fall of the temple, Irish poets and revolutionaries of the dark years, not so long ago, I wonder how low in shame they would hang their heads if they but knew that people of their race and faith are running through the streets screaming, "Down with the Jews!"

Anti-semitic street-corner meetings continued to be held throughout the autumn, police continued to protect the fascists and harass the anti-fascists, and EVM continued to protest— against the police ("the cops gave more protection to Fuehrer McWilliams and his gang of thugs than to the citizens in the vicinity"), the Church ("*Social Justice* is sold openly outside churches . . . what the Jews want to know is where does the Catholic Church really stand on Coughlin?"), and those complacent establishment Jews who would not lead from the front. Again and again, he returns to the question of Jewish–Irish relations. "In the big cities where Coughlin has his recruits it's undoubtedly an Irish crowd. But they're not Irish. It doesn't make any difference what they look like—how Irish their names sound—it's not the real Irish!" He urges Jews not to generalize about the Irish. There can be "no blanket indictment of a people. We have suffered too much on that account ourselves."

In early 1940, EVM recommends the work of the American

League to Combat Anti-semitism, which "after careful investigation seems to me to be the most effective militant agency now in the field." He adds that he will be speaking at the league's "Stop Coughlin" rally and reprints in full its founding statement:

> We shall not leave the scene until your mother and your children, your wife and your sweetheart feel that the danger is over. We shall make American Jewry conscious of their strength, their innate decency, their culture and humanity . . . We seek no gain, no political ascendancy, no honors, no rewards. We are Americans—and being Jews—we shall fight for that Americanism.

In his next column he describes his work with the league as "an eye opener" to the welter of anti-semitic groups and the fractious relations among them. He notes sadly, however, that "to learn about these groups, to know something of their aims and the type of propaganda used, it is necessary to deal directly with the so-called seller of information. A more dastardly crowd is hard to imagine."

Within weeks, EVM was regretting his endorsement of the league, which had announced that members of the Christian Front charged with riot were actually "innocent victims of a plot." Worse yet, the league was holding a public meeting on the alleged "miscarriage of justice" with a representative of Father Coughlin. "Sheer stupidity," EVM huffs, then admits ruefully, "It only goes to prove that one's enthusiasm for a cause sometimes permits support for a group which can be accused of extremely poor judgement." If one of his antagonists—or rivals—had made the same blunder, would EVM have let him off so lightly?

As for others on the left worldwide, fascism posed for EVM a personal and unavoidable test, a confrontation with history and responsibility. He often repeated the story about Henry David Thoreau, who in protest against the Mexican War, which he viewed as a war for slavery, refused to pay his poll tax and was locked up in the town jail. When Ralph Waldo Emerson, the respectable sage, visited his young friend and asked, "Henry, what are you doing in there?" Thoreau is said to have replied, "Ralph, what are you doing *out there?*" For EVM, the anecdote summed up the ethic that compelled him to take a public stand in an era of global polarization, as well as offering justification, celebration even, of his exclusion from the status and success he never ceased to crave.

In retrospect, it has been made to appear a simple choice in a Manichaean conflict. But when war broke out in Europe in 1939, for EVM, an anti-fascist and self-declared "militant Jew," a non-Communist but not an anti-Communist, with a distaste for militarism and a cynical perspective on the motives of great powers, it wasn't so clear-cut.

The Hitler–Stalin pact was signed on August 23, 1939, just as EVM was penning his first column. War between Germany and Britain and France became imminent, and US participation in that war more than a theoretical question. In response, EVM's mind went back to a parallel period: "Us 'old timers' recall 'I didn't raise my boy to be a soldier' and the sudden change to 'Over There'." He wonders "how long will it take for subtle propaganda to sell us all a bill of goods that our place is in the trenches?"

> Sentimentally I would like to go around and envisage a great united front against Germany. It made me feel a bit more secure even thousands of miles away to believe that the Russian army would fight Hitler. But let's be realistic! For months Russia waited upon England and France. Chamberlain fumbled the ball. The Soviet was ready to fight, not just talk, for the Czechs. You know what Munich did.

A week later, after the German invasion of Poland and the Allied declaration of war, his tone seems to change radically: "For years all Jewry has prayed for the day when Hitler and Nazism would fall. THE TIME HAS ARRIVED . . . in or out of the war Jews KNOW where their hearts are in this conflict." Still, he finds he cannot easily bury his one-time "near pacifism." "Before we let our enthusiasm get going, suppose we take off a few days and read some post-war literature." He recommends Dos Passos's *Three Soldiers* and Remarque's *All Quiet on the Western Front*. He quotes Siegfried Sassoon: "I see them in foul dug-outs, gnawed by rats." EVM never shed his antagonism to the army and its ways: "Yes, war is a great leveller . . . it serves to glorify some non-com who should be better labelled a nincompoop. Do you remember what happened to your bunkmate as soon as he got a couple of chevrons on his sleeve?"

> If it comes to a point that we must go, face it as a piece of bad business without any glory . . . all those empire builders as shown in pictures like *Four Feathers* and *Gunga Din*. It is a pleasure to be shot for deah' old England! It's no pleasure folks, just a sordid part of modern life.

This was the period in which modern American Anglophilia (the Special Relationship) was born, displacing the republican Anglophobia that had been a staple of American popular culture until that time. EVM, however, remained—and was to remain—a staunch foe of England, its empire, its class system, and what he saw as its institutionalized hypocrisy. He is appalled that on the day Congress rejects the Wagner bill to admit 10,000 European refugee children (most of them Jewish) as an emergency measure, the *New York Times* carries pictures of upper-crust English children arriving snugly in New York harbor.

EVM found himself in the unaccustomed predicament of not being able to divide the world clearly into two camps and to declare himself a partisan of one and an enemy of the other. He felt this not merely as an American but specifically as a Jew and a leftist.

Violent anti-semitism was hardly confined to the Nazis, and in 1939 it was not yet clear how the Nazi persecution would differ in scale and nature from the wider European anti-semitism of which it was a part. When EVM learns that a Jewish Polish general has been killed in action, he wonders how the man felt "fighting a hated foe for a country that did so little for his people." Despite "the zeal of the Polish patriots" in resisting Germany, "the short life of the Polish republic was not devoid of a great deal of anti-semitism. Polish liberation was not a general cry for freedom for all Poles but rather a fight of one entrenched class against another. Had these patriots given thought to the Jew and their own peasantry the fate of Poland might have been different."

He's also bold enough to ask about Jewish motives in supporting war. "Had Hitler done everything he has done except become violently and actively anti-semitic, without any question the German-Jews would have been as loyal to their fatherland as they were during the Great War. In addition, there would be a great number of Jews in this country who would have pro-German leanings." He says that asking the old question, "Is it good or bad for the Jews?" must give way to asking "whether it is good or bad for mankind." But that doesn't bring him any closer to resolving exactly what position to take in relation to the war in Europe.

Of course, the great disorientating factor of the left globally was the sudden turnabout of the Soviet Union, followed by a change in line from the Communist Party, in the USA as elsewhere. In late September 1939, EVM declares himself "*pactically* uncertain." Though he has "for a great many years been a stout protagonist of the USSR," he confesses he doesn't "get the pact all the way. I certainly don't fully understand the explanation of it by leading Communists!" On the other hand, "I haven't much faith in the 'I told you so' group even now." In particular, he is irate at the way the pact was being used by the red-baiters—the very people who had sided not long before with Franco.

He notes that while the Senate passed with only four against a

$963 million appropriation for the navy, it dithered over FDR's request for $975 million for work relief. "The word 'emergency' fits both situations. Perhaps if we were as enthusiastic about fighting our domestic problems as we are about Japan, some of the economic causes that make for war would vanish." It is a fact, he notes, "that somebody is going to profit on the war." He laments that if one dares to criticize the profiteering of arms manufacturers, "you might be labeled a fifth columnist." Conscription, he believes, is a regrettable necessity, but that doesn't stop him from harping on about its ugliness and class injustice. "If war comes, let's make sure that our generals don't die in bed. Every Congressman and Senator who votes for the draft should at the same time sign up voluntarily."

Even after the invasion of France, Belgium, and Holland in the spring of 1940, EVM remains equivocal:

> To the liberal, it's a tough choice. Chamberlain, Churchill, Reynaud, Daladier aren't much choice as protagonists of real liberty. Ireland, India and when you speak about the benevolent Dutch and Belgians read a bit about Sumatra and the Belgian Congo! It's like facing two locomotives and believing that one has rubber wheels and won't hurt as much as the other. We just must be pro-Ally in spite of all the undemocratic things done by the Allies. We must temporarily forget our own backyard of disgraceful events . . . and beat Hitler!

A week later, he reports:

> My alleged Communist acquaintances have taken me to task for espousing the Allied cause. They claim that I am permitting my Jewish consciousness and extreme emotionalism to overbalance my reason. It has become a question not that I love Hitler less than Chamberlain, but that I do have a grave concern over the fate of all Jews . . . I say, "Beat Hitler first—then we'll remake the world!"

To his Communist critics, he makes the undeniable point: "If perchance Soviet Russia had made a pact with England and was actively presently engaged (a still not wholly impossible situation) in fighting Hitler . . . would there be a single Communist opposing our entry into the war? Decidedly not. I want to be a step ahead!"

By the end of 1940, eight months before the Nazi invasion of the Soviet Union ushered in another Communist volte-face, he seems to have come to a resolution. That war solves nothing remains, to him, "axiomatic," but "peculiarly enough, it does make a difference who your jailer is." He even has a kind word for the British, at least some of them. "It is a magnificent fight the English people are waging," he writes of the Battle of Britain. "But isn't there something that will wake up their top officials?"

In 1939, just as EVM was beginning his *Jewish Review* stint, the family moved into the Amalgamated Cooperative Housing Development in the north Bronx. Here once again Sidney Hillman shaped EVM's destiny. The Amalgamated was the creation of Hillman's Amalgamated Clothing Workers Union, inspired by Vienna's socialist experiments in workers' housing. Though the aim was to help garment workers escape the slums of Manhattan, the Amalgamated was also open to non-union members. Aunt Gert worked as a bookkeeper for the architect in charge of the project, and as a result EVM and family were able to move into a new apartment without having to cough up the usual advance fee. The residents were not tenants but "co-operators," and instead of rent they paid a modest monthly maintenance charge.

Across the street was Van Cortlandt Park, the north end of which formed the city boundary, beyond which lay Westchester County, suburban country. The apartments had a window in every room, cross ventilation, and modern plumbing and they were constructed around courtyards with bushes and flowers and places to sit and play. In addition there were spaces for local enterprises, a cooperative grocery store, a vegetable and fruit market, a shoemaker, a drugstore, and an art studio, where my mother took her first drawing lessons from an instructor paid by the New Deal Works Project Administration. There was also an auditorium for meetings and lectures: the cooperative employed a full-time Educational Director who brought luminaries such as John Dewey and Norman Thomas to speak. "The Amalgamated attracted mainly political idealists of one variety or another," my uncle recalls. "Residents were Communists, Socialists, anarchists, Trotskyists, Laborites, Liberals, and Democrats. If there were any Republicans I did not meet them. Nor am I aware that there were any non-Jews in the Amalgamated."

My mother remembered the excitement of moving into the Amalgamated, but also Olga's warning her not to talk "singsong" like the other kids in the building.

> We thought we were middle class, at least, that's what my mother wanted to think, but in reality *there was no money*. My strongest images are of Mom turning Dad's pants upside down so she could get some change out. My other strong memories are of mom crying because dad was in the park playing pinochle with his cronies which was very déclassé or mom trying to go out the door in her nightgown as she threatened to jump off the roof. She said life wasn't worth living but I pleaded with her and told her that she had to live for me. I was particularly embarrassed about the nightgown.

From his columns you would never know that EVM was married. Among all the names he drops, his wife's is absent. It was about this time that he discovered a doctor's certificate attesting to Gert's virginity (as a child she'd broken her hymen in an accident). He made great play of this and met a furious response from both sisters. As a peace offering, perhaps, he plugged Gert's new business venture in his column, advising readers to visit "Gertrude Salk of Gifts of Character (you should see her exhibit of Swedish pottery) at 40 East 49th Street."

The column, of course, was no money-earner; payment, at best, was in kind. That's how my uncle and mother came to spend the summer of 1940 at Camp Robin Hood in the Catskills: the fee was the camp's payment for its advertising bill in the newspaper. My mother, at eight years old, felt no homesickness. When her parents came to pick her up she cried because, as she explained to a bewildered co-camper, "You'd cry too if you had to go home."

EVM paints a sad self-portrait in an article he published (under the pseudonym "Martin Jannet," using his children's names) first in the National Lawyers Guild magazine, and then in the Communist-guided *New Masses*, where his contribution appeared among articles by Elizabeth Gurley Flynn (one-time Wobbly turned Communist Party leader, jailed under the Smith Act in the 1950s) and Alvah Bessie (later one of the Hollywood Ten, sent to jail in 1950 for refusing to collaborate with a congressional red-hunt). It's not a political polemic, rather a chronicle of a day in the life of "Lawyer Circa 1925"—a lawyer admitted to the bar in 1925, reviewing a disappointing career.

"Lawyer Circa 1925" wakes to find himself besieged by unpaid bills (his wife sleeps late because it enables her to eat less). On the way to work, he buys the *New York Times*, feeling it lends him an "air of respectability," and sees the list of those who have just passed the Bar Exam. He wonders if it was as hard as the one he took and finds himself asking "the biggest question that confronts so many lawyers circa 1925: why have we failed?"

> Things were rotten. No clients, no cases, nothing to do. It didn't help much to know that he had company . . . He bumped into a few of the boys. All lawyers circa 1925 or thereabouts. "How's

things?" "Lousy. You?" "Haven't seen a fee in a year." For a moment lawyer circa 1925 felt that warm spirit of comradeship . . . Well, I guess it isn't altogether my fault—but try and convince HER.

He shares an office with "so many associates that he had to make an appointment to get near a desk." He reads the *Law Journal*. "Trial calendars a mile long. Somebody is getting the business— law is being practised. Where is it going—why past the door of lawyer circa 1925?" He finds himself longing for civil service status with its security, but "pride did not permit one to take the exams years ago." He spends much of the day "trying to look busy." Finally, an envelope arrives for him, from the US District Court. An associate hands it to him, joking, "I told you not to go to that Madison Square Garden rally for Spain." Inside are three checks, money owed from a bankruptcy suit filled in 1931.

There exists no lower form of life than politics . . . Ah but I love it! It's like love. You might be jilted, but you always come back for more!
EVM, 1940

The Hitler–Stalin Pact split the ALP. Soon after EVM's debut as a columnist, the union-dominated right wing, led by Dubinsky and Rose, purged Communists from the leadership of local branches, including several in the Bronx.[7] Candidates for the coming elections were asked to sign a statement condemning the Pact, and when Mike Quill refused, he was removed from the ALP ticket. Two weeks before the election, Communist Party leader Earl Browder was indicted for alleged passport violations. The first incarnation of the House Committee on Un-American Activities, chaired by Martin Dies, was conducting noisy hearings about Communist influence within the unions. On the day before the election, in a speech in Boston, Browder attacked FDR as a tool of Wall Street and railed against British imperialism, but not the Nazis.[8]

In the midst of the faction fight, EVM's first comment on the ALP, in mid-September 1939, raised an entirely different concern about the party's future. "The big political question," he wrote, was the ALP's need for "a more diverse membership."

> No barriers have ever been raised. But it is a tragic fact that its membership has been much too one-sided . . . frankly too Jewish! That's no fault of our people. Seeing a party which interested them they joined in large numbers spurred on by union backing. But to be successful it must show a lot of new and different faces, if you know what I mean.

As a non-Communist, non-trade union ALP activist, EVM saw himself as something of an honest broker. He used his column to inveigh against factionalism and for conciliation in the interests of the common cause:

> Year in and year out I have been upset and not a little annoyed about interparty fights. Stalin, Trotsky, Lovestone, Social Democrats and what have you proved a pain . . . All I did know was that the very causes which each of these factions espoused were the ultimate losers as long as people who should have stood shoulder to shoulder insisted on civil war.

There are times when left groups lean heavily on independents, for legitimacy or for protection. And there are times when they are surplus to requirements or, worse yet, an obstacle to the implementation of the party line. Of course there are independents and independents. Independence from factions can be an excuse for opportunism, as well as for a reluctance to follow a party line. In any case, it seems to be one of the traits I share with EVM. My political activism has often involved and been premised on good relations with left groups many of whose ideas I seriously disagreed with. I could never buy the guilt-by-association excuse for not at least trying to work constructively with left groups in common struggles, though the experience has often been disheartening. Perhaps that's why I empathize with EVM's effort to navigate within the ALP. I also wonder just how much he was kidding himself about his own role. He could see through the self-interested motives of others, but failed to note that they could see through his as well. The very independence that EVM believed would enable him to act as a conciliator—and power broker—within the ALP made him distrusted by both ALP factions. "I never voted a straight ticket," he confessed. "Therefore I never was a good organization man. I think one would have to be entirely moronic to do so."

He was particularly perturbed by the ALP right's cavalier treatment of Quill. "Mike Quill stood up in a thick Coughlinite district for our people. Can we be so devoid of loyalty as to ignore one who fought many of his own misguided people for us?"

Not surprisingly, the 1939 election was a setback for the divided ALP and a comeback for Tammany. Quill stood as an independent, lost his seat, but collected 52,000 votes. EVM now felt obliged to answer queries about just where he stood in the ALP battle:

> My own secret gestapo informs me that some of my readers think I am a Communist. I am not, never have been and probably never will be a Communist. I understand that one of the requirements for membership in that party is rigid adherence to discipline. I can get a thousand affiants to write in bold letters that that alone would be sufficient to debar me! I would no more accept regimentation from Browder than from Flynn or Alex Rose. I am not a red-baiter and will not join in the hue and cry against unpopular ideas. The minority views of yesteryear are the accepted ideals of today!

Though EVM championed the left's presence within the ALP leadership, he was skeptical about its subordination to Moscow priorities.

> Change the situation a bit, have Soviet Russia become embroiled with Germany (ahead of schedule) and reverse its stand and throw in with "imperialist England" . . . Can any honest-to-God left wing ALPite look me in the eye and say that at that time he and the progressive wing will be against conscription? No boys, no soap. You'll all be in favor of a united front . . .

He concedes that while "Roosevelt has veered dangerously to the right" and "despite my aversion to a third term," the "emergency of the situation" demands FDR's re-election. As election day draws near, his support for FDR acquires a more unequivocal, crusading tone, particularly because he has such contempt for the Republican candidate Wendell Wilkie, "the tool of the utilities," and especially those Democrats and Jews who had abandoned the New Deal to back him. Among them was Aunt Gert, who must have known that supporting Wilkie was just the thing to get under EVM's skin. My mother never forgot the arguments.

Though FDR's percentage of the national vote was much reduced from the 1936 landslide, it was still a walkover for him in New York City, where 15 percent of his 2 million votes were cast on the ALP line. EVM was jubilant. He began his first post-election column "There is dancing in the streets!"

> Was there a Jewish vote? I'll say . . . But remember one thing, the Jews didn't vote for Roosevelt as Jews but as Americans along with millions of non-Jews who had the same damn fine reasons. When old Yiddisha mamas came in and asked where was "Roosevelt" and were shown on the miniature machines the spot to pull the lever and they kissed the machines as if they were

mezzuzzas . . . don't tell me there wasn't a Jewish vote . . . and a
perfectly proper exercise of the democratic way.

Despite the triumphalism, EVM was still struggling to find a
satisfactory formula for the collaboration between the Jew and the
American that would require no compromise on either front. He
was able to plow on regardless because of the historical moment.
For EVM, Jewish identity had become a progressive essence,
aligned with the cause of democracy, of America, of the Popular
Front, of labor, of all victims of discrimination. Amazingly, this
alignment remained unbroken even under the great stress of the
Pact years. And though the historical moment passed, the alignment lingered, and provided the backdrop for my own Jewish
upbringing in the 1950s and early 1960s.

6

A Militant Jew

Thanks to his *Jewish Review* column, which was syndicated in Jewish newspapers in Passaic, Pittsburgh, and Patterson, EVM found himself in demand as a speaker, addressing meetings at synagogues and Jewish men's clubs, Hadassah and B'nai B'rith chapters, from Mamaroneck to Long Island. His topics included "The Right to be Wrong" ("the only *ism* this country needs more than a five-cent cigar"), "The Jew in Public Life," and of course the menace of fascism and anti-semitism. One of the most popular talks, and the only one whose script EVM preserved, was "This Assimilation Business."

Here, having recounted his misadventures as a young assimilationist, he describes himself at the age of forty living "in a home which is strictly kosher, and truly so out of deference to others. I have changed my name in order that it is not so distinctly non-Jewish and to avoid my children having to go through the embarrassments that were my own." He now sees intermarriage and amalgamation as utopian illusions. "Cross-breeding should be the hobby of the naturalist and not the aim of mere mortals." What matters is "to become attached to something and militantly carry out such allegiance." Though still an "unbeliever" in the "Bible and Talmudic sense," he pronounces himself unequivocally a Jew: "The only way to become assured of respect is to have it for one's own self, one's heritage, and one's beliefs, and uncompromisingly so."

He recommends Ludwig Lewisohn's novel *The Island Within* in which he says he found a mirror of his own Jewish journey. On EVM's advice, I read the book. The first half is a skilfully told tale of three generations of a Jewish family, moving from east European shtetl through a German city to modern America. But the second half is monstrous. Here the contemporary scion of the immigrant family achieves academic success and social acceptance (he thinks) at Columbia University. He studies the new science of psychoanalysis and sets up a practice in midtown Manhattan. One of his patients is a severely repressed WASP woman, whom he has sex with and subsequently marries. Increasingly, however, he finds himself noticing the emotional gap between his gentile wife and his Jewish family, and finds himself yearning for a deeper engagement with his true self. At the same time, anti-semitism is creeping into the life around him, poisoning old friendships. Then one day the spiritually stunted psychoanalyst bumps into a bearded Chasid on the street, and through him discovers the richness of Jewish folk wisdom, the sufferings of the Jews in Europe, and the hope of Palestine.

Just what did EVM identify with in this racist-cum-psychother-apeutic fairytale, this indictment of the futility and emptiness of assimilation? EVM's was hardly a tale of academic and professional or social success. Nor did his personality bear any resemblance to Lewisohn's icy intellectual getting his ethnic comeuppance. There was, of course, the feeling of being trapped in a passionless marriage (though certainly not to a gentile). What rang true to EVM, I think, was, first, the book's sense of disillusionment with facile "assimilation" in an era of rising anti-semitism, and, second, a conviction that Jewishness was something to be not diluted or tamed but embraced and defended. But I can find no evidence of EVM making the kind of mystical (as opposed to political) investment in "rootedness" that Lewisohn calls for. He was looking not for inner peace as a Jew but for public participation. His problem was not deracination, but multiple tangled roots, tangled politics and a tangled sense of self.

It was in resistance to anti-semitism that EVM, after much searching, found a core, a purpose to his Jewishness. His rejection of assimilation is purely a matter of secular self-definition, or to put it another way, highly political: it has nothing to do with religious, cultural, social or linguistic practices. It consists above all in the unapologetic assertion of his Jewishness in the face of anti-semitism. "Throw off the mask," he cries, sounding like Frantz Fanon or Malcolm X. "We must have respect and the way to get it is to be able to respect ourselves."

EVM's attitude toward Jewishness was of course shaped by his desire to speak to—and be accepted by—an audience. I suspect it was also driven by his need to dramatize his feelings of being an outsider. The paradox was that it was at the hands of fellow Jews that he had first suffered the torments (and pleasures) of exclusion and isolation. And he brought that experience to bear in his views on what was "wrong" with the Jews.

Observing an elderly Yiddish-speaking woman asking for help on a bus in the Bronx and being ignored, and a man with a beard reading a Yiddish paper on a subway shunned, he observes, "The Jewish people seemed to be ashamed of their own." "We prate about prejudice and sometimes act the role of stormtrooper in our own little way. I have no special halo on that score myself." In a column headed "Jewish anti-semitism" he writes:

> With a holocaust* sweeping Europe there still exist Jews who feel they must discriminate against their own to "get in good" with their Christian neighbor . . . assuming a cringing, supine attitude they but defeat their own ends . . . There exist Jewish firms who

---

* EVM wrote this in August 1940. The first use of the word "holocaust" to describe the fate of the Jews of Europe cited by the Oxford English Dictionary dates from 1942, which would place EVM ahead of his time. However, though the persecution of Jews had already reached horrific heights, the Nazis had not yet resolved on extermination. Was EVM's use of the word prophecy or exaggeration? Historical insight or overblown rhetoric? Probably something of both.

refuse to discontinue the sale of Nazi goods. There have always been Jewish firms who have tried to put on a front by discriminating against their own people.

He believes Jews suffer from "a fear complex" rooted in "centuries of persecution from the established order." "We 'take it on the chin' more from a deep-rooted conviction that fighting back is a hopeless task than from any present physical fear." He decries Jewish defeatism and fatalism, which he associates with the idea that the Jews are a chosen people—chosen to suffer. "If we have been chosen . . . let it be for the purpose of fighting for our rights and that of all minority groups. If it is a cross we must carry let it be one for ideals and not self-pity." The greatest sin of the Jews is not standing up for themselves. Echoing the Irish revolutionary James Connolly ("The great only appear great because we are on our knees"), he declares: "Better to die standing than live on one's knees is a slogan we must adopt and quickly."

One of the greatest of Jewish sages, Hillel, centuries ago made the pertinent observation, "If I am not for myself, who will be for me?" If modern Jewry had steadfastly held to this philosophy many pitfalls might have been avoided. First and foremost is the admonition that before a people can hope for outside help in any fight for their preservation, they must be willing to fight for themselves.

Who speaks for the Jews? For EVM, it's too often the wrong people, the "stuffed shirts in Jewry, that clique of moneyed gentry with an in with the powers that be." With Ed Flynn in mind he notes: "The trouble with our political bosses has been that they accept mere membership in some temple or Chevra [burial society] as being a guarantee that the holder of such a post is the representative Jew he claims to be!" He recalls bitterly that "in the midst of the riots in Bronx county a distinguished jurist deplored my suggestion that we FIGHT BACK." Leading Jews have failed "to espouse publicly such issues as birth control, child labor, the Spanish Loyalist cause (*olav hasholem!*), simply because the dominant political group in our country is reactionary."

EVM affects pity for the stymied assimilationist: "Change of name, baptism, intermarriage were some of the devices. Along comes the moody Fuehrer and decrees that all the running away was futile." He urges Jews to see their Jewishness not as a curse but as a blessing: "The tragedy is that a great number of our people do not know themselves and have become the victims of a label rather than its proud possessor." He asks, "How many of us are on the border line? We state our religion. We write the word Jew. And we do so because the Nuremburg Laws indicate that we are to carry this label, but we really might as well write Hottentot."

Yet EVM offers no definition of what constitutes Jewishness, of what makes it more than a label worn in either compliance or defiance. He is far more vividly specific when venting the other side of his feelings of militant Jewishness: his hatred of the enemy. In a column headed "We do not hate enough," he wrote:

Most of our lives we are constantly being reminded that we should love our fellow man. But there are times when we should hate, and put real emphasis in it. You can't just dislike Hitler and the Nazis. You must hate him and them twenty-four hours a day and overtime if possible.

EVM was an ungracious prophet. As events in Europe began to exceed his direst predictions, he bristled with anger at those who had failed to listen.

I wonder how my co-religionists can look me in the eye when they recall how bitter was the road to even get them to listen to a

word agin' Herr Shickelgruber. It isn't very satisfying to know
that if the deluge comes and we are engulfed, we will share the
same cell with Mr Wisenheimer (who thought the Jews should not
band together, who opposed boycotts, who sha-sha'ed and
shuskied) because on such occasions to be able to say "I told
you so" will be meaningless.

This militant Jew overflows with criticisms of Jews. "In these days
of insecurity one has some misgivings about adopting a critical
attitude towards his own people," he begins one column, but he
ends another, "I won't pass up the right to attack what is in my mind
wrong because the victim of my attack is one of my own people."

He complains about unseemly public behavior by Jews on the
High Holidays. "If the modern worshipper finds the service too
long or too boring, shorten the service is my cry! Don't belittle
the occasion by flowing on to the sidewalks." He welcomes the
introduction of English passages into Yiddish plays, following
Haskalah and Zionists in disparaging Yiddish itself: "the kindest
thing one can say about it is that it is and in the nature of things
will remain a jargon."

He notes that litigation for and against Jews is out of all
proportion. "Many times I have heard Jewish lawyers say, 'Give
me one good gentile as a client and I'll trade you for half a dozen
Jews.'" While "the gentile client stands in awe of a professional
man," Jewish clients "do not hold the profession in the esteem it is
entitled to." But the real problem with Jewish clients is that "they
will not take advice even when they pay for it . . . Every Jewish
client is between half and three quarters his own lawyer. He feels
that it is an insult to his intelligence not to be allowed to inject
himself into the court's proceedings . . . and nine times out of ten
cares less for ultimate justice than for satisfaction."

As for rabbis, they "lack backbone" and "kowtow to their
board." "What's the use of a rabbi delivering a sermon replete
with lofty phrases about principles, ideals, leadership, when the

congregation knows that if he had had any of these attributes, he would have resigned the week before?!"

In August 1940 a column entitled "It matters not to the hallowed dead" landed him in hot water. He began it by asking, rhetorically, "When will the Jew learn?" At a neighbor's funeral the undertakers bungled, first forgetting the talith (prayer shawl), then putting it on the corpse in full view of the deceased's family and friends, thus turning "a sacred duty into an act of barbarism." Observing this undignified display, EVM opines that "Old-fashioned Jewry must reform or die!"

> When our older people decry the absence of youth from the cheder and the synagogue have they ever taken stock and tried to reason why? Maybe it is the sorry spectacle that most Orthodox shuls present that is the cause? When it is your sad duty to attend a funeral, remember it's a funeral! Come as a mourner, not as an attendant at a clambake!! Be quiet! Shul is not the place to consummate a second mortgage. A funeral is not the locale to boisterously greet long-lost relatives! We Jews lack discipline and decorum.

Readers took issue, throwing back at EVM many of the accusations he had thrown at others. "From the very beginning of the article there was evident the tone of a defeated Galuth [diaspora] Jew . . ."; "the first point made by the anti-Semite is always that the Jew's manners are not proper, his voice too loud, etc."; "does not Mr Morand know that the real Jew never would reform"; "the Jew is innately disciplined"; "our Jews in Palestine—living a free Jewish life—have shown the world in recent years what role the Jew can play"; and most stingingly: "Yes, when will some Jews learn—learn what it means to be a Jew, and to be proud of being one!"

In response, EVM insists—not very convincingly—that he insulted neither morticians nor Orthodox Jews. "I hold to the belief that if and when criticism can be levelled at our own people it is precisely the duty of our own papers to call attention to our own faults. Charity begins at home—and so does a house-cleaning!"

I've been trying to locate EVM's earliest reference to Palestine. I thought for a moment I'd found it when I came across an enthusiastic review from December 1939 of a musical called *A Nation Without a Home*, which dealt with the plight of "our refugee brethren." But not so. EVM reports, "What got me was the evident enthusiasm of both the actors and the audience to acclaim their love of country and their eternal gratitude for our own brand of democracy. The spirit flows in a mighty wave over the floodlights to the audience and the singing of the Star Spangled Banner in the finale becomes a revival meeting." So at this moment, it's Americanism, not Zionism, that offers the answer to the refugee crisis.

The earliest reference turns out to be from late February 1940, when he reports that "plans have been made for the creation of an Annapolis [a naval academy] in Palestine" and wonders if this may be "the way of the future." During these months, as EVM stumped the Jewish lecture circuit, he came into increasing contact with Zionists. He spoke at Hapoel Hamizrachi (a left Zionist labor group) on "Our Civil Liberties" and was accompanied by a "program of community singing of Zionist songs" (and was advertised as "a lecturer of vast and renowned experience"). He "renewed an acquaintance" with I. L. Wohlman, "a Palestinian journalist of note" visiting New York from Tel Aviv. "If you can hear I. L. Wohlman talk of Palestine as 'home' you can appreciate just how much Eretz Yisrael means to those who have seen the future work in Palestine."

For EVM, the anniversary of the Easter Rebellion of 1916 now invokes "a striking parallel": "when the world stood aghast at British atrocity and double-dealing—a partition of Ireland like unto the scheduled partition of Palestine!" For EVM, as for most Zionists at this time, partition was an unacceptable compromise. Despite Ben Gurion's tactical assent to the Peel Report of 1937, which recommended partition, the assumption was that Eretz Yisrael would or should encompass all of mandate Palestine.

But it was the British government's White Paper of May 1939, which limited Jewish immigration to and land purchases in Palestine, that was regarded as the great betrayal, "tearing up the Balfour Declaration," in the words used by EVM and many others. It weighs heavily in the scale as EVM considers the question of the war. Enthusiasts for the Allied cause are asked: "Be a little more realistic. Who welched on the Palestine mandate? England! Who will give up Jewish rights without hesitation to play politics—England!"

The White Paper of 1939—opposed in the House of Commons by the Labour Party and from the Conservative benches by Winston Churchill—was a concession made necessary by British priorities after the brutal suppression of the Arab Revolt of 1936–39, of which EVM shows, unsurprisingly, no awareness. In contrast to the Spanish Civil War, or even Mussolini's invasion of Ethiopia, the most intense and sustained anti-colonial insurgency of its time was ignored by the left in Europe and North America, and actually denounced by the British Labour Party as "fascist."[1]

Labour Party leader Herbert Morrison, who in the thirties as chairman of the London County Council had replaced slum tenements with high-quality public housing (a role that recalls La Guardia's in New York), was a supporter of Republican Spain, a Zionist and a devotee of the British empire: "The Jews have proved to be first class colonisers," he declared, "to have the real good old, empire qualities, to be really first class colonial pioneers."[2]

The Arab Revolt had begun in April 1936 with a general strike of Arab Palestinian workers that ran for 175 days, throughout which the Zionist trade union federation, the Histadrut, acted as strikebreaker-in-chief. By the strike's end in October, there were

37 British, 80 Jews and 1,000 Palestinians dead. The revolt now spread into the countryside, and for the next two years much of Palestine was in the hands of the rebels, who also controlled significant urban areas, including at times the old city of Jerusalem, and mounted constant attacks on the Iraq Petroleum Company's critical pipeline to Haifa. After the Munich Agreement in September 1938, the British were able to deploy sufficient forces to crush the revolt. Punitive expeditions were mounted against villages, which were also bombed from the air. Mass arrests were followed by torture and hangings. In all this the British were aided by the Haganah, the Jewish military "defense" force in Palestine founded in 1920; it was at this time that its elite unit, later known as the Palmach, came into being under British supervision. Meanwhile the Irgun, the Revisionists' military wing, mounted a terror campaign against Palestinians, bombing marketplaces in Haifa, Jerusalem, and Jaffa.[3]

The suppression of the revolt left five thousand dead, the Palestinians leaderless, disorganized and largely disarmed, while the Yishuv emerged with a strengthened infrastructure and well-trained armed force. Thus the British laid the foundations for the Zionist victory in 1948. But at the time it was the offence of the White Paper that shaped the view of the British held by the Zionist movement worldwide. Of course, in retrospect, the White Paper's limitations on immigration came into force at exactly the wrong moment, as Nazi expansion made the need for some kind of Jewish refuge more urgent. However, it should be noted that, even under the White Paper limitations, more Jews were admitted legally to Palestine (supplemented of course by large-scale clandestine immigration organized by the Zionists) than to either the USA or Britain in the same period.

"The treatment meted out to the Jews in Germany and other European countries is a disgrace to its authors and to modern civilization," wrote George Antonius, pioneer historian of Arab nationalism, in *The Arab Awakening*, published in 1938. But, he added, "to place the burden upon Arab Palestine is a miserable evasion of the duty that lies upon the whole civilized world. It is also morally outrageous." Writing out of a fully informed appreciation of the depths of two coinciding but disparate crises—of Jews in Europe and Arabs in Palestine—Antonius was one of the very few to penetrate its ethical crux.

> No code of morals can justify the persecution of one people in an attempt to relieve the persecution of another. The cure for the eviction of Jews from Germany is not to be sought in the eviction of Arabs from their homeland; and the relief of Jewish distress may not be accomplished at the cost of inflicting a corresponding distress upon an innocent and peaceful population.[4]

The White Paper was opposed by all Zionist currents. Briefly, the Irgun opened anti-British operations. However, with the outbreak of war between Britain and Germany, the campaign was called off. A minority split from the Irgun to form what became known as the Stern Gang (who took their anti-British campaign as far as seeking a pact with the Nazis). It was at this point, in June 1940, that Ze'ev Jabotinsky arrived in New York. However, the Revisionist leader had traveled from Britain to the US not to contest the White Paper but to fire up American support for the formation of a Jewish army to fight with the Allies.

EVM was commissioned to interview Jabotinsky by the *Jewish Spectator*, a quarterly journal edited by Trude Weiss-Rosmarin, a German-educated polymath, feminist and teacher, influenced by Buber, active in Hadassah (the Women's Zionist Organization of America), involved in the Reconstructionist movement and, within the confines of mainstream Zionism, an advocate rf Jewish–Arab co-existence. It seems EVM contacted Weiss-Rosmarin after reading her book-length critique of Freud's *Moses and Monotheism*, in which, among other blasphemies, the founder of psychoanalysis suggests that Moses was Egyptian, not Jewish,

and that it was this Egyptian who taught the Jews their monotheism, before being murdered by them. In his column EVM
praises (and admits he's intimidated by) Weiss-Rosmarin's intelligence and scholarship, and her modesty in person. She has, he
is certain, demolished Freud, demonstrating that "here he has
strayed far from his territory of expertise." But still, EVM
confesses, there's something he finds "intriguing" in the notion
of the great leader of the Jews being a non-Jew, an outsider.

At this stage, EVM's exposure to Zionism had largely come
through the mainstream Zionist Organization of America and the
Labor Zionists, both of whom viewed Jabotinsky as a dangerous
pariah, an authoritarian nationalist with fascist leanings. At first
glance, it's strange that EVM should have been eager to meet the pre-
eminent leader of the Zionist right wing, sire of Begin, Shamir and
Sharon. But EVM viewed Jabotinsky principally as the organizer of
the Jewish battalion that fought with the British in World War I and
as a founder of the Haganah. Jailed by the British but released after an
international campaign, Jabotinsky had broken with mainstream
Zionism in favor of a more militant—or at least more frankly
militarist—strategy. EVM would have known him as a champion
of the boycott and and opponent of the Ha'avara. He also saw
Jabotinsky, and I suspect was drawn to him, as an intellectual and
literary figure ("the translator of Dante") who had turned himself
into a warrior, a fighting and uncompromising Jew.

As a right-wing nationalist, Jabotinsky found common ground
with Mussolini, and for some years his Revisionist organization
found a home in Fascist Italy.[5] Its youth wing, Betar, was
organized on paramilitary lines and sported brown shirts, and
initially its German supporters welcomed Hitler's rise. However,
Jabotinsky himself consistently opposed Nazism and rebuked
those among his followers who sought common ground with it.

"This is the time for blunt speaking," Jabotinsky told the press
conference on his arrival in New York. "I challenge the Jews
wherever they are still free to demand the right of fighting the

giant rattlesnake, not just under British or Polish or French labels. But as a Jewish army. Some shout that we only want others to fight, some whisper that a Jew only makes a good solider when squeezed in between gentile comrades. I challenge the Jewish youth to give them the lie." It was a typical Jabotinsky performance, blending coldly calculated Zionist interest with a rawly emotional appeal to Jewish chauvinism (and wrapped up inside it, Jewish shame and guilt).

The ranks of American Revisionism were in those days slim, yet Jabotinsky received telegrams of support from Senator Claude Pepper of Florida, a New Deal liberal who was later to reinvent himself as a staunch anti-Communist, while maintaining throughout an enthusiasm for the Zionist cause, from Yale President Charles Seymour, a WASP "scholar and gentleman," and from one Francis R. Coudert, a Republican state senator who was soon to become a prime target of EVM's wrath.[6]

At their interview, EVM is at first disappointed by Jabotinsky, who he thinks "could be passed by in a crowd." On closer examination, however, he detects "a face that indicates a great deal of hidden resourcefulness." EVM introduces his subject as "one of the most outstanding critics of the British government. I knew that while I was talking to him, his son was in a British jail [in Palestine]. Yet this man was here not only to aid Jews, but to help the Allies." When EVM asked him how he reconciled this contradiction, Jabotinsky "pondered for a moment, no doubt knowing the universal interest of such a question." No, he had not forgotten his differences with the British but "shifted them from the front part of [his] head to the back." Certainly, "promises had been broken," but he reminded EVM that "prior to the last war, Palestine had but 65,000 Jews, today almost half a million." England takes "three steps forward and two back."

EVM points out that American Jews who joined the proposed Jewish army could be found guilty of breaking the Neutrality Act. "I am not advocating breaking the law," the Revisionist replied, but "Jews who have their hearts set will find a way"—an evasive formula typical of this "blunt speaker." Who then would join this Jewish army? "Palestinians," Jabotinsky answered, "Jews in 'no man's lands' and refugees. Anyone who desires to enlist even before his country becomes a belligerent."

EVM asked again about Jabotinsky's new alliance with his old enemies. "I see that you have reverted to this question," the interviewee duly noted. "Apparently you labor under the delusion that I have a utopian faith in England." No, what EVM labored under was the delusion that Jabotinsky was an anti-imperialist. Jabotinsky was, explicitly, a Western supremacist. "We Jews have nothing in common with what is denoted 'the East' and we thank God for that." Despite his periodic clashes with the mandate authorities, and his collaboration with Mussolini, he always saw the British empire as Zionism's necessary partner, and the future Jewish state as a European bulwark in the Middle East. Jabotinsky recognized that the indigenous population had no reason to welcome colonizers and every reason to resist them. Therefore the only realistic route to a Jewish state was to compel their submission through the "Iron Wall" of military power. When critics questioned the ethical basis of his vision, he argued that the key ethical decision had already been made: when one chose to become a Zionist. After that, questions of means became secondary. "A sacred truth, whose realization requires the use of force, does not cease thereby to be a sacred truth." In many respects, Ben Gurion and the Labor Zionists adopted Jabotinsky's analysis and strategy, without committing the tactical error of making them plain.

EVM knew his next question would be "a delicate one." How would his subject react? "Boldly I queried, 'What about the charge that Revisionism is fascist in scope and design, and that you, Mr Jabotinsky, are an advocate of fascism?' Wearily, Jabotinsky observed that he 'knew no interview would conclude without that question. However, I appreciate your frankness in putting it to me so bluntly.'" He then described "the cry 'fascist'" as "the first and favorite term of abuse utilized the world over to deceive the public. It is deliberately and absolutely false when applied to Revisionism." It was, rather, his mainstream critics who represented the "anti-democratic trend in Jewish nationalism."

Like all Jabotinsky's assertions—apart from those regarding his new-found friendship with Britain—EVM leaves Jabotinsky's disingenuous evasion of the fascist accusation unchallenged. Gertrude Weiss-Rosmarin, however, felt that Jabotinsky did need to be challenged, though not on this point. In an editorial appended to EVM's interview, she declared that "while Mr Jabotinsky's Jewish patriotism and courage is to be admired," his proposal for a Jewish army must be rejected. "The Jews of America are law-abiding and patriotic citizens. Their fate is entwined with that of all America's faithful citizens. Should the United States be compelled to enter the war, American Jewry will certainly do its share as Americans."

A month after his interview with EVM, Jabotinsky died at a summer camp run by Betar, the Revisionist youth wing, in upstate New York. Observers at the time believed, wrongly as it turned out, that the hopes of Revisionism in the USA had died with him.

My mother liked to tell us that she'd learned the phrase "white chauvinism" before she was six years old. For EVM, the black struggle for equality in the USA was not only a mirror for the Jews, but a political and personal touchstone. "Any Jew who treats with indifference or scorn a colored person hasn't any right to expect a decent life himself," he writes. "When I think of some of my co-religionists who promiscuously use the term 'nigger' or who consider the Negro an inferior type—then I feel that that type of Jew deserves a harsh fate."

For twenty years, EVM was an associate and supporter of James S. Watson, a barrier-breaking African-American lawyer, one of the first to be admitted to the American Bar Association, who was later to serve as a judge on the Manhattan Municipal

Court bench. His friendship with Watson was a source of pride and sometimes frustration for EVM—not surprisingly, as Watson was a cautious reformer. In 1940, despite an exceptional record on the bench, Watson was initially denied nomination for re-election on the Democratic ticket in favor of the local Tammany leader's protégé. EVM—along with the New York County Bar Association—was outraged. A Citizens' Non-Partisan Committee to Re-Elect James S. Watson was formed. Its co-chair was Adam Clayton Powell, Jr., then a rising star in Harlem politics,* and one of its backroom masterminds was EVM. In the end, Watson secured the nominations of both the Democrats and the ALP and won re-election easily. Years later, EVM recalled: "I managed a campaign for Judge James Watson, one of the first Negro lawyers to make the bench. I worked in Harlem, and found more factions among the Negro people than the Jew or the Irish can boast."

In August 1940, EVM began a new, twice-weekly radio program called *The Jewish Review Commentator*. Among the studio guests on his first shows was a journalist from the Zionist Organization of America "who depicted life in Dachau concentration camp," a campaigner organizing safe conduct to Mexico for Spanish refugees, and two notables of the Yiddish stage. Topics included the Alien Registration Act, the draft laws, and the recent deaths of three prominent but very different Jews—Trotsky, Jabotinsky and Max Steuer, a celebrity trial lawyer notorious for his no-holds-barred defense of stock swindlers, municipal grafters and gangsters, and in particular for his role in getting the Triangle Shirtwaist factory

---

* In 1941, Powell, backed by the Democrats and the ALP, became the first black member of New York City Council. In 1944, he was elected to Congress—having previously swept Democratic, ALP and Republican primaries. For the next two decades, he enjoyed national celebrity as the flamboyant "Congressman from Harlem." After World War II, he broke with the ALP and took up the anti-Communist crusade. Over the years Powell amassed a remarkable legislative record (on civil rights, labor, education) and a wide array of enemies, who used his lavish lifestyle and casual approach to public and private finances to have him expelled from Congress in 1966. He fought a court battle to win reinstatement but was finally unseated by the voters of Harlem in 1970.

owners off a manslaughter charge following the death of 146 workers in a sweatshop fire.* (*Time* described him as "a brilliant, inconspicuous, hawk-faced Austrian Jew.")

But the major theme of the program was the exposure of anti-semitic hate groups and their supporters. Here EVM's guest experts were journalists from the brief-lived *Friday* magazine, which had tried to place adverts for its scoops on anti-semitism in the mainstream and Jewish press, only to find its business refused. "When I heard that our leading Yiddish newspapers were among those who turned down the ad I was amazed," EVM writes. "Did our brethren weigh the question of fat advertising contracts against the fate of Jewry and decide in favor of their pocket-books?" He blasts the same Jewish papers for accepting ads for Ford motor cars and notes the attempts to whitewash Henry Ford by press agents. "The Yiddish press cannot attack Ford the man and take his money for advertising. Ford is bad medicine for the Jews. You can't sugar-coat him." Ford's Dearborn *Independent* had published "The Protocols of the Elders of Zion," and Ford himself had publicly endorsed a range of anti-semitic myths. Considering what he calls "the hush hush policy of certain leading Jews," EVM recalls the role played in the past by the Court Jews, bankers who loyally managed the finances of Europe's aristocratic rulers, regardless of their policies toward Jews in general. They "danced to the tune of pay, of ransom," EVM seethes. "It is because I revolt against that way of life that I have decided to expose our Modern Court Jews."

It was heavily hinted to EVM that if the *Jewish Review* stopped running attacks on Ford, it would be rewarded with advertising. A senior executive at *Forward* called EVM to urge him to think again. "To refuse Ford's ad," he warned, "would create a pogrom—for Ford would lose business, discharge men, and tell them it was the

---

* The fire at the Triangle Shirtwaist factory in 1911 raised public awareness of sweatshop conditions, and sparked a rapid growth in unionism among New York's largely Jewish garment workers.

fault of the Jews." EVM says that on hearing this his "hair stood on end. Here was the Court Jew, paying for protection yet again. Haven't we learned what appeasement has done to the world?"

In 1940, the philosopher Bertrand Russell was offered a professorship at the City College of New York—the city's most renowned and radical public college (with, at that time, an 80 percent Jewish student body). Christian clerics fomented a backlash, denouncing Russell as an advocate of "free love," "communism," and "atheism." Under pressure, La Guardia cancelled funding for the post and Russell's invitation was rescinded. Soon after, the state legislature set up the Rapp–Coudert committee to investigate "subversive activities" in publicly funded schools and colleges. Coudert was the same state senator who had just sent his best wishes to Jabotinsky— even while defending the newly established Vichy regime in France. EVM had already rebuked him for sponsoring a bill to strengthen the church's role in public education. But it was in his role as inquisitor and crucifier of Morris Schappes (pro-nounced Schapp-*ees*) that Coudert became a name ranked by EVM along with Coughlin, Dies and Lindberg in the infamous roll call of American fascists. And not without reason. Here's Coudert explaining his committee's approach to the City College faculty: "Now if your dog had rabies you wouldn't clap him into jail after he had bitten a number of persons—you'd put a bullet into his head, if you had that kind of iron in your blood. It is going to require brutal treatment to handle these teachers."[7]

Beginning in September 1940, the Rapp–Coudert committee subpoenaed and interrogated more than 500 teachers and students. On March 6, 1941, it was the turn of Morris Schappes, a much-admired City College teacher, to testify. He admitted that he was a Communist Party member, but when asked to name other party members at City College, he named only four, three of whom had died in the Spanish war and one who had already left the college. At Coudert's request, district attorney Tom Dewey secured an indictment for perjury. Schappes was arrested on March 18, 1941, tried and found guilty.

On July 3, EVM published "An appeal to Justice Jonah J. Goldstein," the Tammany nominee who had tried the Schappes case and was at that moment deliberating on the convicted teachers's sentence. EVM began by telling the judge he should have disqualified himself from the case. "Perhaps, with so many other of our leading Jews, you have fallen victim to that fanciful and grotesque proposition that a Jew must lean over backwards—that a Jew must show to the world his distaste for Communism—to prove to the world that a Jewish judge could impartially administer justice where a fellow Jew was involved." EVM himself had attended every session of the Schappes trial and had helped prepare the National Lawyers Guild's *amicus curae* brief on the case. In his view Schappes's "alleged perjury" had been forgotten in a "mass of irrelevant material"; the prosecutor had tried communism and the Communist Party, not Schappes. "Read a little history," he admonishes Goldstein:

> Has it occurred to you that as a member of a minority group— even in this grand and glorious land—your sitting on the bench is the result of years of struggle waged by some of the so-called rebels of yonder years? Do you think that honor and high place have come to the Goldsteins because the Couderts and Coughlins wished it? Schappes is of that breed who swim against the tide . . . Hast thou forgotten Jeremiah, Micah, Hosea? Canst recall Bar-Kochba?

Goldstein sentenced Schappes to one and a half to two years in prison. Afterwards, the martyr met with his supporters. EVM left a brief, unpublished note of the occasion:

> Schappes had a bit of a quiver in his voice as he suggested, a la
> Thoreau—"if I'm in jail—what will you people be doing out?"
> Everyone looked a bit teary. Max Yergan spoke as if his heart
> would break . . . The funny part of all this is that Morris is much
> braver and more resourceful than his friends.*

The Rapp–Coudert committee eventually led to the dismissal
from City College of fifty staff and students, including Schappes's friend Yergan, a pioneer in the teaching of black studies. It
was probably the largest political purge of a faculty in US
history. And it had repercussions for EVM in the Free Sons of
Israel. He had availed himself of the pages of the *Bronx Flash* to
publish an article about the Schappes case blasting both Coudert
and Goldstein. The article elicited a barrage of complaints,
particularly for its disrespectful tone in regard to Judge Goldstein, and a fraternal furore ensued which EVM, at least,
referred to as "the Affaire Morand." Shortly after the article
appeared, the District Grand Master sent registered letters
regarding EVM's unpaid dues to two lodge officers ("high-
grade morons," in EVM's view), who then urged brothers at a
lodge meeting to suspend him for being in arrears. EVM
responded with an irate letter of protest to the offending Grand
Master, which begins, "Were I to appear in person, I'm sure our
respective comments would becloud the issue." He is particularly indignant about the "disclosure of the facts connected with
my loan," which he describes as an "act of reprisal" and a
"flagrant violation of all ethical and fraternal concepts." He
immodestly avers that apart from Schappes himself, "no one in
the city knows more about the case than I do."

* In prison, Schappes studied Hebrew and Jewish history. In 1946 he was part of a group
of party activists who founded the magazine *Jewish Life*, which became an unofficial
party organ. In 1958, it was relaunched as *Jewish Currents*, with Schappes as editor, a post
he held for forty years. The magazine broke with the Soviet Union, and after 1967
moved closer to Israel and became one of the earliest vehicles for critiques of "black
anti-semitism" and "left-wing anti-semitism."

I have no quarrel with your difference of opinion as to what I wrote. I would not retract a word. I believe that the Schappes case and the Coudert committee are involved in the entire question of anti-semitism in the public school system . . . it is high time that the Free Sons stopped pussyfooting on important issues. Substitute Dreyfus for Schappes.

Reminding the Grand Master of his work on behalf of the lodge and his devotion of "many columns to you personally," EVM concludes ruefully: "I realize that Felix Frankfurter's espousal of the Sacco–Vanzetti case kept *him* off the United States Supreme Court bench for years—my espousal of the Schappes case will probably keep me on a *park bench* for just as long."

7

In Ancient Palestine

*That the Jews assumed a right Exclusively to the benefits of God will
be a lasting witness against them & the same will it be against
Christians.*

William Blake, "Annotations to Bishop Watson's
An Apology for the Bible in a series of Letters
Addressed to Thomas Paine" (1798)

EVM was fond of quoting Isaiah, Hosea, Jeremiah. He liked to
place himself in a prophetic lineage as an agitator against
complacency, standing up for truth in opposition to mighty
forces. The prophets occupied the center of his idea of ethical
Judaism, and in this he shared common ground with many. It's
long been customary to trace Jewish social activism back to the
prophets, whose legacy has been claimed by Reform and Reconstructionist Judaism, by trade unionists and civil rights
marchers, and by both Zionists and anti-Zionists.

I first encountered the prophets in Sunday school, in highly
selective anthologies that emphasized their ethical injunctions and
their promise of Zion to the children of Israel. Later, in university,
I encountered them as literary geniuses and, soon after, as source
material for masterpieces of Western art, especially by Donatello,
whose *Habakkuk* (sculpted for the campanile of Florence's cathe-
dral) embodied my idea of a prophet, a stern, lean (and bald) man,
tense with the duty of truth-telling. I had already imbibed,

without realizing it, something of the tradition through the poetry of Allen Ginsberg and the songs of Bob Dylan, which led me to William Blake, and his troubled lifelong pursuit of a prophetic mission that was at once poetic and political. And I found the familiar imagery in an unfamiliar light in reggae, where the old metaphors were revitalized in the context of contemporary struggle. My Sunday school background alerted me to the spiritualized (and ganjified) black "Zionism" of the songs of Marley and Tosh.

It was Blake who drew my attention to Numbers 11:29: "*Would to God that all the Lord's people were prophets.*" He appended it as a bold-lettered motto under the text of the poem that has come to be known as "Jerusalem" (part of the larger illuminated book he called *Milton*). In the Torah, the people are wandering in the wilderness of Sinai, and as usual they are complaining; they want to eat meat. Moses, who cannot feed them, complains in turn to God: "I cannot carry all these people by myself; it is too much for me." God instructs him to gather seventy elders and officers of the people into a tent where he will bestow the spirit on them so that they can share Moses' burden, and in due course he makes the seventy "speak in ecstasy." However, two men who had not been chosen to attend the tent meeting "had remained in the camp; yet the spirit rested upon them . . . and they spoke in ecstasy in the camp . . ." Such unauthorized behavior alarms Joshua, who asks Moses to restrain the two. To which Moses replies, "Are you wrought up on my account? Would that all the Lord's people were prophets, that the Lord put his spirit upon them!"

The biblical scholar Robert Alter has cited this passage as an example of "radical spiritual egalitarianism."[1] For Blake, it had wider implications: public witness and the exercise of the imagination were linked democratic obligations, to be fulfilled in defiance of state, church and marketplace. Certainly, what the passage suggests, and at the heart of the Torah, is that there can be no official boundaries to the prophetic, that it cannot be circumscribed by institutions, that it is not the prerogative of elites or the property of either state or temple.

It also implies that prophetic authority is plural, which in turn implies dispute and even discord among prophetic visions. The more you read the prophets, the harder it is to find a category to contain them. Prophecy is a genre of Hebrew literature, so rich in rhetoric and metaphor that its power seems able to survive almost any translation. But that's not all it is. Prophets also appear in the historical books of the Bible and play a major role at various turning points in Israel's history. They are all public speakers, confronting kings and priests without compromise, jailed, scorned and exiled for their pains. They are embedded in the national and international developments of their era, sharing with their audience their own reading of past, present and future. What's more, they don't just speak in words, they embody their message in their lives and actions. Elijah's mission begins with leaving Israel to live among the alien poor. Hosea marries a whore and names his three children "Jezreel" (the site of atrocities committed by Ahab and Jezebel), "Unloved" (or "unpitied"), and "No people of mine." Jeremiah walks through the streets with a yoke on his back.

The words of the prophets as we know them are the result of successive and variant redactions over hundreds of years. In some cases it seems that passages denouncing contemporary mores and foretelling doom were composed while the Judaic kingdoms were in existence and their elites were prospering, whereas passages of consolation promising future redemption for the people as a whole were composed in the aftermath of disasters, notably the exile to Babylonia. But it's not only texts that are internally inconsistent, it's people, and indeed historical moments. The poetry of the prophets is marked by mood swings, it excels at both darkness and light, at both violence and tenderness. It feeds the glorious human appetite for seeing the mighty brought low ("How are you felled to earth, O vanquisher of nations!"—Isaiah 14:12). It inaugurates the literature of the persecuted, the marginal, and it has been giving them succour ever since.

llan Halevi described "prophetism" as "the morality of history thrown in the face of politics. It emerges at times when masses of men are torn by the history of empire from their traditional modes of existence."[2] As the Bible makes amply clear, the history of ancient Judea was one of repeated crisis. During the 200-year period of the *Nevi'im* (the Hebrew word translated as "prophets"), the boundaries of both northern and southern kingdoms expanded and contracted, and by its end both had disappeared. These were relatively small states that only fitfully exercised authority over the wealthy cities of the coastal plain, and throughout their histories they were enmeshed in a shifting web of alliances with the great imperial powers of the day. Not surprisingly in that context, the question of alliances with and reliance on great powers is a major prophetic concern.

The prophets' common theme is the superiority of spiritual commitment and personal morality over ritual and lip service, and this they share with other "protestant" schools of religious thought, from Buddha through the Bhaktis of south Asia, the Sufis of the Islamic world and Saint Francis in the west. Like these others, their teachings were to become encrusted in the very ritual and lip service they decried, as the institutions that claimed their mantle sought to tame an urgent and by definition incomplete testimony and reconcile it with an official paradigm.

In the Bible, a prophetic dynasty runs parallel to the political ones, an alternative lineage of dissent. The early prophet Samuel only reluctantly blesses the introduction of a monarchy, and subsequent prophets nearly all set themselves in opposition to the existing state, often not only warning of but wishing for its destruction. For the most part, the prophets hailed from the Levite caste; they were not poor men, though they often championed the poor; they did not incite or lead popular rebellions. Some seem to have yearned for a restoration of the pre-monarchic, more egalitarian clan society.

Certainly, nearly all saw monarchic, military, inegalitarian statehood as corrupting, a wrong turn in Israel's historic road:

> Where now is your king?
> Let him save you!
> Where are the chieftains in all your towns
> from whom you demanded:
> "Give me a king and officers"?
> I give you kings in my ire,
> and take them away in my wrath.
>
> (Hosea 13:10–11)*

The prophets wrestle with their burden and rail against it. It's
not just their Cassandra fate that they bewail but the vision of
human suffering with which they are burdened. Their eyes have
been opened and it hurts, not least because it is so difficult to
reconcile that suffering with divine justice and mercy. At the start
of his mission, Habbakuk wails:

> How long, O Lord, shall I cry out
> And you not listen,
> Shall I shout to you, "Violence!"
> And you not save?
> Why do you make me see iniquity
> Why do you look upon wrong?—
> Raiding and violence are before me,
> Strife continues and contention goes on.
> That is why decision fails
> And justice never emerges;
> For the villain hedges in the just man.
>
> (Habakkuk 1:2–4)

* All quotations are from the Jewish Publication Society translation, 2004.

The prophets deserve their reputation as witnesses against social injustice; they insist that the fundamental measure of a nation is not its military strength or wealth but the way it treats its own people. It is Jerusalem, not Sodom or Gomorrah or Babylon, that Zephaniah denounces: "Ah sullied, polluted, overbearing city! . . . The officials within her are roaring lions; her judges are wolves of the steppe . . . her prophets are reckless, faithless fellows, her priests profane what is holy" (Zephaniah 3:1–4). But some of the prophets' assumptions and deepest wishes cannot be reconciled with social justice as we understand it today. While their activity has a democratic thrust—they offer an alternative to official authority—they themselves are anything but democrats. Many are icons of intolerance. The Book of Kings describes how Elijah triumphed in his battle with the 450 prophets of Baal on Mount Carmel. Having demonstrated his superiority through a trial-by-ritual-sacrifice, Elijah, dedicated sectarian that he was, seized the 450 and slaughtered them to a man.

The monotheism of the prophets is militant. Like other monotheisms, it has its liberating and its tyrannical sides. What unites all the biblical prophets is their intolerance for the syncretism that characterized popular religious practice of the day, and at times held sway in the royal courts. Archaeologists have shown that small statues of Baal or other deities were common household items across the territory ruled by the Judaic kingdoms. People persisted in visiting "the high places" and offering sacrifices there not to Yahweh but to the older clan gods.[3] In opposing this "backsliding" the prophets sometimes stood in opposition to the monarchies and sometimes in alliance with them—and the relative assessments of the kings chronicled in the Jewish Bible broadly reflect where they stood on the issue of suppressing syncretism. So here the prophets appear kin to the Salafis, who wish to purify Islam of (often Sufi-inspired) folk accretions, notably saint worship, or to the Catholic and Protestant clergy in Europe determined to wipe out vestiges of pagan ceremony.

The prophets also subscribe to the theory of collective and inherited guilt, that the sins of the fathers are indeed visited upon the sons—a biblical doctrine which Thomas Paine singled out as "contrary to every principle of moral justice." At times, their visions of vengeance are genocidal. They want women to be supine and fulminate against the wearing of jewelry, cosmetics or colorful clothes. The Taliban are as much their heirs as civil rights marchers. There's a thin line between the prophet and the demagogue.

Some prophets do promise the territory known as Palestine to the Jews, though the borders are fluid. They do promise that the Jews will dispossess or rule over others, that it is indeed their destiny to do so. Isaiah (14:1–2) prophesies that the people of Israel will be settled on their own soil "where strangers shall join them . . . and the House of Israel shall possess them as slaves and handmaids on the soil of the Lord. They shall be captors of their captors and masters to their taskmasters." Zephaniah predicts doom for the Philistines, the etymological ancestors of the Palestinians:

> Gaza shall be deserted
> And Ashkelon desolate
> Ashdod's people shall be expelled in broad daylight;
> And Ekron shall be uprooted.
> O Canaan, land of the Philistines,
> I will lay you waste
> Without inhabitants.
>
> (Zephaniah 2:4–5)

And so it came to pass, in the twentieth century. Modern Ashkelon is built on the Arab town of Al-Majdal, inland from the remains of the ancient coastal city of the Bible. In November 1948, when it was captured by Israeli forces, it was an Arab town of 11,000 and had been assigned to the Arab state under the UN partition plan. By October 1950, only twenty Arab families

remained and the former Arab houses had been occupied by
Jewish immigrants. When Ashdod—also assigned to the Arabs
under the UN plan—fell to the Israelis in October 1948, most of
its 4,000 residents fled. Benny Morris records that among those
who remained behind, 300 flew white flags from their homes—
but all were expelled to Gaza.

Amos, one of the premier voices for social justice in the Old
Testament, was a favorite with Labor Zionists and especially with
Ben Gurion, who ordered the expulsion from Ashdod. But the
Zionists' take on Amos is a highly selective one. The "sheep breeder
from Tekoa" (not a poor shepherd but a propertied man from a
village five miles south of Bethlehem) prophesied from 783 to 743 BC,
the earliest of those whose poetry is preserved in the Bible. His
opening oration (Amos 1:3–3:2) is dramatic and panoramic, a
sweeping purview of the region and its malaise, an indictment of
the barbarism of the nations. He foretells destruction for Damascus
because it "threshed Gilead with threshing boards of iron" (Gilead,
east of the Jordan river, was a disputed area, frequently changing
hands in this period), for Gaza because "they exiled an entire
population, which they delivered to Edom," for Tyre because "they
handed over an entire population to Edom, Ignoring the covenant of
brotherhood," for Edom because "he pursued his brother with the
sword and repressed all pity," for the Ammonites because they
"ripped open the pregnant women of Gilead in order to enlarge their
own territory," for Moab because "he burned the bones of the king
of Edom to lime." Note that Amos denounces the nations for crimes
against humanity, notably war crimes, not crimes committed
specifically against the people of Israel.

In the dramatic and ethical climax of the oration he turns from
the foreigners to Judah and Israel, and they too are condemned to
the fate of the nations. Judah is doomed "because they spurned
the teaching of the Lord and have not observed his laws, they are
beguiled by the delusions after which their fathers walked." The
indictment of Israel, the northern kingdom—soon to be destroyed

by the Assyrians—is more severe. Israel will be struck down "Because they have sold for silver / Those whose cause was just, / And the needy for a pair of sandals." Added to the crimes of exploitation and injustice are a host of blasphemies: "father and son go to the same girl," wine is drunk in the house of God, the prophets are ordered "not to prophesy." Amos (or God through Amos) most definitely "singles out" Israel. He demands from it a higher standard, not so much of behavior as of accountability:

> You alone have I singled out
> Of all the families of the earth—
> That is why I will call you to account
> For all your iniquities.

The revolution here is the argument not only that all the nations of the world are subject to the judgement of God, but specifically that Israel is not exempt. There are universal standards.

> This is what the Lord showed me:
> He was standing on a wall checked with a plumb line
> And He was holding a plumb line.
> And the Lord asked me,
> "What do you see, Amos?"
> "A plumb line," I replied.
> And my Lord declared:
> "I am going to apply a plumb line
> To my people Israel;
> I shall pardon them no more."

(Amos 7:7–9)

The plumb line is the universal standard, determined not by self-interest but by the law of gravity, always and everywhere the same. Measuring contemporary Israel by that standard, he turns his fury on the Jewish state and its pretensions:

> I loathe the Pride of Jacob
> And I detest his fortresses
> I will declare forfeit city and inhabitants alike.

Prominent among those marked for destruction are the ancient counterparts of today's deregulated global capitalists:

> You who devour the needy,
> Annihilating the poor of the land,
> saying, "If only the new moon were over,
> So that we could sell grain;
> The sabbath, so that we could offer wheat for sale,
> Using an ephah [unit of weight] that is too small
> and a shekel that is too big,
> Tilting a dishonest scale,
> And selling grain refuse as grain."

This is more than an indictment of a corrupt monarchy or an indolent ruling elite: Amos points the accusatory finger at the rich and the specific forms of their exploitation of the community. Unlike the plumb line, their units of measurement cannot be trusted.

Amos's prophetic career climaxes with his vision of the total destruction of the kingdom and the temple. Here there is no relief even in dispersal: "if they go into captivity before their enemies, there I will command the sword to slay them. I will fix my eye on them for evil and not for good." Then comes a passage that demands to be read as a rebuke to Zionists:

> To Me, O Israelites, you are
> Just like the Ethiopians—declares the Lord.
> True I brought Israel up
> From the land of Egypt,
> But also the Philistines from Caphtor
> And the Arameans from Kir.

> (Amos 9:7)

In other words, you are no closer to God than any other people; this land does not belong exclusively to you; the others who dwell in it are also here by God's will. Expect no exemptions, no special prerogatives, no matter what you've suffered.

There's a coda—a happy ending—in which God declares, "But I will not wholly wipe out the house of Jacob . . . I will plant them upon their soil, / nevermore to be uprooted." But this appears, on stylistic and other grounds, to be a later addendum.[4] The redactors needed to fit the jagged, incomplete prophetic testimony into a cyclical narrative of national suffering and redemption.

Jeremiah presents even more complex discomforts for Jewish chauvinists than Amos. If he prophesied today, he'd be condemned as a self-hating Jew. The major theme of his forty-year public career (627 to 586 BC) was the inevitability and justice of the destruction of the Jewish state and the imperative of abject surrender to Babylon. His prophetic independence from state power was used to advocate subordination to a foreign power. At times it's hard not to see him as a quisling, scurrying around the country inculcating defeatism at every turn. As a result, he was at various times barred from the temple, banished from Jerusalem, imprisoned, and castigated as a traitor. He was locked in conflict with the pro-Egyptian faction at court, who were dominant during Jehoiakim's reign, but he clearly enjoyed support from its opponents within the court and other notables.

Jeremiah was a member of the priestly caste, but from a line of former chief priests expelled to the provinces at the time of Solomon. In his earliest prophecies (609 BC) he denounces the whole of Jewish society:

> For from the smallest to the greatest
> They are all greedy for gain;
> Priest and prophet alike,

They all act falsely . . .
saying "all is well, all is well" when nothing is well.
(Jeremiah 8:10)

The collective sin is irredeemable: reform cannot come from within, but only through conquest from without. Because the people of Israel have failed their God, he is raising "a great storm" in the north that will annihilate them. Babylon is the instrument of the Lord's justice, and Jeremiah's poetry resonates with the awesomeness of its world-spanning destructive power. While he heaps indictments on the Egyptians, he rarely notes or seems concerned about the crimes of the Babylonians. In the name of God he declares:

I herewith deliver all these lands to my servant, King Nebuchadnezzar of Babylon; I even give him the wild beasts to serve him. All nations shall serve him, his sons and his grandsons . . . the nation or kingdom that does not serve him—King Nebuchadnezzar of Babylon—and does not put its neck under the yoke of the King of Babylon, that nation I will visit—declares the Lord—with sword, famine and pestilence, until I have destroyed it by his hands. As for you, give no heed to your prophets, augurs, dreamers, diviners, and sorcerers, who say to you, "Do not serve the king of Babylon." For they prophesy falsely to you . . .

(27: 7–11)

Jeremiah's advice—at every turn—boils down to this: "Serve the king of Babylon, and live!" (27:17). In 593 BC, a rival prophet, Hananiah, prophesies in the temple that the Lord will break the yoke of Babylon and restore Jerusalem within two years. Jeremiah replies in the name of the Lord: "I have put an iron yoke upon the necks of those nations, that they may serve King Nebuchadnezzar of Babylon—and serve him they shall!" Jeremiah prophesies Hananiah's death, and in rapid course the prophecy is fulfilled, a narrative QED that puts an end to many prophetic disputes.

In 597 BC, Nebuchadnezzar captured Jerusalem and deposed King Jehoiakim, whom he deported, along with other notables, to Babylon. Jeremiah's letter to the first wave of exiles—the first diaspora—is a call for "assimilation" and became one of the foundational texts of Reform Judaism:

> Build homes and live in them, plant gardens and eat their fruit. Take wives and beget sons and daughters; and take wives for your sons and give your daughters to husbands, that they may bear sons and daughters. Multiply there, do not decrease. And seek the welfare of the city to which I have exiled you and pray to the Lord in its behalf; for in its prosperity, you shall prosper.
>
> (Jeremiah 29:5–7)

It's a markedly different view from the one taken in Psalm 137, in which the Jews weep "by the rivers of Babylon."

> Our captors there asked us for songs;
> our tormentors for amusement.
> "Sing us the songs of Zion."
> How can we sing a song of the Lord on alien soil?
> If I forget you, O Jerusalem,
> let my right hand wither.

As for Babylon, the psalmist offers "a blessing on him who seizes your babies / and dashes them against the rocks." Not surprisingly, there were leading Jewish exiles who objected strongly to Jeremiah's advice and called for action to be taken against him as a false prophet.

In the midst of the Babylonians' final siege of a once-again rebellious Jerusalem, in 588–87 BC Jeremiah was arrested by the Judean authorities while trying to leave the city, then beaten and imprisoned. "The officials said to the king, 'let that man be put to death for he disheartens the soldiers, and all the people who are left in the city, by speaking such things to them. That man is not seeking the welfare of this people, but their harm'" (Jeremiah 38:4).

When Babylonian forces finally seized the city and began its destruction and the deportation of notable families (the poor majority remained), they freed Jeremiah from prison and offered to reward him with comfortable relocation to Babylon. He chose to stay—with Babylonian approval—and joined the fearful remnant of Hebrews. "Do not be afraid of the King of Babylon," he urged and warned them against taking refuge in Egypt, which he said would be destroyed by Babylon (a prophecy that didn't pan out). His fellow Hebrews, however, did not trust Jeremiah; they saw him as a "Chaldean" agent, disregarded his advice, and made their way to Egypt.

Jeremiah is not preaching Gandhian non-violent resistance; he opposes all forms of resistance to Babylonian domination. Like the *Bhagavad Gita*, his poetry counsels submission to a violent world order and offers consolation in faith. I've heard him described as a "revolutionary defeatist," a reference to Lenin's view that the main enemy is always at home, that the defeat of one's own ruling class by anyone is to be welcomed. One of the continuing strengths of the prophets is indeed their sense that the main enemy is at home, that self-examination and self-criticism—collective and individual—are the foundation of any truly ethical stance. (See EVM: "Charity begins at home, and so does house-cleaning!") But Jeremiah wanted to see his own ruling class replaced not by a subordinate class, but by an even more distant and despotic foreign power. His message was that Jews simply have no alternative but to do as they're told and wait for the tide of history to deliver them.

Jeremiah may have been an Uncle Tom and objectively he was a tool of the Babylonian empire. But was he a self-hating Jew? In so far as he taught that the Jews got what they deserved—in the form of the Babylonian conquest—he'd qualify under most working definitions of our day. Yet this was the poet who authored some of the great verses of Jewish (and human) redemption, who painted the golden age of the future as vividly as the horrors of the present. He remains uncontainable.

Unlike much else in the Bible, Jeremiah, Amos, and the best of the other prophetic books have continually renewed their appeal to human imaginations. But it did not prove easy to accommodate these awkward customers within the secular worldview of Enlightenment rationalism. The pioneers and martyrs of the Enlightenment were themselves prophetlike: they defied power and parochialism to speak universal truths, to advance the cause of humanity. But they did so with a type of critical self-consciousness alien to the ancients.

Spinoza argued that "the prophets were endowed with unusually vivid imaginations, and not with unusually perfect minds." He noted that all nations and religions produced prophets, that it was a human and not a Jewish category. The prophetic books of the Bible were a source of moral precepts, but of little else, and certainly not any kind of historical authority. "Although certain passages of Scripture plainly affirm that the prophets were in certain respects ignorant," defenders of the all-knowingness of the prophets "would rather say that they do not understand the passages than admit that there was anything which the prophets did not know; or else they try to wrest the scriptural words away from their evident meaning."[5]

In *The Age of Reason*, Tom Paine observed that "mystery, miracle and prophecy" were the three principal means used "to impose upon mankind." He regarded the Bible as a whole as "a history of wickedness that has served to corrupt and brutalize mankind." But he was at pains to separate the actual words of the prophets from the uses made of them. "The word prophet was the Bible word for poet; and the word prophesying meant the art of making poetry." Paine was wrong here—you can't reduce *nevi'im* to "poet"*—but surely he was right that "in many things, the writings of the Jewish poets deserve a better fate than that of being bound up, as they now are, with the trash that accompanies them, under the absurd name of the word of God." The cardinal error was that "the flights and metaphors of the Jewish poets . . . have been erected into prophecies, and made to bend to explanations at the will and whimsical conceits of sectaries, expounders, and commentators."[6]

Blake admired Paine as a political activist but rejected his deistic materialism. He agreed that prophets were poets—the greatest poets—but then he also thought that poets—the greatest poets—were prophets, and that it was the separation of poetry and prophecy that was the bane of the age. So he saw Paine himself as a prophetic figure: a man who gave himself to his "energetic genius," through whom "the Holy Ghost . . . strives with Christendom as in Christ he strove with the Jews." In response to Paine's sarcastic dismissal of miracles, Blake asks:

> Is it a greater miracle to feed five thousand men with five loaves than to overthrow all the armies of Europe with a small pamphlet? Look over the events of your own life & if you do not find that you have both done such miracles & lived by such you do not see as I do. True I cannot do a miracle thro experiment & to domineer over & prove to others my superior power, as neither could Christ. But I can & do work such as both astonish & comfort me & mine. How can Paine the worker of miracles ever doubt Christ's in the above sense of the word miracle?[7]

Unless you embrace the incomplete, inconsistent, provisional nature of their testimony, the prophets can be a dangerous indulgence. In my experience, the prophetic strain in Marxism

---

* *Navi* has also been translated as "proclaimer." Its etymological root (shared with the Arabic *nabi*) denotes hollowness or openness: the prophets as vessels.

and the left has a decided negative side: the monopoly claim on truth, the clinging to hopes of historical vindication, self-selection by self-righteousness. And then I look at EVM's career as a prophet: he proved to be right about one vital matter—the threat of fascism—but was left disorientated when he tried to replay that prophetic triumph in other arenas and eras.

8

The War in the Bronx

The US finally entered the war a week before my mother's tenth birthday. "I thought World War II must be a blessing since my father had an actual job and I remember he had a salary of about $200 a month," she wrote, recalling "an overwhelming thrill to be an American . . . the enemy was so easy to hate and we didn't even know the full story of the concentration camps until it was all over." For her, EVM was a hero, an air raid warden, an antifascist who'd been proved right about Hitler. But really his war was less than glorious.

In early 1942, he applied unsuccessfully for a commission in the US army in the Judge Advocate General's Department (in his application he noted that prior to the war he had urged the department to establish special courses to prepare civilian lawyers for wartime duties). However, war led to a rapid expansion of federal employment; Gert became an inspector for the newly established Office of Price Administration (OPA), which set and enforced maximum retail prices. She worked in the cheese and nuts division (as my mother recalled, "heaven help any shopkeeper who didn't toe the line"). Through Gert, EVM was hired as an OPA assistant investigator in November 1942 (hence the $200 a month). He spent thirteen months in the job and, as was later to become apparent, it was not a happy experience. In July 1943, he applied for a job with the Fair Employment Practices Committee.

The FEPC had been created by FDR two years earlier in order to forestall a march on Washington called by union leader A. Philip Randolph, who threatened to bring a quarter of a million African-Americans to protest against racial discrimination. In mid-1943, FDR increased the FEPC budget, establishing a network of field officers, and EVM applied for one of the new jobs.

In the note EVM submitted in support of his application, he stresses his long-time fight against discrimination, and his "particular interest in the Negro problem," evinced by his involvement in the Scottsboro case and in the Watson re-election campaign. Through his writings and "hundreds of public addresses throughout the years" he has "never failed to support any cause or movement aimed to destroy discriminatory practices." The FEPC, he notes, should not be a mere wartime expedient but must "become a permanent part of the economic structure of our government."* He also states that his current assignment with the OPA was only accepted "on the basis of possibility of transfer to grade of attorney. Acceptance of position at this salary a definite compromise and as part of my contribution to the war effort." This was not true, the OPA salary of $2,600 per annum being, as my mother recalled, a significant improvement on EVM's earnings in private practice.

EVM joined the FEPC in December 1943. At the same time, the Office of Emergency Management, the larger wartime department that supervised the FEPC, asked the FBI to investigate EVM to determine his suitability for employment. J. Edgar Hoover duly ordered the investigation and the FBI reported back in March 1944.

Thanks to the Freedom of Information Act, I was able to secure a copy of this report—with names of informants and other details blanked out. It's the main piece of documentation I have about

---

* Others, notably Eleanor Roosevelt, agreed. After the war, she was active in support of a bill to create a permanent FEPC, but the Senate blocked the measure and the FEPC died in 1946.

EVM that does not come from inside the leather case. In its own way, it's as starkly revealing about EVM, and his times, as anything he himself chose to leave behind.

The FBI interviewed dozens of people about EVM: people who'd known him in his years as a lawyer, in radio, in the Free Sons of Israel, in the Amalgamated, and in the OPA. Opinions were sharply divided, sometimes hostile, sometimes admiring, frequently ambivalent. One of EVM's employers from the twenties recalled "a bright young man whose only drawback was that he talked too much." An informant from the radio industry described EVM as:

> A man of decided views on political, social and economic questions and also dogmatic and irritable in his discussions. The applicant also had a Jewish persecution complex and walked around with a chip on his shoulder, virtually defying anyone to suggest that the Jews were not being mistreated. He would engage in antagonistic discussions involving the Jewish question upon the slightest provocation.

This informant felt that EVM "is the type of person who thinks the world owes him a living and does not think he should have to work for it." Another said EVM "definitely has Communistic tendencies and it certainly would not take much more for him to qualify as a Communist." He added caustically that EVM "was not brilliant and clever as some people had described him but merely a radical and boisterous talker."

An informant from the Bronx lodge of the Free Sons of Israel "stated that the subject is intelligent and clever and he feels that he is of good character and integrity and is a loyal American . . . He feels the applicant lacks a certain amount of judgment but feels he would make a satisfactory employee." Bronx Judge Harry Stackell (whose name is not blanked out because he was one of EVM's nominated referees) called EVM "a loyal Amer-

ican" of "ability and integrity . . . always ethical in his
practising of law before his courts," who "on many occasions
has represented clients without pay, and even on these occasions
has shown a genuine interest in the cases regardless of the lack
of a fee." His old friend Judge James Watson also vouched for
EVM, calling him "ethical, of good character, integrity and
ability" and "a loyal American." Referring to the *Jewish Review*
column, Watson noted that it "favored minority groups, but the
nature of the column was nothing un-democratic." Martin
Frank, the Bronx DA who had known EVM for eighteen
years, described him as "having ability, integrity and energy"
but noted that he "completely lacks diplomacy." Other informants described EVM variously as "a very capable speaker and
could give entertaining extemporaneous speeches for almost any
occasion," as "possessing no executive ability," and as having
"a peculiar personality which rubs everyone the wrong way,
unless they are closely acquainted with him." Another noted
that "he has a somewhat morbid delight in taking an individual's weak points and 'riding' him about these weak points
until the individual has become his enemy."

But it's his former colleagues at the OPA who speak most
damningly of EVM. They charge him with "reviewing files in
which he had no connection whatsoever and then contacting
investigators" to get them to "go easy on the subject." "He
always attempted to build up the defense of the subject rather than
a prosecution." The most serious charge involved the purchase of
nylon hose, a wartime luxury. EVM was accused of "using a form
of pressure" to purchase said hose at ceiling prices (as opposed to
the more prevalent black market prices) from a person under
OPA investigation. One colleague said EVM "was too 'foxy' to
have anything pinned on him and that he did not actually know if
his attempt to suppress OPA cases resulted in his obtaining
monetary consideration or not." The same man described
EVM as:

super-sensitive on the Semitic question and is always on a Jewish crusade. On any occasion where a case involves a member of the Jewish race he immediately jumps to the conclusion that it is a deliberately anti-Semitic act . . . If he is hired by the Government in any capacity it would be a detriment to the Government and the war effort.

The FBI itself highlighted EVM's role in the Schappes Defense Committee, which had been investigated by the House Un-American Activities Committee, and was regarded by the FBI as a Communist front.

EVM was presented with a digest of the accusations and asked to submit an affidavit in response, which he did in March 1944. Like his letters to Dr Paul, to Olga and to the Grand Master of the Free Sons, this is a resentful, often grandiose, sometimes pedantic non-apologia *pro vita sua*. It's one of those "Here I stand, I can do no other" declarations of which EVM was so fond, and like the others, unintentionally self-revealing.

At the outset deponent wishes to state that he believes that his political philosophy is entirely consonant with democratic principles and has taken a militant part in every liberal and progressive movement for the past twenty years. Deponent is not, never was and does not contemplate becoming a member of the Communist Party. Deponent's aversion to regimentation precludes the possibility that deponent would ever join any political party that would require strict compliance with rules and regulations.

(Years later, my mother wrote: "My dad never joined the party. To this day I'm not sure if he was so goddamn independent in his thinking or he was watching his own ass which I later realized was a big problem for him.")

EVM details his involvement in the Schappes case ("Deponent's only interest was that of a liberal who believed that

Schappes had been convicted because of his opinions") and then
sums up his response to the charge of being a subversive:

> If being an ardent Administration supporter; a believer in minority
> rights; holding a burning interest in militant anti-fascist activities;
> a firm believer that we missed the boat during the Spanish conflict;
> any feeling that FEPC is the last bulwark for Negro and Jew; if
> having been a staunch supporter for Irish freedom, the liberation
> of India and one hundred and one causes lost or otherwise in
> which deponent has shown some interest is to be considered
> subversive; your deponent must do a bit of plagiarizing and say
> with Patrick Henry, "If this be treason . . ."

Clearly, this part of his self-defense he relished. On the accusations made by colleagues at the OPA, however, he concedes that
it is "exceedingly difficult to answer categorically all of the insane
charges concerning my conduct in the OPA. The only thing I
would plead guilty to is the fact that I definitely believe that I was
not temperamentally suited to be an Investigator." He denies he
reviewed other investigators' files or pressed for leniency for any
offender. As for the nylon hose, he had indeed purchased it at
ceiling prices, but had not been aware at the time that the seller
was under investigation and did not in any way use his position to
influence the price of the sale. He can't resist pointing out that
"when deponent came to the OPA office, the fact that he was able
to purchase nylons at ceiling prices interested many of his co-
workers," including those now making the charges against him.

He concludes the affidavit with a tale. On assignment in
Binghamton in upstate New York, EVM found himself drinking
with two local OPA staff members on St Patrick's Eve. "Having
imbibed too freely of liquor, [they] gave vent to their emotions,"
declaring that the OPA was "lousy with Jews and Communists,"
that FDR "ought to be assassinated," and that "the whole New
Deal stank." EVM says he "sobered them up" but chose not to

report the incident. However, months later, he was told by his senior manager that his rating of "very good" had been lowered to "good" as a result of a report from the OPA office in Binghamton. EVM protested, and his "very good" rating was restored.

> This is the only occasion that deponent ever raised the question of anti-semitism, and as a matter of fact, explained to the chief investigator that he had purposely not reported the incident to him because of the fact that he was not a Jew and deponent disliked very much raising a religious issue under any circumstances. The gratuitous statement that deponent is "super sensitive on the Semitic question and is always on a Jewish crusade" is without foundation in fact. There is a vast difference between taking a militant position as a member of minority race and walking around with a chip on one's shoulder.

In 1943, Sidney Hillman launched the CIO Political Action Committee (CIO-PAC)* to support pro-labor candidates in congressional races. For Hillman and other New Dealers, it was part of a larger strategy to spread the ALP model outside New York. However, the ALP itself was once again in the midst of a faction fight. While Hillman had welcomed the left back into the fold after the Nazi invasion of the USSR, Dubinsky, Rose and the Socialist Party old guard remained hostile (a bitter antagonism that went back to the early twenties). The Alter–Ehrlich affair in spring 1943—the execution of two Bundists by the Red Army—exacerbated tensions, especially after Hillman, out of deference to wartime allies, failed to show up for the memorial meeting for the slain socialists held in New York.[1]

---

* In the late 1930s, the Congress of Industrial Organizations, whose founders included Hillman and Dubinsky, brought 3 million hitherto unorganized workers into the US labor movement, including in critical industrial sectors such as auto, rubber, steel and electrical. Communist Party members played a significant role in the campaign.

Hillman offered the CP a deal: their members would remain within the ALP fold but would not occupy visible positions. The CP, which at this time was temporarily liquidating itself into a "pressure group" called the Communist Political Association, readily agreed. When Hillman assured FDR that the Communists would be kept out of top office, the President added his tacit backing. Dubinsky and Rose mounted an across-the-board challenge to the Hillman–CP faction in the ALP primaries in March 1944. They took out advertisements in the *New York Times* charging Hillman with being an agent of the Communists and calling for an ALP that was truly liberal and democratic. Despite the large ILGWU membership eligible to vote, especially in the Bronx, the Hillman–CP forces swept to victory in all five New York boroughs. (The Red Army was popular and was being cast by the US media in a heroic light.) Dubinsky, Rose, and the right wing then formally broke from the ALP and established the Liberal Party, which was to play a role in New York city politics for decades.[2] EVM had counseled conciliation between the factions, but when the split came, he stayed with Sidney Hillman.

Hillman was at this point not only the leader of the Amalgamated Clothing Workers, the chairman of the ALP and the CIO-PAC, but also Roosevelt's war production supremo. The tale that Roosevelt had responded to a proposed nominee for vice-president with the words "Clear it with Sidney" was a source of pride for Jews but also succour for the right-wing opponents of the New Deal who wished to paint it as a "Jew Deal," a left-wing Jewish conspiracy. According to his biographer Steven Fraser, Hillman

loved the whirl of Washington power politics, but it was after all a milieu of gentile gentry saturated in anti-semitism. No matter how agnostic, even irreligious, he might appear, no matter how aloof he held himself from the worlds of Jewish labor and Zionism, Hillman remained tainted, and he knew it. As the psychological regimen needed to survive in this atmosphere of intrigue and covert operations grew ever more gruelling, Hillman confessed, "I must work harder. If I fail it will be the failure of the Jew Hillman."[3]

Kovno, in which both Hillman and EVM had found themselves forty years earlier, had been occupied by the German army the day after its invasion of the USSR. The Jews were soon compelled to wear yellow stars, and within a month 30,000 had been evicted from the main city and forced back into the old Slobodka ghetto— eighty years after they'd been liberated from it by Alexander II. Jewish institutions in the main city—hospitals, orphanages, synagogues, libraries—were then destroyed. In the weeks following September 15, 1942, 10,000 Jews were taken to the old Czarist forts and murdered. By December, there were only 16,000 Jews left in Slobodka. In the spring of 1944, as the two factions of the ALP fought it out in New York, and EVM composed his affidavit, the Red Army advanced from the east, and the Nazis stepped up the pace of annihilation. Between July 8 and July 11, nearly all the remaining occupants of the ghetto were executed or deported to concentration camps. German troops then incinerated the entire ghetto. The Red Army entered Kovno on August 1, 1944.[4]

All this became known in the USA—and to EVM—only later. As a reader of the *New York Times*, EVM would have seen the January 1943 story headlined "Harsh Nazi Rule in Baltic States," which referred to a report of two hundred executed in Kovno.[5] His heart surely would have beat more heavily when he read a piece, in January 1945, headlined "10,000 Kaunas Jews slain in one night," quoting a French officer in Cairo who'd been with the Red Army when it entered the city some months earlier at which time "absolutely nothing remained of the Ghetto area."[6] A month later, a report showed that in 38 localities liberated by the Red Army in the last six months, "not 1 percent of Jews" remained: the report referred specifically to Kovno, where only 574 out of 30,000 Jews had been found alive.[7]

For years I've gazed at it, hanging on the the wall above my desk, a framed copy of EVM's campaign flyer from the 1946 congressional election. His slogan: "In The Roosevelt Tradition." His record: veteran of World War I, lawyer on behalf of the community, fighter against the Christian Front, opponent of discrimination, columnist and broadcaster. Member: National Lawyers Guild, National Association for the Advancement of Colored People, Jewish War Veterans, North American Committee to Aid Republican Spain, Non-Sectarian Anti-Nazi League, Free Sons of Israel, Zionist Organization of America. His program: rent control, emergency housing construction, a national Civil Rights Bill, an anti-lynching law, a permanent FEPC, abolition of the poll tax, social insurance and a national health care system, an increased minimum wage, the abolition of "secret diplomacy" and advocacy of "mutual understanding and good will in Russian–American relations."

The 1946 mid-term elections were the first popular verdict on the then un-elected president, Harry S. Truman. The Republicans were resurgent and the left discontented. In New York, the ALP backed New Deal Democrats for governor and senator. But in the congressional races the ALP ran candidates of its own against right-wing Tammany Democrats. In the Bronx, Ed Flynn had decreed that no Democratic candidate would accept nomination on a minor party ticket (that is, endorsement by the ALP or Liberals was ruled out). That probably suited the ALP grassroots, who'd been restrained from an outright challenge to the Flynn machine during the war years.

It certainly suited EVM. The Amalgamated lay in the 25th Congressional District, with a population of 366,000, the largest in the state. Since 1934, its congressman had been Charles Buckley, a building contractor, intimate with the Catholic hierarchy and a Flynn man (and later his successor as Democratic boss of the Bronx). EVM's long-time vehemence against the Flynn machine may have made him an attractive candidate. His Jewish record would also play well, especially against an Irish Catholic (though pro-Zionist) incumbent. EVM was acceptable to both Hillman and the CP, and there may also have been hopes that he could appeal to old garment trade Socialists wooed by the Liberal Party. In any case, stitching up the ALP slate for the 1946 elections—including EVM's nomination to contest the 25th CD—was probably one of the last things Hillman did before his death on July 10, 1946, at the age of fifty-nine.

A week later, my mother sent EVM a postcard from a summer camp in Highland, New York. "Daddy, please do not decline from Congressman. Pretty please. You don't realize what you can do for the people of this country and I am not being prejudiced because you are my pop. If all our politicians were like you everything would be swell." I doubt he ever had the slightest intention of declining nomination. In August, EVM's name duly appeared on the ALP primary ballot—unopposed, as were all ALP nominees that year. The factional wars had been resolved by the departure of the Liberals, and both the unions and the CP preferred to agree slates behind closed doors.

However, neither the unions nor the CP would have been delighted that the first thing EVM did after securing the ALP nomination was to set up an Independent Citizens' Committee for the Election of Edward V. Morand to Congress. Its sponsors were relatives, neighbors, lodge brothers and small businessmen. It solicited cross-party support, issued appeals to voters, paid for advertisements. None of which could have endeared EVM to the ALP machine.

I know from my experience in the British Labour Party that candidates run the gamut from lofty indifference to the mechanics (and to the foot soldiers) to obsessive interference in the dirty details (and with the foot soldiers). I suspect EVM was firmly on the latter end of the spectrum. He seems to have penned most of the propaganda himself. It certainly has more punch and personality than other ALP campaign material. An appeal from the

Independent Citizens' Committee begins with the salutation: "Dear Fellow Politicians." Am I wrong in suspecting that the following could only have been composed by EVM himself?

> Ed Morand has been the champion of the under-privileged and the proponent of liberal legislation for more than twenty years. No one has given more of himself in the cause of a Jewish National Homeland—in the fight against discrimination . . . No one man by his pen has done more to arouse all people in the common fight against fascism. His has been truly a prophetic role and were his words heeded many of the catastrophies that beset the world this last decade might have been avoided.

Nor could ALP organizers have been impressed by his repeated declarations of political independence: "We are not hog-tied to any party." "Principle should transcend political ties. I doubt if I have ever voted a straight ticket in my life." "You know as sure as black is black that no one, no group can change my philosophy of life. It has been tried before and it did not work." It's a characteristic EVM mixture: a proud statement of personal integrity that was also aimed to allay concerns among non-Communist liberals.

Congressional campaigns in New York in those days were fought on street corners and from the backs of sound trucks, an art at which EVM was said to excel. He inveighed on rent control and the need for new housing, and against "patronage, trickery, and corruption" (namely, Flynn), and he attacked Dewey over his failure to act on the "Mississippi-style" police killing of two black veterans in Freeport, Long Island. There were meetings at Jewish War Veterans posts, chapters of the League of Women Voters, and the (CP-dominated) Jewish People's Fraternal Order, where EVM spoke with Quill and ALP state assemblyman Leo Isacson. He was an invitee to the big closing campaign luncheon downtown at the Hotel Commodore, with Henry Wallace, former Vice-President and current Secretary of Commerce, as guest speaker.

EVM made his personal entry into the fray with a column in the *Jewish Review* entitled "We run for Congress." He confesses: "It is a unique experience. Heretofore, we have spent two decades stumping for others and for other causes," but the rest of the column is a declaration that EVM will continue to be EVM:

THERE ISNT A SINGLE LINE THAT HAS EVER APPEARED IN THIS COLUMN THAT WE WOULD RETRACT OR A SINGLE CAUSE FOR WHICH WE HAVE FOUGHT THAT WE WOULD SHY AWAY FROM TO CAPTURE ONE VOTE OR 50,000 VOTES AND YOU KNOW IT!

His readers also know, he adds, that he "hates Franco's guts," supports strict separation of church and state, and is "against any form of partition in Palestine." He concludes: "These are the times that try men's souls. The bells are tolling. As the teenagers would say, 'Are you hep?'"

The theme of the ALP congressional campaign was that the FDR legacy was in peril. In one of his last public speeches, in May 1946, on the tenth anniversary of the founding of the ALP, Sidney Hillman had warned that "the forces of reaction which fought President Roosevelt in his lifetime are now engaged in a desperate effort to rob the people of the heritage he left us." The ALP charged Truman with betraying the FDR legacy on both the domestic and the international fronts. Friendly US–Soviet relations were the centerpiece of ALP foreign policy, but second only to that—and coupled with it—was a commitment to the Jewish cause in Palestine. The ALP demanded the opening of both Palestine and, crucially, the United States to Jewish refugees. It called for withdrawal of British troops and a UN mandate to establish a "free and democratic Palestine."

Great Britain has loosed a reign of terror against the Jewish people in Palestine and has proposed partition to foster antagonism

between the Jewish and Arab peoples and to play each off against
the other as a manoeuvre in imperial policy.

With the defeat of Nazi Germany, Haganah joined Irgun and
the Stern Gang in a guerrilla war against the British, during which
railways, police stations, RAF bases, and bridges across the
Jordan were bombed. On June 18, the kidnapping of British
officers precipitated a crackdown. The Jewish Agency offices in
Jerusalem were raided; across Palestine 2,500 Jews were detained.
On July 22, the terror campaign reached a climax with the
bombing of the King David Hotel in Jerusalem, where the British
Secretariat was located. Some 91 people were killed, including 28
British, 41 Arabs, 17 Jews, plus Armenians and Greeks.

On July 31, Cabinet member Herbert Morrison addressed the
House of Commons on British anti-terror operations in Palestine.
He lamented "the refusal of the Jewish population in Palestine to
cooperate with the forces of law and order." The bombing of the
King David Hotel had proved that "the curse of Hitler is not yet
fully removed. Some of his victims fleeing the ravaged ghettos of
Europe have carried with them the very plagues from which they
sought escape—intolerance, racial pride, intimidation, terrorism
and the worship of force."[8] Thus the one-time champion of the
Jews as empire builders became one of the first to draw the
analogy so many would now prohibit.

That same month, a young Trotskyist named Tony Cliff wrote
a despatch from Jerusalem in which he argued that "Between the
imperialist master and his Zionist servant there are both common
and antagonistic interests." He noted that at the very moment the
demand for the evacuation of British forces was sweeping the
region, Britain was "concentrating its army in Palestine on the
grounds of defending the Arabs from Zionism." The British
benefited and promoted antagonism between Arabs and Jews,
which blocked real possibilities of labor unity in a number of
industries. Yet even as the Zionists waged their war against the

British, they stepped up their campaign against the Arab population.

> In these very days a picket of some scores of Zionists is posted at the entrance of the Arab market beside Tel Aviv to prevent Jews from buying Arab products. The beating of Arabs, throwing of petrol on the products of the fellaheen (peasants) who dare to offer their wares to Jewish customers and similar acts are everyday occurrences.

Cliff stressed that Zionist terror's aim was not to expel British imperialism. Even after the mass arrests, the Jewish Agency had affirmed that "Jews in Palestine are ready to defend themselves, but this does not mean that they are against the maintenance of a British Army in Palestine to guard the just interests of the British Empire." The immediate goal of the war against the British was to pry open Palestine to the mass immigration of European Jews. Cliff notes ironically that in professing to be pro-British and loyal to the empire, the Zionists shared common ground with their arch foe, Haj Amin al-Husseini, the Mufti of Jerusalem, a feudal grandee once patronized by the British, now in exile after a period of cooperation with Hitler.[9]

None of this was visible in the Bronx. When the British warned the Yishuv that "continuance of indiscriminate murder and condoning of terrorism lead only to the forfeiture by the community of all right in the eyes of the world to be numbered among civilised peoples," EVM couldn't contain his indignation at the audacity of the threat. "If to be numbered among those who are allegedly civilized—the English who rule—'tis better that we share the world with aborigines." Perhaps responding to Morrison's condemnation of the Jews in Palestine, EVM writes, "What irks the officials more than anything else in this conflict is that no member of the Jewish community will aid in the capture of any Jewish 'terrorist' . . . England cannot find a Judas in the land where Judas roamed." Two years later, he reflected: "We may in public have remained a bit silent at some of the 'terroristic aspects' of the Stern Gang. We never have doubted the patriotism of its members or the dastardly deeds of both Britain and Arabs which called forth some of its unorthodox and unprecedented exploits."

In the wake of the King David Hotel bombing, these exploits continued unabated. Markets and cafés were bombed, police officers and British soldiers were assassinated, captured, flogged. Money for these operations came in part from bank robberies and extortion, and in part from the USA.

On September 4, 1946, a show called *A Flag is Born* premiered on Broadway. It starred Paul Muni and a 22-year-old Marlon Brando as concentration camp survivors setting off from a blasted Europe to Palestine. It was written by Ben Hecht, with music by Kurt Weill, and was produced by Peter Bergson, a Revisionist Zionist who had been with Jabotinsky when he came to the USA in 1940 and campaigned during the war for emergency measures to save European Jews. In 1946, Bergson was running the American League for a Free Palestine, which raised money and political support for the Irgun. *A Flag Is Born* ended with Brando addressing the audience:

> Where were you—Jews—when the killing was going on? You Jews of America, you Jews of England, where was your cry of rage? Nowhere! Because you were ashamed to cry as Jews! A curse on your silence . . . And now you speak a little, your hearts squeak—and you have a dollar for the Jews of Europe. Thank you. Thank you.

In a six-month tour of the USA, the show raised $400,000 for Irgun.[10]

On September 12, 1946, in the midst of the election campaign, Henry Wallace sharply criticized his own administration's foreign policy in a speech at Madison Square Garden, where thousands of

ALP activists gathered under the auspices of the National Citizens Political Action Committee, effectively a wing of Hillman's CIO-PAC. The speech made the front page of the *New York Times*, led to Wallace's firing from the Cabinet eight days later, and ultimately his campaign for the presidency in 1948. Initially, its significance was its public attempt, from within the Democratic Party, to resist the developing bi-partisan Cold War policy. The *New York Times* story was headlined "Wallace warns on 'tough' policy toward Russia." But it's striking that the article itself begins by reporting that Wallace "warned last night that the British imperialistic policy in the Near East combined with Russian retaliation would lead the United States straight to war unless we have a clearly-defined and realistic policy of our own."

Wallace argued that concessions were being made to reactionary Republicans as a result of which State Department policy—which he characterized as anti-Russian and pro-Arab—was dictated by the British Foreign Office. Wallace's belief that the British tail was wagging the American dog was myopic. But in one respect he proved prescient. "Our primary objective," he said, "is neither saving the British empire nor purchasing oil in the Near East with the lives of American soldiers. We must not allow national oil rivalries to force us into war."

According to the *New York Times*, Wallace was heckled by Communists when he insisted that Russia had to meet America "halfway," and again when he denied American imperialistic interests in China. *The Daily Worker* was initially critical of the speech, but the CP quickly reassessed its position and the ALP praised Wallace for making "American foreign policy a major issue in the 1946 election campaign."

So it was not without significance that EVM was chosen to pen the foreign policy section of the Bronx ALP campaign newspaper, distributed across the borough in October 1946. "The foreign policy of a nation is truly its conscience before the world," he writes, adding that sadly, "our foreign policy throughout our history has repeatedly belied our democratic way of life." He weighs into State Department career diplomats who support reactionaries in China and the Philippines and who "have worked hand in hand with the British Foreign Office to defeat every attempt to secure justice for the Jewish people in Palestine." They needed to be replaced "with men who do not have big-stick imperialist ideas."

EVM said he was proud not to have the support of the right-wing *Daily News*. But his pulse must have quickened when, two weeks before the election, the New York daily *PM* endorsed his candidacy, printed a photo of him and noted, "Morand is somewhat of a maverick in the ALP because of his efforts to get a united ALP–Liberal coalition working." *PM* had been established in 1940 as a left-wing, anti-fascist tabloid featuring sharp political coverage and high-quality photographs and carrying no advertising—to ensure its writers were free to speak their minds. Its circulation hovered between 150,000 and 200,000, always somewhat short of what it needed to break even, making it reliant on subsidy from the millionaire Marshall Field III. Nonetheless, it spoke to and for the popular front and its community in the city, and its endorsement was a plum prize.

A week later, however, the desire for unity with the Liberals of which EVM was an advocate undermined his own candidacy, and in the pages of *PM*. La Guardia used his weekly column to air his thoughts about the congressional election in the district where he lived:

In my own district, the 25th Congressional (Bronx), I am not going to vote for the present Congressman, who is a political palooka. His record is one of uselessness and absenteeism. His Republican opponent . . . would be most anti-New Deal and would follow the reactionary leadership of the Republicans in the House . . . Therefore, the voter in this district must choose between the American Labor and the Liberal Party candidates. Here is another instance of how unfortunate it is that the liberals in our city are divided.

As if La Guardia's fence-sitting wasn't aggravating enough, three days before the election *PM* revised some of its own congressional endorsements.

> *PM* originally made up its mind that the Flynn issue was so great that we would endorse a minor party candidate, Morand of the ALP, against the worst of the Flynn Congressmen, Buckley . . . in the last few days, however, it has become increasingly clear that the fight for control of Congress may be very close. The stakes are great . . . Therefore *PM* is revising its opinion and has decided to hold its nose about Flynn and back the four Democrats running in the Bronx—even Buckley.

I can imagine EVM's frustration at *PM*'s "lesser of evils" volte-face. As it turned out, the newspaper's endorsement probably gave Buckley his slim margin of victory. After a recount, the incumbent edged out his Republican rival by a mere 337 votes. EVM placed third with 25,575 votes, 18.5 percent of the total. The Liberal came fourth with 15,000, 11.5 percent. It was a bad night for the Democrats, in the Bronx, the city and the country. The Republican landslide did indeed result in one of the most reactionary Congresses ever, famous for the anti-labor Taft–Hartley Act. In Manhattan, Marcantonio clung on, with Democratic backing, while former state Senator Coudert (backed by Dewey) swept to his first congressional victory in the affluent East Side "silk stocking district." Nonetheless, the ALP's position was strengthened; 355,000 voters backed the party across the city. The Democrats could not win in the state without their backing, or so some ALP commentators concluded.

A week after the election, EVM received a letter from Julius Lichtenfeld, who had been the treasurer of the Independent Citizens' Committee—and one of Ed's pinocle pals. He stated baldly that he disliked the ALP and that he'd become involved with the campaign solely "with a view to furthering the career of a great character—one Edward V. Morand, who I always believed could achieve increased greatness if he were a proponent of the principles he genuinely believes in and which are inconsistent with those subscribed to by the party for which he was the standard bearer in the late lamented election."

Two years later, reflecting on the vicissitudes of party politics, EVM recalls "Quill's runout of his own congressional candidate (myself) in the 25th Congressional District. His support for Buckley the Democratic incumbent. His refusal to allow his own candidate an opportunity to speak in the district off the TWU sound truck." EVM attributed this betrayal to his rebuking Quill for calling Colonel Charles Keegan, then US military governor of occupied Bavaria, a fascist and an anti-semite.

My uncle—then aged nineteen and already embarked on his lifelong vocation as a labor organizer—absented himself from EVM's 1946 campaign. Instead, he worked for Marcantonio, "the more electable candidate." My mother seems to have believed until the votes were counted that EVM was going to win, and that the family would be moving to Washington.

> I was so proud of him when he stood on sound trucks in his campaign for Congress and when he wrote columns and had a radio program, but he never knew when to shut up and leave me some privacy and dignity. Whenever I had a date he would say something to the guy about making me walk so many feet behind, like they did in China. I literally begged him to stay locked in his room when any boyfriend called for me.

Part Three

9

Nakba

When you're surrounded by mirrors on every side, you lose your ability to see, and the monster of history makes you its prey.

Elias Khoury, *Gate of the Sun*[1]

EVM returned to the pages of the *Jewish Review* in the first week of February 1948, by which time the bi-partisan Cold War policy had taken grip with the Truman Doctrine and US intervention in the Greek civil war. In December 1947, Wallace had announced his intention to run as an independent candidate for President. The plan was to build a countrywide progressive coalition along the lines of the ALP in New York State.

The Wallace campaign was to prove a watershed event for the US left, splitting the labor movement, polarizing anti-Communist liberals against both Communists and anti-anti-Communists like EVM, and isolating the ALP. Strangely, however, in the many thousands of words EVM published between February and September that year there's almost nothing about Wallace or the ALP.

Another event had intervened: the UN vote for the partition of Palestine in November 1947, precipitating five months of civil war, followed by seven months of war with the Arab states, resulting in the political dispossession of the 1.3 million non-Jews who made up the majority of the population of mandate Palestine. EVM commented on these events, not mainly as a columnist (though "It's on the Tip of My Tongue" made occasional appearances) but as an editorialist. Each week the *Jewish Review* would carry at least two and sometimes four pages of bold-headlined editorials. They were unsigned but far from anonymous. EVM adopts the editorial "we" as if born to the manner, speaking now as an American Jewish partisan of the infant Jewish state, but with emphases and obsessions that are unmistakably his own.

It's when it comes to 1948—what actually happened, its meaning, morality and long-term implications—that anti-Zionists part company, decisively, not only with Zionists but with the majority of the Jewish diaspora. And it's where I part company, decisively, with EVM. Reading his take on events as they unfolded, I'm horrified, but also compelled; it's a slow-motion, close-up view of a man of conscience committing a colossal historic error. As always with EVM, the global conflict houses a more intimate world populated by doubts and demons. His first editorial begins with a declaration:

> We have truly come to the end of the road. The barricades are manned—the drawbridge lifted—and silently Haganah waits. It is a bit different from the days of the gas chambers. Men, women, and children are standing on their feet—and they are armed! . . .
> This time, no matter what happens, Jewry goes down fighting!

He notes with pride (and history makes the phrasing multiply ironic) that "Palestinians are staying, fighting and if need be dying—but they will not give up their land." What's needed in this moment of crisis are "arms, money, and a mass crusade to break the embargo of our fake neutrality." Despite the daunting odds, he urges readers to face the future with confidence: "Haganah—100,000 strong—are standing ready."

EVM overstated the strength of Haganah, which at this time was probably 35,000, but nonetheless he fully subscribed to the view that what was happening in Palestine was a David-versus-Goliath struggle. His writings testify to the effectiveness of the Zionist public relations strategy, in which the Jewish settlement in Palestine was portrayed as threatened with imminent annihilation at the hands of vastly superior forces, the numberless Arabs pressing in from all sides. "If we lose Israel there is no hope for the People of the Book," EVM warns, and he predicts "another holocaust" should Jewish forces not prevail in Palestine. Pressing the case for urgent donations to the United Jewish Appeal Palestine fund, he reminds readers: "There are 700,000 Jews in the Bronx, half of what once lived in Warsaw. Do you know what a shambles they would turn your Medina into if they breach the walls?" (Medina, city or nation in Hebrew, was then common parlance for an urban area, its Arabic background apparently forgotten.)

While this picture was being painted for the world at large, privately the leaders of the new state assessed their position in a much more optimistic light. In February, Ben Gurion wrote to Moshe Sharett, his foreign minister, that not only would the Yishuv be able to defend itself, it would move on to "take over Palestine as a whole—I am in no doubt of this. We can face all the Arab forces."[2] Until May 1948, the Palestinians could muster just 4,000 fighters against a Jewish force at least seven times that size. The odds evened out after the mandate ended on May 15, when armies from Jordan, Egypt, Syria, and Iraq got involved; still, that left 25,000 Arab soldiers facing 35,000 Jewish soldiers, whose numbers dramatically increased in the following months, thanks to new immigrants: up to 65,000 by mid-July and 96,000 by the end of the year. The Arab armies fighting in Palestine were also enlarged, but throughout the conflict they remained outnumbered by the Jewish forces.

Crucially, the Jewish forces were better organized, better led and better equipped. The Arab League didn't come up with even a nominal joint plan of action until the end of April—two weeks before the mandate was to expire. They refused to allow the establishment of a provisional Palestinian government or to provide money or weaponry in significant quantities to Palestinian guerrillas. It wasn't until May 12—three days before the great invasion of Zionist legend—that the Egyptian parliament approved sending a military force. Far from being up against a united foe with a clear aim (the eviction of the Jews), Israel faced an array of vacillating regimes with second-rate armies pursuing separate and sometimes rival political and military agendas.[3]

In 1946, EVM had been vehemently anti-partition, along with most Zionists (and most American leftists), who interpreted the Balfour Declaration as promising the whole of mandate Palestine to the Jews. However, in midsummer 1947, the Zionist leaders accepted the principle of partition, which they saw as a necessary stepping stone toward the larger Jewish state they still envisaged. Thus the UN vote for partition in November was everywhere hailed (or denounced) as marking the realization of the Zionist dream. Partition, writes EVM, was originally "but a ruse to wipe us out while statesmen deliberate" but it has now become an existential necessity: "without partition Jewry will not survive." Only a Jewish-majority state in Palestine can now save the Jews, all the Jews, even if they live elsewhere: "We refuse to remain a minority dependent on the sufferance of others." The defense of partition becomes the political question to which all others must be subordinate. "Partition was itself a compromise." There was no more scope for concessions. "We must definitely take a stand against any further loss of territory."

In 1947 there were 1,293,000 Arabs and 608,000 Jews in Palestine. Jews thus made up 32 percent of the population, though they owned only 6 percent of the land. Under the UN plan they were given 55 percent of the country, including the most economically developed areas, not least the citrus-growing plains. In the proposed Jewish state there would be 498,000 Jews and 407,000 Arabs—not including 90,000 Bedouin. In the proposed Arab state, there would be 725,000 Arabs and 10,000 Jews. Jerusalem, where the remainder of both Jews and Arabs lived in about equal numbers, was designated as an international zone. When the fighting finished in early 1949, the Jewish state had acquired 78 percent of mandate Palestine. Some 18 million of the 26 million dunams of land in this area passed from Arab into Jewish hands. The Arab state envisaged under the partition plan never came into existence. Instead, the remaining 22 percent of Palestine, the West Bank and Gaza, were controlled by Jordan and Egypt respectively. Thus 180,000 Palestinians found themselves a minority within the expanded borders of the Jewish state. And 700,000 to 900,000 had been made refugees.

In the midst of this largely one-way process of destruction, displacement and plunder, EVM's constant cry is "no retreat!" He seems to have entirely lost his former distaste for war and militarism. There's no hint of the ambivalence that marked his response to the outbreak of World War II. And any hint of ambivalence on anyone else's part is denounced. He's disparaging of those Christians who profess concern about the impact of the war on the "sanctity of holy places," notably in Jerusalem. "We cannot subscribe to the theory that men must die rather than destroy a house of worship or a shrine used by the enemy as a machine gun nest," he writes, sounding eerily like a US officer in Fallujah. The rhetoric often turns bloodthirsty:

England cannot understand that for a life taken by British soldiers—British soldiers must pay with their own lives. England cannot understand that for every Jew turned over to the Arabs for murder—an equal number of English will die.

For EVM, the Haganah and Irgun (he is equally fervent in his endorsement of both) have at last laid to rest doubts that the Jew would be able to "gird his loins and meet the challenge." He notes that even Jewry's traditional "appeasers" have, in this moment of crisis, "come to the realization that only by force of arms will the new state of Israel survive. The enemy has picked up the weapon, let him know that Jewry knows how to handle it."

In this war, there seems to be only one kind of victim, Jewish:

"Armed men have crossed the border of Palestine," he writes. "Aircraft has bombed Tel Aviv. Ambulances have been blown to bits." The last is a reference to an attack on a Hadassah medical convoy in which seventy-five nurses and medical personnel were killed. EVM seems unaware that the attack on the convoy was widely seen as a reprisal for the April 9 massacre at Deir Yassin, in which Irgun slaughtered hundreds of Palestinians within sight of a British base. Ben Gurion disowned the action but it was in keeping with his strategy. On April 6, three days before Deir Yassin, he'd told a Zionist meeting:

> We will not be able to win the war if we do not, during the war, populate upper and lower, eastern and western Galilee, the Negev and Jerusalem area, even if only in an artificial way, in a military way. . . . I believe that war will also bring in its wake a great change in the distribution of Arab population.[4]

"Two—four—six—eight, A Jewish state in '48!" was the chant on April 11, as EVM joined a Jewish War Veterans-sponsored parade of 250,000 down Fifth Avenue. "There is no turning back for Jewry," he exclaims. "It's partition and nothing else." As a long-time critic of the JWV, he's delighted to be able to say "Well done!" But he can't refrain from adding: "Had this parade, as originally planned, been held on a weekday with a stoppage ordered on the part of labor—New York City would have stood still. We wonder why that plan was allowed to fizzle out."

For EVM, never before had Pesach seemed so resonant. "*Manishtanah halaila hazeh* . . . why is this night different?" Because "this year . . . we have by our sacrifices created that which Moses set out to do—make a nation and give status to those who were but slaves." As Jews in America conduct their seders and count out the ritual ten drops of "blood" (wine, marking the ten plagues visited on Pharaoh), they must "think of Egypt and Germany and the blood that this very night runs rampant in Jerusalem." He sees the birth of Israel associated with "a renaissance of fervor, a renaissance of spirit for the glory that was Israel's" across the diaspora.

Nonetheless, he continues to view Jewish prospects in Palestine as bleak. "No one in his right senses would hold the situation other than most precarious. Surrounded by hostile bandit chiefs, deserted by a Mandate power under the guise of implementing a freedom they refused to sanction and have done everything to prevent— double-crossed by the greatest democracy on earth . . ." Yet on the day he wrote this, April 22, Haifa—Palestine's biggest port—fell to Jewish forces. Haganah had been shelling the Arab quarters for weeks while the Irgun machine-gunned Arab workers in broad daylight. Within days of the Jewish conquest, all but 4,000 of Haifa's 70,000 Arabs had left. About half jumped into boats and made their way to Acre (which fell to Jewish forces on 6 May), Tyre and Beirut. Yes, it was Jews who were pushing Palestinians into the sea in 1948, not the other way around. Over the next few months, Jewish immigrants were settled in and given legal title to the homes of Haifa's Arab refugees. On April 25, the Zionists attacked Jaffa. By the time they completed the conquest of the city on May 14—the day before Israeli independence was declared— only 4,000 Arabs remained out of a population of at least 50,000.[5] EVM demonstrates no awareness of any of these events.

He greets the birth of the Jewish state on May 15 reverentially: "Baruch habo—blessed is thy coming . . . we are here by God's will as proxies for the six million dead, many of whom rest much easier in their graves to know, as they must, that a Jewish state is born." This is "the bar mitzvah of our people—today we have become men and are a nation." But he notes, "this has been no easy birth. In the land where Caesar roamed Judea has come about by a Caesarian operation. The spirit has been borne by Jeremiah. The midwife at the event is Hadassah. And the surgeon Haganah." EVM reports jubilantly "a monster rally," 22,000 strong, at Madison Square Garden celebrating the establishment of the Jewish state.

Ten days after the declaration of independence, in his first mission as head of state, the newly designated President of Israel, Chaim Weizmann, visited Truman in Washington. Weizmann wanted the arms embargo lifted, and a loan from the US to pay for munitions and emergency relief for immigrants. The meeting was private, but afterwards Weizmann told reporters that Truman had "left him with some hope" that Israel's requests would meet with a positive response. He took the opportunity to assail British policy, and in particular Britain's role in the Arab Legion (the army of Transjordan). "It is almost inconceivable" that Jerusalem "should be invaded by Arab hordes under the leadership of a Christian nation. It was taken by Richard the Lionheart and these people are trying to give it back to a vandalistic group." On a more conciliatory note, he added that if a truce was agreed, Israel would be willing to evacuate Jaffa "because it doesn't belong to us."

Weizmann expressed confidence about getting the US loan: Truman, he told reporters, "said there was no trouble about that because the Jews paid their debts."[6] EVM—along, it seems, with everyone else—registered no qualms about the Jewish stereotyping. What irritated him was the implication that the Jews owed anybody anything. What he wanted to hear from Truman was an acknowledgment of the "debt owed to the Jews by the world and whether and when it will ever be paid."

EVM dedicates a large proportion of the column inches at his disposal to denunciations of enemies, among them the State Department, critics of partition, overcautious, defeatist or apathetic Jews, and—lowest of the low—anti-Zionist Jews. Arabs, of course, are numbered among the damned but actually rarely mentioned. They are referred to in passing as "Arab marauders" or "robbers," never of course as Palestinians (the label applied to Jewish settlers). Once, and once only, he refers to them as "Moslems" and therefore "fanatical." "Whenever the term Arab League is used," EVM advises, "the reader should substitute the words oil, [Secretary of State] Forrestal, Great Britain." For EVM, the Arabs are incapable of independent thought or action, and are in the end merely tools for the prime enemy of the Jews: Britain, now under a Labour government, with union leader Ernest Bevin installed as foreign secretary.

In February 1948, the *Jewish Review* carried an article entitled "Yiskadal V'yiskadash," under the byline "Pat Fogerty." The author tells us that on a recent visit to Borough Park in Brooklyn, he spotted an old friend of the family, a Catholic priest, going into the YMHA (Young Men's Hebrew Association) to attend a memorial service for one Moshe Pearlstein, a local youth killed in Palestine.* "I know little about Zionism," he admits, "but I know enough about England (after all, the name is Fogerty) and I know plenty about war . . . I come from a long line of people who fought and died at the hands of these same misguided Tommies who are turning their backs while Arabs kill." He is moved by the service, by the intoning of the cantor:

> As I sat there my mind went back to 1918. I was up at Camp Devens. How old? Just eighteen. What did I know—well, for cannon fodder your IQ really isn't important. Jews I knew because I came from Borough Hall . . . I shared to my discredit a popular supposition that Jews just wouldn't fight. To be perfectly frank, Jews were cowards. I spoke my mind to a bunkmate. I said some uncomplimentary things—that's when I got my ears pinned back—but good. As usually happens, we became inseparable buddies . . . I learned a lot about the Jew. I learned he could really fight.

* Moshe Pearlstein was one of the celebrated Convoy of 35—thirty-five soldiers of Haganah who were killed on January 16, 1948 while attempting to resupply the Gush Etzion kibbutzim, outposts in a predominantly Arab area assigned to the Arab state under the UN partition plan. The area was incorporated into Jordan after the ceasefire, and only fell under Zionist control in 1967.

"Moshe Pearlstein died in Palestine," Fogerty concludes, "but he was All American to me." It was a tag line that—among many other details—suggests at the least the heavy editorial input of EVM. Here he reconciled the Jew, the Irish, the American, and set them all against the English. And even Camp Devens found a place in the mythic web EVM wove around himself.

EVM praised Judge Sylvester Ryan for suspending sentence on six young men caught in possession of TNT destined for Palestine. "Maybe he closed his eyes and remembered a couple of grandpappys who stood before a British court long before Chaim Weizmann perfected TNT and were adjudged criminals for merely blowing up a few Englishmen! Personally we would like to feed some to Bevin." He is delighted to report "that more than a score of Irishmen are aiding Haganah."

For EVM, England embodied old Europe: hierarchical, snooty, undemocratic, politely anti-semitic, and cynically imperial. "England followed a divide-and-rule policy centuries before Hitler . . . India, Africa, Ireland and Palestine. The sun truly never sets on England's perfidy." Neutrality and non-intervention—"from Spain to Palestine—from China to Ethiopia" always served a single end: "The obliteration of small nations who stand in the way." "Pharaoh is still Pharaoh and England is still England." By displacing the Palestinians and making the British the prime enemies, EVM was able to treat the war in Palestine as a classical national liberation struggle, whose opponents were all, by definition, reactionaries.

Of course, EVM had got the Irish analogy upside down. Sir Ronald Storrs, the first British Governor in Jerusalem, argued that a Jewish homeland in Palestine "will form for England a 'little loyal Jewish Ulster' in a sea of potentially hostile Arabism." This remark appeared in Storrs's best-selling memoir, *Orientations*, published in 1937. Here he distilled his decades of service to the empire, in Egypt, Arabia, Iraq, Northern Rhodesia, and Cyprus as well as Palestine, and his view of the relationship of the Jewish settlers to that empire was at the time shared across the British political spectrum, however incongruous it may have appeared to EVM. Nor were the British, at this juncture, quite the "cool and calculating schemers" EVM imagined. They had just overseen a bloody partition in south Asia. Their principal concerns were to maintain their economic and military presence in Iraq and Egypt, where British-sponsored royal rulers were under pressure from popular anti-colonialist opposition, and at the same time to consolidate the new junior partnership with the US superpower in the Cold War. The country was in debt and the program of the Labour government called for massive domestic investment. British policy in regard to Palestine, between 1946 and 1948, was an expression of weakness.[7]

The Soviet Union and the US had been partners at the UN vote on partition, but that didn't stop US and British policy makers from seeing the Middle East as a prime battleground with the Soviets. The US voted for partition but would not supply or support the means to enforce it. A UN force on the ground would have to include the Soviets or their allies, a development that under no circumstances could be permitted. So it was left to the British, who said from the start that they could not enforce the plan. You can see why they resented the Americans. While the US government insisted that 100,000 Jews be admitted to Palestine, the US itself was prepared to admit only a negligible number. Meanwhile the US press was denouncing the British, and the US government was allowing fundraising on US soil for the purchase of ships and arms to be used against both British and Arabs.

Labour Party policy was pro-Zionist. In 1944, the Labour conference had passed, without a single challenge from the floor, a resolution that included a proposal for a transfer of the entire Arab population to neighboring states (the Zionist leadership feared it made too explicit something that was best left unmentioned, and distanced themselves from the proposal).[8] Bevin sought to balance the commitments to Zionism with broader British interests, exactly as previous foreign secretaries had done, going back to the Balfour Declaration, which could never be reconciled with Britain's agreements with France or its pledges to the Arabs. Was the Foreign Office driven by anti-semitism, as EVM and many others believed? Given the upper-class nature of the milieu, it would be surprising if anti-semitism wasn't commonplace. However, the FO viewed all the various peoples whose fate it determined with condescension. In fact, anti-semitism was a significant factor in British policy mainly in so far as it bolstered Zionism. The same Balfour who promised a Jewish homeland had piloted the Aliens Act of 1905 through Parliament, slamming the door on east European Jews in the midst of a wave of pogroms and repression. For Balfour, a desire to restrict Jewish entry to Britain was easily reconcilable with a belief that Zionism was "of far profounder import than the desires and prejudices of the 700,000 Arabs who now inhabit that ancient land." Churchill believed that "a Jewish state under the protection of the British crown . . . would be especially in harmony with the interests of the British empire," not least because he saw Zionism as an antidote to Bolshevism, the Jewish disease.[9]

During the course of the mandate, Britain had given the Jews in Palestine unique license to build a state-within-a-state. The Zionists controlled their own labor markets, schools, industrial and agricultural concerns, and enjoyed an exceptional degree of political license (which enabled the Yishuv to establish diverse media, as well as trade union and welfare organizations). Crucially, it was allowed to develop an armed force. This state-within-the-state enjoyed official recognition through the Jewish Agency, which negotiated directly with the British on behalf not only of the Jews of the Yishuv but world Jewry as a whole.

Under the British, 368,000 Jews emigrated, legally, to Palestine between 1920 and 1945; Jews expanded from 11 percent to 31 percent of the total population. Despite the immigration limitations imposed by the White Paper of 1939, and the violent conflict of 1945–46, Britain kept more of its promises to the Jews than to others in the region. In the end, its greatest breach of faith in regard to Palestine was its failure in 1948 to meet its obligations under the mandate to protect the civilian population. A British army of 70,000 for the most part stood aside as Jewish forces proceeded with the ethnic cleansing of territories both within and outside the UN-allotted borders of the Jewish state. This abdication of responsibility proved vital for the Zionists.

Strangely, the withdrawal of British troops on May 14, 1948, did nothing to placate EVM's ire. In fact, it is only after that, in June, that he dedicates pages of the *Jewish Review* to calls for a boycott of British goods. "Every communiqué attests to the fact that Jews are being killed by British-made weapons." Therefore, all supporters of Israel should "avoid seeing British films. Don't fly British planes. Give up scotch. Don't buy socks or clothes made out of British wool . . . don't patronize any store that sells British goods." As in the case of the anti-Nazi boycott of the thirties, EVM acknowledges that "unfortunately, innocent people suffer through the imposition of a boycott." In particular, he writes, British Jews may suffer retaliation. But "can we ask them to give less than their brethren on the firing line in Israel?" Since the boycott is "a holy war against the prime aggressor of the Jew—Great Britain," if you fail to join it, "you are a party to the murder of your brothers in Palestine."

Even a proposal to revise the arms embargo to allow Israel "the right to self-defense" leaves EVM deeply unsatisfied. "Israel as a sovereign state has a right to arms for defense and offense whenever the situation decrees either. A sovereign state has police powers that extend beyond its borders. It has the right to anticipate aggression and strike first to prevent a full-scale war." Thus, the one-time "near pacifist" and scourge of imperial arrogance became a prophetic herald for the lawless doctrine of pre-emptive war.

In response to pressure from the US, a four-week truce between Arab and Israeli forces was declared on June 11, 1948.

"Bevin asks the House of Commons to be patient and to give the Palestine belligerents time to think!! Did his countrymen need time to think at Dunkirk? Does he think Haganah needs time to think at the Wailing Wall?" For EVM, the truce is unprincipled because it has been "foisted upon the victim and the aggressor with equal force." He views the coming negotiations with distrust. "What is there to be negotiated? There is only one conceivable settlement—that the Arabs lay down their arms against Israel." The war had so far gone well for the Zionists, but EVM was wrong in declaring "Haganah did not need a truce. Haganah and Israel need a decision not a breathing spell." In fact, the first truce turned out to be entirely to Israel's advantage. Though successful, the new Israel Defense Force was stretched; time was needed to consolidate and resupply. Decisively, in the middle of the truce, Israel received a massive arms shipment from Czechoslovakia, in defiance of the UN embargo. Jordan, Egypt, and Iraq all depended entirely on the British to supply their armies, but the British respected the embargo and temporarily suspended their treaty commitments with the three regimes. So when the first truce came to an end, the Israelis were able to go on the offensive. They advanced further into territory designated for the Arab state, capturing the towns of Lydda and Ramle on the Tel Aviv–Jerusalem road. Here they killed 250 Palestinians and expelled almost all the rest—40,000—at gunpoint.[10]

During the first truce, it was mooted that Abdullah, king of Transjordan, might assume the role of mediator in the conflict, a notion EVM found abhorrent. "His is but an oil pipeline kingdom . . . carved out of lands that ethically [sic] and geographically belong to and should form part of Palestine." EVM correctly spots that Abdullah was motivated by a "desire to annex part of Palestine to Transjordan to make his state larger" but could see no reason why Jews should support his ambitions. Zionist strategists disagreed.

In his assessment of Abdullah as a British client, EVM was on the mark. He had been placed on the throne of the newly created emirate by the British in the wake of World War I, a reward for services in the military campaign against the Ottomans. His army—the Arab Legion—was equipped by Britain and led by British officers. But what EVM failed to grasp was that Abdullah was the Zionists' best friend in the region. From 1921, he had maintained contact with the Zionist leadership and had even invited Jewish investment on his side of the Jordan. In November 1947, Abdullah reached a private agreement with the Zionists to carve up mandate Palestine. His armies would cross the Jordan but would not cross or contest the borders of the Jewish state. In other words, he would be allowed to annex the West Bank to his kingdom (which is what happened and is how Transjordan became Jordan), while the Jewish state would take the remainder.

Abdullah blocked Arab troops moving through his territory to aid the Palestinians because he feared they might stage a coup against his own regime. In March, his prime minister met secretly with Bevin in London, where they agreed that the Arab Legion would enter Palestine at the end of the mandate but would restrict themselves to the area demarcated for an Arab state. Bevin was pleased; he had no other cards to play. This was the only way he could get partition implemented on the ground, deter Arab wrath, and preserve a British presence in the area. From then on, the tacit Abdullah–Zionist deal became the cornerstone of British policy. Here was one thing the Zionists, the British, and the leaders of the Arab regimes could agree on: the undesirability of an independent Palestinian state.

The Arab Legion was easily the strongest, most battleworthy force on the Arab side. After May 15, the Arab Legion crossed the Jordan river but, as promised, did not encroach on the areas allotted to the Jewish state. Abdullah's main concern was ensconcing his own rule in the Arab territories he occupied. He expelled the Arab Liberation Army (guerrilla volunteers) from

Hebron and Bethlehem. In the end the Arab Legion engaged in no significant battles with the Zionists—with the very significant exception of Jerusalem and its approaches. Here there could be no agreement. The UN and just about everybody else wanted the city internationalized. But the Zionists could not accept a Jewish state without Jerusalem, and Abdullah could not cede Jerusalem to the Jews without losing all face in the Arab world. So it was in and around Jerusalem that there was a protracted battle in which neither side could prevail and which ended with the partition of the city. Apart from that, Abdullah, who was the titular chief of the Arab armies, did everything possible to obstruct battle and block coordination.[11]

For EVM, Abdullah had "one redeeming feature . . . his well-known personal animosity for the Mufti," a man EVM describes as "a war criminal" who "openly consorted with Hitler and . . . would, if permitted, initiate a pogrom." When I read this, I thought, Ah, I knew EVM would get to the Mufti at some point. The Mufti was now in Egypt, acknowledged but also excluded by the Arab League. The unacceptability of a Mufti-led Palestinian state was common ground between Abdullah, the rest of the Arab League, the British, and the Zionists.

The Mufti was by no means the only anti-colonial leader to dally with the Axis. Subbash Chandra Bose, the one-time President of the Indian National Congress and to this day celebrated across India as the incarnation of militant patriotism, met Hitler and recruited an Indian National Army that fought with the Japanese against the British in Burma. Moroccan nationalists, spurned by the leaders of Popular Front governments in both Spain and France, also turned up in Berlin during the war, as did Irish Republicans. And of course Zionists—both mainstream and Revisionist—repeatedly made their own compromises with the Nazis. World wars make strange bedfellows: they are multi-dimensional conflicts, in which the global and the regional, the tactical and the strategic all jostle, and matters of principle are easily sacrificed or misconstrued—which is why EVM's own feelings at the outset of World War II were so decidedly mixed.

Throughout 1948, events in Palestine were making themselves felt in US politics, not least in the Bronx. In February, an ALP candidate won a shock victory in a special election in the 24th Congressional District, adjacent to the district in which EVM had run in 1946. EVM was not the candidate, which may have disappointed him. What's certain is that he had no liking for the man who was, Leo Isacson, the former state assemblyman, born on the Lower East Side and described by *Time* as "a young, good-looking and aggressive labor lawyer."

The district's population was 55 percent Jewish, 18 percent black, and the rest Irish, Italian and Puerto Rican. It was, in *Time*'s words, "a disheartening area of crowded walk-up tenements, blackened, blind-walled factories and littered streets" and had long been regarded as a Flynn fiefdom. But sensing an opportunity, *Time* reported, "the Wallace–ALP forces behaved like hungry politicians." Marcantonio stumped non-stop for Isacson, and was frequently joined by Paul Robeson, singer, actor, activist, and, at the time, after heavyweight champion Joe Louis, the most well-known black man in the country. An army of left-wingers imported from all corners of the city rang doorbells and "harangued the voters in English, Yiddish and Spanish." And what they harangued them about, along with the nickel fare and rent control, was Palestine. "Over and over Isacson hammered home the contention that Harry Truman had ducked the Palestine issue."

Isacson succeeded in converting a 15,000 Democratic majority into a 10,000 margin for the ALP. The upset was reported nationwide and was greeted ecstatically by Wallace supporters. The time was ripe: the progressive constituencies that had supported FDR were ready to break with Truman and the Democrats. Thus the Wallace bid for the White House took off, at least in New York, in a mood of buoyant optimism. Isacson's victory did not turn out to be a bell-wether in the way the left thought at the time, however, though it did herald the ballot box power, among Jewish voters, of the Palestine issue.

Wallace's charge that, when it came to the Middle East, the State Department was a tool of the British Foreign Office was widely echoed on the left. EVM accuses the State Department of "sabotaging, stealing, tricking and murdering partition!" He goes further than most when he asserts, "We know that those who hold the leashes at the State Department think no less of hunting Jews than for possum." His worst premonitions seemed to be borne out when, on March 19, the US representative told the UN Security Council that the US was suspending support for the partition plan. In light of the "chaos, heavy fighting and much loss of life," the US now proposed a temporary UN trusteeship to maintain peace and give the Arabs and Jews another chance to reach an agreement.

EVM fulminated at "this new decree: No partition . . . a *ukase* that makes any of the Czar's pale in importance. Blood is on the hands of Truman, Marshall, Forrestal, Bevin and Loy Henderson [US Under-Secretary of State] and all the great and little stooges and satellites among the nations." Truman justified the policy reversal by referring to the bloodshed in Palestine, to which EVM responds thus: "To be sure a medium of violence was to be expected. The cold hard facts suggest that many lives might be lost. Jewry was willing to pay that bill." The real reason for the change in US policy, EVM argues, is oil, which "has smeared the honor of our country long enough . . . United States policy wrecks partition for oil and military bases." He notes that the forces undermining partition are the same ones pushing the US toward war with the Soviet Union. Such a prospect must be rejected by "any sane individual who did not wish to commit suicide even in the company of the rest of the world." The first step in stopping the march to nuclear Armageddon "is a reversal of Truman's trusteeship (which is really only a step towards re-imposition and continuation of the British mandate). We must stop the spread of the Truman doctrine of unilateral American imperialism to Palestine."

Much space in the *Jewish Review* is given over to the fate of the Jewish vote in the upcoming elections and in particular to the difficulties that the reversal on Palestine created for Ed Flynn. EVM warns that unless the White House changes course on Palestine, Jewish voters in the Bronx will bolt the Democratic stable, though he shies away from specifying the alternative, a vote for Wallace. "What we want to know is how far will Flynn go to insure partition in Palestine. Is he willing to create partition in the Bronx and turn against the national administration?" In Congress, Buckley, EVM's rival in 1946, sponsored a motion against the arms embargo, and won EVM's praise—a measure of how far from parochial political concerns the anti-Tammany scrapper had now drifted.

EVM seems not to have shared the rosy view of Wallace's prospects, nor the excitement over the ALP's election success. In an incomplete memoir he wrote in 1948, called "So You Want to Be a Politician," EVM tells us that Isacson, "the fair-haired boy of the Bronx ALP," was "hated by his outward supporters," and that Marcantonio in particular "thinks his congressional colleague is in his own words a 'schmoo', the current vernacular for 'dope.'"

The Wallace campaign was unwelcome in the extreme for a number of hitherto close allies of the CP, especially in the unions. Among those who broke with the left at this juncture, publicly and sensationally, was Mike Quill. On April 7, six weeks after the Isacson victory, he denounced the CP, Wallace's Progressive Party, and the ALP at a Transport Workers Union rally at Manhattan Center. The slogan for the night was "wages before Wallace." Quill held a copy of the *Daily Worker* over his head and tore it to shreds, declaring, "That's what I think of them." The immediate cause of the breach was the ALP's support for retaining the nickel fare, which stood in the way of the TWU's wage claim. The proximate cause was the Wallace bid for the presidency and Quill's belief that this would isolate him and his union. Quill soon joined the red-baiting chorus, but he remained, politically, on the left of the labor movement, and never in the Democrats' pocket.[12]

"So You Want to Be a Politician" is redolent with EVM's disillusionment not only with the ALP, but with party politics in general. "I have seen the scramble for jobs from that of street painting inspector to the Supreme Court. I have promoted many deals myself and have been as quickly forgotten by the very men I helped elect." He recalls that, over the years, he has seen independents in the ALP (including himself) "double-crossed" by all the factions: the ILGWU, the Amalgamated and "the Reds." He was particularly embittered by "Marcantonio's feud" with Mayor William O'Dwyer, a liberal Democrat elected to succeed La Guardia, with ALP support. "I was on the inside of some of the negotiations that have never seen print." According to EVM, early in 1948, Marcantonio and Robeson visited EVM's friend Jim Watson to persuade him to run as ALP candidate for the Surrogate Court of New York County—which EVM describes as the "richest judicial plum in the world." Marcantonio had the electoral arithmetic all worked out: how Watson could take Manhattan, district by district. It was agreed that Watson would approach the Democrats for a deal, with EVM "personally calling Paul O'Dwyer" (the mayor's brother, a civil rights lawyer and later an anti-Vietnam War congressman) "to be sure to relay to the mayor that the Democrats could have the endorsement if they would play ball." Sadly, "the deal was all set and just didn't jell."

After Watson dropped out, the Surrogate's job became a battleground between Marcantonio and O'Dwyer, who failed to agree on a series of compromise candidates. O'Dwyer denounced Marcantonio as a "Stalinist" and backed a Democratic challenger in his congressional district. At a Wallace rally at Yankee Stadium, Marcantonio taunted O'Dwyer as "whirling Willie" and "flip-flop Willie," though according to EVM it was Marcantonio himself who did the "flip-flopping" over the Surrogate's job.

Wallace's ten-month nationwide presidential campaign had seen him break convention and defy intimidation by speaking before integrated audiences across the South. He finished it in the Bronx, touring the borough with a motorcade of 100 cars on election eve. Just before midnight, he addressed a meeting of 3,000, telling them a vote for Truman would be wasted because Truman would lose, whereas a vote for the Progressive Party was a protest against "the war and anti-labor policies of Wall Street."

The Wallace forces had talked of getting 10 million votes. On election day, their candidate received only 1,157,328 (2.37 percent), slightly fewer than voted for the Dixiecrat Strom Thurmond, who won four Southern states outright. Only in five states did Wallace secure more than 3 percent. His best return, by far, was in New York, where he won 8.25 percent of the vote and cost Truman the state. Of all votes for Wallace nationwide, 36.5 percent were cast in New York City; his 106,000 votes in the Bronx were as many as he received in the whole of the industrial Midwest.

However, even the Bronx result was a disappointment, with Wallace well beaten by both Dewey and Truman. Isacson lost the seat he'd briefly held, defeated by a joint Democratic-Republican-Liberal candidate. "For local offices the ALP has lost, almost completely, balance of power position," reported the *New York Times*. Only Marcantonio, standing for the first time solely on the ALP line, squeaked in with 36 percent in a four-way race. The *New York Times* was distressed by the result and urged that, next time round, the joint strategy deployed against Isacson should be adopted to remove Marcantonio. Only two years before, the paper had called for his re-election.[13]

The Progressive Party campaign of 1948 proved to be the last gasp of the American popular front. It was also the first taste of left-wing politics for a new generation of activists. My uncle, my father and my mother all worked for Wallace. While the campaign drew my father and mother into the CP orbit, it left my uncle with what he calls "post-1948 traumatic stress syndrome"—a lasting skepticism about third-party politics in the US context. The illusions that surrounded the Wallace campaign are certainly a warning, even today. It's too easy for the left to overestimate the spread or the depth of its support, to mistake its desires for facts on the ground, to believe its populist rhetoric echoes a reality. The fate of the Wallace campaign also warns about the dangers of allowing a broader coalition to fall under the manipulative sway of sectarian organizations like the CP. Nonetheless, the objective conditions that gave birth to the hunger for a third party in 1948 are still with us: the absence of real political alternatives, on both domestic and foreign issues. Not least when it comes to Israel and Palestine. That's just what Henry Wallace warned about, except that the bipartisan consensus to which he and the left objected was, in those days, in their eyes, anti-Zionist.

There was, inevitably, the enemy within. The Jews, as ever, were plagued by division.

> While the Roman legions were massed outside the walls of Jerusalem—when it was evident that a breach in the walls meant extermination—Jews could not agree. Within the temple walls, factions opposed other factions. The Arabs are outside the gates— verily they are holding the remaining wall of what was Israel's temple. And what do we do? Just divide and divide again into factions.

EVM is outraged that B'nai B'rith and the American Jewish Committee have withdrawn from a planned American Jewish unity conference. "It is our firm belief that the AJC could never be part of a united front for Jewry." These Jews "live on the other side of the tracks and won't cross." He excoriates what he sees as their long, shameful record of self-serving short-sightedness. "Our Deutsche Yehuddim exert an unhealthy and unprogressive influence on all of Jewry because in the main they foot the bill." (While EVM liked to scold other Jews for engaging in racial stereotyping, he frequently gave himself free rein to indulge in those stereotypes that appealed to him.) "The hour is near when American Jewry must rid itself of the Court (moneybags) Jew—who wants his dollar to control opinion."

> In these perilous times a kid-glove policy of not offending anyone or any party cannot be countenanced. There can be no rail-sitters with the world on fire. As American Jews in this hour of despair you are either with us 100 per cent or we must count you as an enemy.

Among those whom EVM classed as "enemies of the Jewish people" was Virginia Gildersleeve, who as Dean of Barnard College between 1911 and 1947 had been among the most prominent champions of women's rights in academia. Under her aegis, the numbers of Jewish students at Barnard swelled (she barred restrictive quotas). She campaigned for Al Smith and FDR, and during World War II for Russian war relief. In 1945 she was the sole female among the US delegation to the San Francisco Conference that drew up the UN Charter. Gildersleeve was responsible for the insertion into the Charter of two vital, progressive aims: "higher standards of living, full employment, and conditions of economic and social progress and development" and "universal respect for human rights and fundamental freedoms for all without distinction as to race, sex, language, or religion." All of this made her a respected figure in liberal circles, but when she opposed partition she was attacked, in the *New York Times* as well as the *Jewish Review*, as an anti-semite.

Gildersleeve later described Zionism as "a movement which was to plunge much of the region into war, sow long-lasting hatred and make the Arabs consider America not the best-liked and trusted of the nations of the West . . . but the most disliked and distrusted."[14] In early 1948 she helped found the Committee for Justice and Peace in the Holy Land, to lobby for peace and equal rights and by implication for the reversal of partition. She was among the earliest campaigners in the US for the Palestinian refugees. All this prompted EVM to "wonder what comfort the dear Dean gets out of the news of Jews murdered every day."

But Gildersleeve, at least, was not Jewish, and therefore was spared the wrath EVM visited on anti-Zionist Jews, who were lacerated in an editorial entitled "The Jewish Quislings." "Quisling," EVM notes, may be a new word from World War II, but it is an ancient phenomenon among the Jews, "from Josephus to the American Council for Judaism."

The American Council for Judaism was founded by dissident Reform rabbis after the Central Conference of American Rabbis had voted in 1942 to support the establishment of a Jewish army. Initially, the ACJ's aim was to preserve Judaism from Zionism, to reassert the non-national, religious identity of the Jews and specifically the democratic and universalist credo of Reform. The dissenters were shocked by the character assassination to which they were subject by their Zionist opponents, including Stephen Wise. As Rabbi Elmer Berger, the ACJ's co-ordinator and for six decades an uncompromising opponent of Zionism, observed, the experience was a wake-up call: to the anti-democratic character of Zionism, to its willingness to abandon all scruple in debate, and to its insistence on monopoly representation of Jews.[15]

EVM dedicates a full column to an attack on the ACJ's leading public spokesperson, Lessing Rosenwald, art collector and heir to the Sears-Roebuck fortune. EVM calls Rosenwald (several times) a "fool," one of "the select Jews" who "live apart from Jewish National Life." He accuses him of putting "a false emphasis on his so-called Americanism at the expense of his Jewish heritage." He is incensed by Rosenwald's article, "The Fallacies of Palestine," which had just appeared in *Collier's Magazine*: "Rosenwald's most glaring lie is his assertion that nine out of ten Jews do not know what the Palestine situation is about. That false statement—made in a magazine which has a preponderance of Gentile readers—is but typical of the man and his alleged mind."

EVM had little to worry about. The *Collier's* article proved to be the high watermark for anti-Zionist Jews in the US media. Although the ACJ did draw support from Jews in the south and west (including wealthy Jews like the owner of the famous Neiman Marcus store in Texas), it was unable to make significant inroads among the more numerous Jews of the eastern seaboard, not least because it had no links to Jewish labor. Former Bundists, as Norman Thomas complained to Berger, were now "too busy working for the Zionist movement" to spend time building socialism in the USA.

As Berger later confessed, a major weakness for the ACJ was that its opposition to Zionism was mainly theoretical and theological. "Looking back," he wrote, "I remain appalled at how little any of us knew about what was really happening in Palestine between November 1947 and May of 1948."[16] Like many others, the ACJ assumed the Arabs would win a quick victory in the war and the upshot would be another wave of refugees, Jewish refugees, who would have to be admitted to the USA. Berger was to dedicate much of the rest of his life to keeping himself informed about Arab and Palestinian viewpoints and experiences, through which his opposition to Zionism matured and hardened.

Through the long years from the 1940s until 1973, I waited—not always quietly or patiently—for my rabbinical colleagues to include Palestinian refugees in their frequent declamations of the universality of truth and justice. I chafed, very often, at the exception for the state of Israel they made in their moral codifications. I watched, sometimes bemusedly, as they paraded their anti-war sentiments in the context of Vietnam but found all the usual pretexts to justify Israeli militarism. I felt a strange combination of sadness and near-amusement as I witnessed their participation in the civil rights battles in the United States while they were silent—and perhaps ignorant as well—about the near-apartheid practised by the Zionist infrastructure in the Zionist state.[17]

In the early years Berger, Rosenwald, and the AJC were confident their efforts would bear fruit. They wrongly assumed that, for American Jewry, Zionism would be a brief, passing enthusiasm, an emotional response to Hitler. They also assumed, wrongly, that Zionism and support for Israel were inconsistent with what they look to be "American" ideology—linked with the univers-alist ideology of Reform—and incompatible with American economic and political interests.

In New York, two young American Jews had been busted for stocking arms for shipment to Jewish forces in Palestine. That they were prosecuted under the Sullivan Act (an early gun control measure) strikes EVM as irresistible irony, given that "plenty of Sullivans" (i.e. Irish people) "were up to their necks for caching arms" to fight the British.

> Is it a crime to cache arms to send to the fighting Jews in Palestine? State Department fiat and Sullivan law notwithstand-ing—we say NO! It was against the law to throw the tea into Boston harbor, to hide behind a fence and shoot a redcoat . . . We say that these boys are made of the stuff that patriots are made of and we need more of them . . . Imagine the headlines if they read like this: Lafayette arrested in arms cache!

For EVM, Zionism and Americanism seem a natural pairing: "1776 and 1948 for the Jews of the world have much in common. Not least is the historic fact that the colonists of America and the colonists of Palestine sought to break the infamous bonds which tied them to England." The Jewish state is a cause equivalent to that of "our own thirteen colonies." He responds to calls for a ceasefire by asking "Could there be a truce at Valley Forge? Benedict Arnold rides again at the State Department." He insists there is no issue of "dual loyalty. American Jewry is proud of what is happening in Palestine and is willing to share the cost in money and lives." Nonetheless, "American Jews have no intention of forsaking this land for any other. We do not think in terms of hyphens."

But at this very moment the category of "Americanism" was being reshaped, defined in relation to its alleged antithesis, "un-Americanism." An EVM column from April 1948 headlined "It is later than you think!" was not, for once, about Palestine but about the domestic threat to civil liberties. "The witch-hunt is on—and is gathering in intensity every day." The hearings and tribunals and guilt by association "make one feel sick at heart at being an American." "We are certain as we sit at the typewriter this hot and sultry day that we are passing through a period comparable to that which ushered Herr Hitler on the scene." An example of the attach on civil liberties is the hated Nixon–Mundt Bill, which required Communist Party members to register with the Attorney General, denied them passports, and barred them from federal employment. EVM warns that it will be used not only against Communists but against Jews, Negroes and liberals, and even those "advocating a new state for the Jews in Palestine."

In a widely publicized speech, Stephen Wise had criticized both the US and the USSR over their race to war. "The highest patriotism," he declared, "is loyalty to the human race." He was attacked by both left and right. EVM defended the speech. "It is not anti-Soviet to suggest that there exists as much possibility that some group of nudniks in the Kremlin could stir up war sentiment any more than it is in error to suggest that this same brand of nudniks can and are attempting to stir up a war right here at home."

EVM notes with contempt the formation of an American Jewish League Against Communism and sneers at those who want the Jew to be seen to "do something" about Communism. "Each decade the anti-Semite finds a new word to scare you away," he warns. "Just now Communist is the naughty word." Those Jews who go along with "the witch-hunters and the boys who sing the Star Spangled Banner at the top of their voices" are guilty of "appeasement." How could any self-respecting Jew "have broken bread with the very people who would not hesitate to blot us out"—the nativist right wing? Safety for the Jews lies not in attacking the Communists, EVM insists, but in "making every effort to support civil liberties" for all people—the very strategy the Zionists rejected.

Concurrent with the anti-left hysteria, EVM sees another and related threat to freedom. The DeWitt Clinton principal, heir to Dr Francis Paul, had banned *Gentlemen's Agreement* and *Focus* from the school library. Both were popular novels dealing with anti-semitism in American society. According to the principal, the problem was that *Gentlemen's Agreement* made light of extramarital sexual relationships and *Focus* was offensive to the Roman Catholic Church (by suggesting that Catholic priests were involved with the Christian Front). EVM was contemptuous. "Voltaire's *Candide* has more sex in one chapter than all of *Gentlemen's Agreement*." He reminds the principal that *The Merchant of Venice* is on the DeWitt Clinton curriculum, despite its anti-semitism. Somewhat inconsistently he also notes, apparently with approval, that teaching the play has recently become optional in the New York City system, and that at one high school teachers had ruled it out of the classroom. Soon after, the New York City school system banned the *Nation*, after complaints about an article critical of the Catholic hierarchy. (Eleanor Roosevelt led the campaign to get the ban rescinded.)

> A vast barrier has been set up. Logic and reason are of no avail. A spiritual halo is placed over every controversial question. You never get a chance to argue the matter out as it should be in a democracy. The first crack out of the box and you are told, shush, you are attacking the Church.

His concerns about the relation between religion, state and civil society—historic anxieties among Jews in the USA—extended to the new Jewish state. "We would decry any attempt on the part of Jewry in Palestine to make Judaism a state religion and to parochialize its educational institutions." He criticizes a proposal from the Rabbinical Council of America that American Jews should accept the Chief Rabbinate of Israel as the world's central Jewish authority. While he exults in the Zionist-driven "spiritual renaissance" of Jewry, he is convinced that "in the new state of Israel there must be no state religion. To do otherwise is to set the clock back a thousand years." EVM, like most of the Zionist leadership in the US and Palestine, was a secularist; but it was a secularism tied to a religious identity and tradition (not least the biblical tradition that declares Palestine the land of the Jews), a conundrum that neither Israeli lawmakers, Zionist ideologists nor rabbis have been able to resolve.

EVM had been a fierce proponent of immigration and immigrants' rights since he campaigned for Al Smith in the 1920s. Once again in 1948, proposals to admit refugees to the USA, including people still trapped in displaced persons' camps in Europe, three years after the end of war, were rejected by Congress following what EVM calls a "sordid" debate. "For clear and convincing chauvinism and anti-foreign sentiment," it had no equal. He blames both anti-semitism and "an isolationist fear of contact with that which they know little about." And he blames the Jews:

> The tragedy lies in the fact that many of us, descendants of those who came here but a short span ago, sit listlessly by and permit the raucous voices of the hinterland to dictate policy. We American Jews have been most negligent in rising up to fight the barrier against immigration. Statute after statute has been introduced to make entrance here on a par with an exclusive club. We have the resources. We have the room—for a million more immigrants . . . There can be no real peace in the world unless immigration barriers are removed. To love thy neighbor it is necessary to meet and know him.

As EVM wrote these words, hundreds of thousands of Palestinians were in flight from their homes. Belatedly, some concern about the fate of the refugees began to be expressed in the British and US press. For EVM, however, it was just another British ruse:

> The British Foreign Office supplies both the "canned tears" and the "pitiful victims" for whom the tears may be shed . . . This time the object of their sympathy is the poor and lowly Arab (with whom they have had absolutely no contact for centuries) as represented by some effendi with social connections. The British Colonial Office is concerned with Arab DPs [displaced persons] and has cried aloud at their plight. That 11,000 Jewish DPs are confined at Cyprus by these same British officials has escaped their attention for many months.

In fact, the British did even less (virtually nothing) for the Palestinian refugees than for the Jewish ones. And despite EVM's not unreasonable claim that Britain's attempt "to cry pity for Arab marauders matches all its prior performances as the champion international hypocrite among nations," what screams out from these pages is his own inconsistency on the rights of refugees. It's not cynical and calculated, like the Foreign Office's, it's just blind, but in its own way more disturbing.

How did the champion of the refugee and the immigrant come to gloat over a forced mass exodus? How did the skeptic about patriotism turn into a super-patriot, albeit for another country? The path to 1948 spirals back through EVM's life and times. The holocaust. The anti-fascist struggle. Changing his name and wanting always to be associated with the Jewish people. A lifetime of anger at the Jewish establishment and a lifetime of craving their acceptance and recognition. Tammany, World War I, Camp Devens. The Irishman his father and the Jew his mother and his famous mixed heritage. Where would he have been without the British empire to knit it all together?

EVM was a victim (and propagator) of false analogies. Spain, Ireland, India, World War II. He defined the war in Palestine as a continuation of the struggle against fascism, anti-semitism and a Nazi-like enemy. Even his references to the Maccabees, indigenous insurgents against a foreign power, are misplaced. Having been a prophet in the wilderness on Spain and anti-semitism, EVM now recast himself in the role he liked and needed. Taking a stand, fighting for a noble cause, championing the underdog—these were his addictions, and the Zionist cause fed them. Here he could be gloriously uncompromising, at a safe distance.

His grand crusade was both world-historical and intimate. It was an assertion of his vexed Jewishness, and of his strangled individuality (both of which he unwittingly subordinated to an ideology more restrictive and reductive than the ones from which he was seeking to escape), a vehicle for his grievances and aggression, his fear of violence and his shame of that fear, the redemption of his ambivalent military record, an exercise in manliness and military valor by proxy. All this was in keeping with the old Zionist promise of a new Jew, a healthy, vigorous, un-neurotic Jew, cleansed of self-hatred and defeatism—and just as hollow.

It also has to be said that EVM's passion for Palestine was an expression of a long-standing internationalism: that so many of us allow injustice to overwhelm people in distant lands while we get on with our workaday lives had been for him a source of perpetual indignation. The tragedy was that in this case he completely misidentified which people were being overwhelmed by injustice, and who was committing it.

Of course, little accurate information about the impact of Zionism on people other than Jews was available in New York at the time. Still, there remains, in EVM's and the left's responses to events in 1948, a fatal failure of imagination. A failure to imagine the people on the receiving end of your dreams. It's a failure rooted in Western and white supremacy, a network of unexamined assumptions that has proved much more ineradicable and insidious than anti-semitism. EVM's writings of 1948 resound with it, and offer inadvertent testimony to the racist character of the Nakba and Nakba denial.

Sometime during the summer of 1948 my mother had her nose "fixed." She was sixteen and heading off to college in the autumn. The decision was entirely her own. She later said that it was motivated by a desire to be more conventionally pretty, and since people at college wouldn't know her with her old nose, she wouldn't have to explain anything to anyone. What EVM made of this I have no idea. But it's pretty obvious where she acquired the self-consciousness about her nose. "I left for college from the Greyhound Terminal and Dad took me there," she recalled. "He announced, loud enough for everyone to hear, that he had two pieces of advice. 'Don't join the Communist Party and don't get pregnant.'" By the time she graduated, four years later, she had done both.

10

Diasporic Dimensions

Only a few years have passed since the defeat of Germany and our democracies are displaying that complacency which made the rise of Nazidom and Hitlerism possible. And again the core of the trouble is the so-called "non-interference-in-foreign-affairs" principle. A case in point is what is happening to the Jews in Moslem countries. Ever since the Arab League declared war against Israel in defiance of a United Nations decision, the Jews in those countries have been subjected to pogroms, horrors, blackmail, threats of extermination and confiscation of property in the good old Nazi style.

Jewish Review, October 1948

In writing the above, EVM was responding to (and copying analogies from) statements issued by the American Jewish Committee and the Israeli government which claimed that Jews in Arab countries, notably Egypt, were being subject to a reign of terror. At the time, critics within the AJC, as well as State Department and FO officers, regarded the propaganda blitz as inaccurate and exaggerated. "Rulers of Arab countries are planning to confiscate Jewish property as indemnity for Arab losses in the war, throw Jews into camps and give their homes to Arab war exiles from Israel," wrote EVM. What was happening at that moment was nearly the reverse: Jews were expelling Arabs, confining them in camps, confiscating their property, and handing it over to Jewish immigrants. In accusing their Arab foes of this very behavior, the Zionists—with EVM in tow—were not only grossly abusing the Nazi analogy but laying the basis for another false analogy.

This is the analogy in which it is made to appear that Oriental Jews were swapped for the Palestinians—the "transfer" idea of old reworked—and the Nakba morally cancelled out.

At Sunday school we learned about the "Sephardim"—under which rubric all non-Ashkenazi Jews were grouped. It seemed an exotic offshoot, outside of history, as were all Oriental phenomena. Dimly, we were given to understand that the Sephardim were "Spanish Jews"—though they had not lived in Spain for nearly five hundred years. Thus was blotted out much diversity and history: Berber Jews and Arab Jews (with significant differences between Mashriqi and Maghrebi Jews), Ladino-speaking Jews in northern Italy, Turkey and the Balkans, Persian and Mahratti Jews, the "Portuguese" Jews of Holland and southern France. We learned more about the Ethiopian Jews than about the far more numerous—and Jewish in the classical rabbinical sense— Arabic-speaking Jews, even though one of these was Maimonides, the prince of Jewish philosophers.

Until modern times, Jews in the Arab world lived under a system that combined institutionalized discrimination and institutionalized protection. Though distinct, they formed an integral part of the Arab world—economically, culturally, intellectually. In the Crusades, western European Christians fought and slaughtered both Jews and Muslims, and were resisted by both Jews and Muslims, not least in Jerusalem itself. The Arab–Jewish symbiosis—cultural, philosophical, musical, culinary—evinced a degree of participation by Jews in the wider society, albeit within the confessional framework, that did not take place in Europe until the Enlightenment. Periodically Jews suffered mob attacks or were threatened, along with other minorities and dissident Muslims, by fundamentalist regimes (to escape one of which Maimonides left Cordoba first for Fez and then for Cairo, where he was welcomed at Saladdin's court). But there is nothing in the history of the Jews in Arab lands comparable to the Jewish experience in Europe in the late nineteenth and twentieth centuries.

Or is there? EVM thought so. Indeed in 1948 there were 800,000 Jews in Arab countries, 6 per cent of all world Jewry. Twenty-five years later, all but a few thousands had departed, about two-thirds for Israel.

Like the Palestinian victims of the Nakba, many of the Jews of the Arab world suffered fear, terror, poverty, and displacement. But beyond that, the analogy does not work. The Jews left Arab lands not in a matter of months, as the Palestinians left their homes, but over a period of thirty years. They did not leave as a result of a coordinated policy imposed by military force. They were actively recruited by the Zionist movement and the new Jewish state, and given financial incentives to leave their homes. Apart from Iraq in 1950, the official policy of all the Arab states, and of most Arab nationalists, was to retain the Jewish population, not expel it. Though there were sporadic attacks and bombings, Jewish quarters and villages were not subject to ethnic cleansing or anything like it. The national movements in Iraq, Morocco, Egypt and elsewhere defined Jews as equal citizens of the nation, in theory at least, and certainly they always enjoyed recognition and rights denied Arabs by the Jewish state in Palestine. They also enjoyed a degree of freedom of choice not enjoyed by Palestinians, in regard to when and how they would leave, and where they would go. Many chose not to go to Israel, preferring France or Canada or the USA. The largest numbers of Jews came from places Palestinian Arabs could not reach: Morocco, Yemen, and Iraq. At no time were Jews in Arab countries subject to the military government imposed on Israeli Arabs until 1965. This was not an exchange of populations, or of sins, but a succession of events. It was a response to the Nakba and to ongoing Israeli policy.

Iraq was home to the oldest and one of the most well-established Jewish communities in the world. On the eve of partition in

Palestine, there were perhaps 140,000 Jews in the country, 2.6 percent of the population. They were overwhelmingly urban—concentrated in Baghdad and Basra—Arabic in language and culture, more likely to be literate than other Iraqis, strongly represented in commerce and the professions. Between 1919 and 1948, during the course of the British mandate, fewer than 8,000 Iraqi Jews migrated to Palestine. Even in the first two years after the birth of Israel, only 2,000 followed them. Then, between the summer of 1950 and the summer of 1951, almost the entire community—more than 120,000 people—decamped to Israel.[1]

Jews had suffered violence under the Nazi-leaning Iraqi government of 1941, but in the years following World War II they were confident and investing in the future, building schools, libraries and synagogues and setting up businesses. They supported and benefited from the liberalization of 1946, and many in the younger generation turned to the left, principally the Communist Party. Out of this emerged the Anti-Zionist League, dominated by young Jewish Communists.

The AZL drew a clear distinction between Judaism and Zionism, which it analyzed as a "colonialist" phenomenon. Like the European emancipationists they argued that "Jews have no other cause than that of their surrounding societies"—and they did so under similar circumstances: as part of a broader national and democratic movement. The crucial difference was the changed context of global struggle between imperialism and its victims, a struggle in which, at that moment, in that region, Palestine was central.

The AZL saw Zionism as a threat to both Jews and Arabs. It called on the UN to terminate the British mandate "to enable the Palestinian people to exercise their right to establish their own democratic state in which all people, without prejudice to their race or religion, can live equally." The AZL published a daily newspaper with a circulation of 6,000 and drew lively crowds to its events, much to the chagrin of the Zionists, who could rouse little interest among Iraqi Jews in these years.[2]

As elsewhere in the Arab world, the government used the war with Israel as a pretext to crackdown on opposition of all stripes. In July, Zionism, along with Communism and anarchism, was outlawed. In September 1948 the AZL was dissolved and its activists were arrested, charged with both Communism and Zionism.

In New York, the Soviet Union's support for the partition of Palestine had been a boon for the left. In Baghdad, and across the Arab world, it was a disaster. The Iraqi Communist Party, with its Jewish members in the lead, had appealed to Stalin to "lend support for the cause of Palestine when it comes before the United Nations . . . the right of its Arab people to independence is unambiguous and their question is unrelated to the plight of the Jewish displaced persons."[3]

For the corrupt Iraqi government, in the pockets of Britain and the US and under pressure from the nationalist tide, Soviet support for Israel was a godsend: Jews along with Communists could be used as whipping boys. Ministers and their press minions questioned Jewish loyalties and issued menacing statements. Jews were driven from their jobs and subject to harassment.[4] Defending their record to the US State Department in November 1948, Iraqi officials insisted, correctly, that the treatment of Jews in Iraq compared favorably with the treatment of Arabs by Israel. Nonetheless, they also embraced the idea of exchanging Iraqi Jews for refugees from Palestine.[5] As Abbas Shiblak, historian of the Iraqi Jewish exodus, observed, "frequent use of this analogy by Arab officials, far from countering Zionist arguments, probably strengthened the Zionist case."[6]

Despite obvious unease, observers of Iraqi Jewry in 1949 detected no widespread desire to leave. There was a belief that with the armistice and peace in Palestine, life would return to normal. But at the same time, Zionists, funded by Israel, stepped up their activity and their propaganda. The Chief Rabbi, Sassoon Khedouri, an anti-Zionist, recalled this as a period in which "American dollars were going to save the Iraqi Jews—whether

Iraqi Jews needed saving or not." Unable to restrain the Zionists, Khedouri resigned in 1949. In London, the *Jewish Chronicle* supported Khedouri. "Those Baghdadi Jews with anything to lose dislike Zionism because it has brought them misery . . . On the whole, Islamic tolerance has enabled Baghdadi Jews to flourish as a centre of learning and commerce. They and their kind would like to stay." They certainly preferred their homes to "immigrants' camps in Israel, where they believe people are not particularly friendly to oriental Jews."[7]

In March 1950, the Iraqi government issued a Denaturalization Law which would permit those Jews who wished to leave for Israel to do so on the condition that they forfeit their Iraqi citizenship. Initially, the law was welcomed by much of the Jewish community. It offered Jews an irrevocable choice but promised to clear the air. At the same time, Iraqi officials were negotiating a "transport agreement" with Mossad representatives. Under this deal, the Iraqi government placed total responsibility for the evacuation of Iraqi Jews in Israel's hands. It also placed the business of the evacuation—via Cyprus—in the hands of a US company, much to the annoyance of the British. Nonetheless, both British and US governments were happy with the "transport agreement" which fit in with the "transfer" schemes that had long accompanied Zionist and Western visions of the future. Significantly, it gave the Zionist faction among Iraqi Jews the *de facto* support of the Iraqi government as well as of Israel, the British and the Americans. The local Jewish community was not consulted.[8]

Initially, only small numbers of Jews applied to emigrate under the new law. Then on April 8, 1950, a hand grenade exploded near a Baghdad coffeehouse patronized by Jews. No one was killed. The next day 3,400 turned up to register for "denaturalization," three times as many as in the entire previous three weeks. A further incident took place on January 14, 1951, when another hand grenade, this time near a synagogue, killed two Muslims.

That was followed by bombings of the US Information Center and a number of Jewish-owned businesses. The exodus swelled.[9]

In June 1951, Iraqi police uncovered a Mossad-sponsored "spy ring" and charged it with responsibility for the bombings; the accused were found guilty in November. The Israelis have never admitted any involvement in the Baghdad bombings, but over the years evidence has been published in support of the Iraqi charges. What's more, it is an admitted fact that Israeli intelligence sought to employ precisely the same terrorist tactics a few years later, in Egypt.[10]

In contrast to the relatively homogeneous Iraqi Jewish community, Egyptian Jewry was diverse. Even many of those who had lived in the country for generations retained foreign nationality, a legacy of Ottoman and British rule. In 1947, there were 75,000–80,000 Egyptian Jews. Among them were a substantial minority of 20,000 indigenous, Arabic-speaking Jews, including a Karaite community, most of them impoverished. The majority of Egyptian Jews were Sephardim, who had arrived in waves, beginning with Maimonides in the twelfth century, augmented after 1492 by exiles from Spain, and in the 1860s by Jews from cities across the Mediterranean attracted by the Suez Canal boom. This had also drawn to Egypt a small Yiddish-speaking Ashkenazi community (until the 1950s, there was a Yiddish program on Egyptian state radio). The prominent business houses and recognized community leaders were Sephardim, some of whom had made their way via Istanbul from northern Italy, held Italian nationality and spoke Italian or a Judeo-Italian at home. This heterogeneity and cosmopolitanism were not unique to the Jews but characteristic of Egyptian society. Among Cairo's prominent trading communities were not only Jews but also Greeks and Armenians.[11]

As in Iraq, the Zionists for many years found slim pickings in Egypt. The Sephardi Chief Rabbi, who served from the 1920s until his death in 1960, was an anti-Zionist. In 1944, Rene Qattawi, a wealthy businessman and leader of the Cairo Sephardim, informed an American Jewish delegation that Zionism fulfilled no need for Egyptian Jews: "Egypt is our homeland and Arabic is our language."[12] As in Iraq, May 1948 was seized on by a weak government as an excuse to jail opponents, including Zionists and Communists. On July 15, Israeli planes bombed residential areas of Cairo with extensive loss of life. Five days later, a "revenge" bombing in the Karaite quarter killed twenty-two Jews. Over the next three months, further incidents followed, notably explosions targeting Jewish-owned department stores. These were attributed to the Muslim Brotherhood, which was banned at the beginning of December 1948. By the end of the month, the prime minister had been assassinated by the Muslim Brotherhood and in retaliation the government had killed Hassan al-Bana, the organization's spiritual leader.[13]

Claims made by Zionists that Jews in Egypt were being subject to an official pogrom were challenged by Salvator Circuel, president of the Cairo Sephardim and owner of one of the bombed department stores. He told the American Jewish Committee in October 1948 that the recent anti-Jewish outbreak was caused by "the existence of Israel and the defeat of the Arab armies" and should not be interpreted as a general attack on Jews.[14] As for the tales of Jews being thrown into camps, among those rounded up by the government in May were some 300 Zionist and 300 Communist Jews, altogether 1 per cent of Egyptian Jews. In contrast, when the US was at war with Japan nearly the entire Japanese population of the West Coast of the USA was interned.

As a result of the instability and the attacks, during 1948–49 some 20,000 Jews left Egypt, 14,000 of them for Israel. More than 55,000 remained. From July 1949 the political atmosphere improved. Most Egyptian Jews assumed the crisis was over. They were further reassured by the return to power of the constitutional nationalists in 1950. The leaders of the Free Officers' coup of 1952 went out of their way to express respect and support for the Jewish presence in Egypt. The new president, Naguib, revived the slogan of the 1919 revolution: "Religion is for God. The nation is for all."[15] Nasser, who replaced Naguib in 1954, pursued a more pan-Arabist politics that eventually led to increased conflict with Israel and the West. But of far greater impact on the security of Egyptian Jews was the exposure of Operation Susannah by Egyptian police in December of that year.

Susannah was the code name for a spy ring involving Egyptian Jews established by Israeli military intelligence. Their plan was to bomb the United States Information Service library, as well as train stations and cinemas in Cairo. At the time of the arrests and during the trial, Egyptian ministers and the state prosecutor stressed that the Egyptian Jews as a whole were not on trial and that most were loyal "sons of Egypt." Soon after the trial concluded in 1955, British Labour MP Maurice Orbach visited Cairo and described daily relations between Jews and others as "friendly." Jews continued to serve in the police. On Yom Kippur the state radio broadcast the Kol Nidre. But Orbach also noted that Egyptian Jews felt "grave anxiety."[16] What they wanted and needed was peace between Israel and Egypt. They didn't get it. On October 29, 1956, in an attempt to reimpose Western control over the Suez Canal, nationalized earlier that year by Nasser, British, French and Israeli forces mounted a combined attack.

British, French, and Jewish property was confiscated. British and French nationals, among them many Jews, were expelled. A thousand Jews were detained. From 1952 to 1956 only 4,918 Jews had left Egypt. Between November 1956 and March 1957, 14,000 left; another 19,000 departed over the next decade.[17]

In the Draa valley, in southern Morocco, flanked on one side by a densely green date palm oasis and on the other by the crumbling, rust-brown, high pisé walls of what had been the Jewish quarter of the now-abandoned ksar (fortified village) of Tamnougault, I read a newspaper report of the recent Israeli assault on the Gaza town of Beit Hanoun. A residential area had been shelled, and nineteen people had been killed, most of them women and children, most of them in their sleep.

Legend has it that the Draa valley was once home to a mighty Jewish kingdom. Certainly, when the Arab conquerors reached Morocco in 700 AD, they found among the indigenous Berber inhabitants large and widespread communities of Jews. Their numbers were increased by Jewish refugees from Spain who arrived between the thirteenth and sixteenth centuries. Well into the second half of the twentieth century, Morocco remained home to a large, distinctive and diverse Jewish community. There were Arab-speaking and Berber-speaking Jews. There were dark- and fair-skinned Jews. There were Jewish scholars, poets, slave traders and bandits. Some Jews were wealthy but most were poor. There were Jewish merchants, courtiers and doctors, Jewish barbers, peddlers, peasants and laborers, and Jewish artisans—jewellers, metal workers, masons, ceramicists whose contribution to Morocco's rich tradition of decorative art is immeasurable.[18] Jewish musicians were conduits for Morocco's classical tradition of Andalusian music, swaying between plaintive elegance and affirmative exuberance. Though its lyrics touch on religious themes, this is a secular music, and above all a music for weddings. The more lavish the wedding, the bigger the orchestra, and until the early 1970s those orchestras contained disproportionate numbers of Jews.

As People of the Book, Jews in Morocco enjoyed subordinate but protected status. While they enjoyed autonomy in managing their own community affairs, as individuals nearly all Jews interacted on a daily basis with the Muslim majority through commercial, civic and personal relationships. Evidence of centuries-long intermingling can be found in religious and secular literature and in the shared custom of saint worship. Uniquely in the Jewish world, Moroccan Jewry venerates wise men, martyrs, and miracle workers by building shrines around their graves and marking the anniversaries of their deaths by festivals known as *hiloula*, which devotees celebrate with singing and feasting. The *hiloula* is clearly a Jewish counterpart to the Muslim *moussem*. Indeed, a number of saints are jointly venerated by Jews and Muslims, and in remote areas Muslims have traditionally acted as the custodians of Jewish tomb-shrines.[19]

As European influence spread in the course of the nineteenth century, some Moroccan Jews enjoyed the status of foreign protégés, acting as intermediaries between the colonial powers and the local population. This trend was strengthened by the educational work of the Alliance Israélite Française, through which the Moroccan Jewish elite came under French cultural influence. However, when most of Morocco passed formally to French rule in 1911, the French decided not to permit Moroccan Jews to adopt French citizenship, unlike in Algeria and Tunisia (where most Jews became French citizens*). This was partly because the Sultan, insisting that the Jews were Moroccans, would not concede to the French a significant bloc of his people. The decision also owed something to French anti-semitism, which was widespread among the colonists and in the army.

During World War II, Jews in Vichy-administered Morocco fared better than Jews in any European country under Axis control—much better than in France itself. The populace resisted attempts to round up Jews, and the Sultan declared, "The Jews remain under my protection and I refuse to allow any distinction to be made among my subjects."[20] The only significant assault on a Jewish community in modern Morocco took place in Oujda in 1948, under French rule, and was condemned by the nationalists.[21] Meanwhile, Zionist and Israeli organizations, with French approval, began mounting well-resourced recruitment drives among poorer Jews in rural areas.

At the time of independence in 1956, there were some 250,000 Jews in the country, living in communities in the cities of the coasts and plains, in the Atlas Mountains and in southern oases

---

* And the vast majority emigrated to France, not Israel, after decolonization.

like the Draa. The 1956 constitution assured equality between
Jews and Muslims. Three Jews were elected to Parliament,
including a rabbi. A Jew was appointed Minister of Posts and
Telegraphs.

However, the new government soon moved to block emigration to Israel, banning Zionist organizations and denying passports to Moroccan Jews. The policy was motivated partly by
commitments to the Arab League and the Palestinians, and partly
by self-interest: the country's Jewish population was considered
an essential part of its economic fabric. But the emigration
restrictions backfired, making Jews feel trapped and vulnerable,
thus enhancing the allure of Israel. Mossad organized a secret
emigration network. The Moroccans came under pressure from
Eisenhower and American Jewish organizations. Between 1961
and 1964, King Hassan II negotiated with Mossad and American
Jewish organizations for the discreet emigration of some 100,000
Jews to Israel. (In return for this, vast sums of money were
deposited in his Swiss bank accounts.)

The trauma of the 1967 war led to the final wave of emigration.
Amid calls for a boycott of Moroccan Jewish businesses (calls that
were not supported by any of the main political parties), the
Palace continued to proclaim its traditional role as protector of the
Jews. Police ensured that Jewish schools and institutions were
unmolested. Nonetheless, almost half the country's remaining
Jews emigrated in the ensuing four years. By 1971, the Jewish
population had dropped to 35,000.

It was then that the Jews of Tamnougault left, *en masse*, for
Israel. Soon after, the other inhabitants moved to new houses on a
plateau above the old fortified village. These days, the ksar is on
the tourist route (Brad Pitt and Cate Blanchett filmed part of
Babel there) but still evocative. As you explore the labyrinth of
passageways, chambers, stairs and rooftops, you pass suddenly
from dark to light, from inner to outer. The plain, plastered
synagogue is minute, and roofless. The mahia vat is strategically

positioned at the entrance to the mellah, the Jewish quarter. Mahia, a luscious firewater distilled from dates or figs, is a Moroccan Jewish speciality. Indeed, within traditional Moroccan society, it was the exclusive privilege of the Jews to produce and sell mahia. The vat is at the entrance to the mellah for the convenience of Muslim neighbors.*

The thirty-year-long emigration of Moroccan Jews was not a response to persecution or specific threats of violence. There was no breakdown in daily relations between Jews and other Moroccans. Village by village, community by community, Jews were induced to leave by Zionist recruiters, aided by the international climate, and, ironically, a mystical and decidedly pre-modern strain in Moroccan Jewry, among whom pilgrimage to Palestine (and the chance to die there) was long established as a Jewish equivalent to the Muslim Haj. Today, there remain only about 5,000 Jews in Morocco, mainly in Casablanca. As Haim Zafrani, doyen of Moroccan Jewish studies, wrote, "They went up to Zion in messianic fervour and found no warmth in the welcome they received in the land of their fathers."[22] In Israel, Moroccan Jews, along with others from the Arab world, were used as muscle power to build new "development towns" and reinforce border settlements. Regarded as second-class Israelis by the Ashkenazi Zionists, they suffered discrimination, poverty and for many years the denial of their distinctive culture, which has nonetheless survived.

In the mid-1970s, Hassan used Moroccan Jewish intermediaries to win US support for his annexation of Western Sahara. At the same time he invited Moroccan Jews who had emigrated to return to Morocco, and small numbers did. With Saudi Arabia's backing, Hassan positioned himself as a "broker" between Israel and the

---

* There is now a specifically Jewish tourist trail in Morocco, aimed at well-heeled American Jews. I was browsing in an antique shop in Fez and asked about some glazed ceramic tiles. When the owner informed me that it was a Jewish design fashioned by Jewish artisans, I must have shown an extra flicker of interest, because he promptly asked, "*Vous êtes de Florida?*"

US on one side, and the Arab world on the other. In doing so, he leaned on the Jewish link between Morocco and Israel. He encouraged Israelis of Moroccan origin to visit the old country and they have been doing so ever since, maintaining links with family, friends and villages, taking part in *hiloulas* and always finding a warm welcome.[23] Israelis of Russian or Polish descent would view any similar return to their roots with chilly trepidation. In contrast to eastern Europe, in Morocco today the loss of the Jewish population is widely lamented. There is a proud awareness that Morocco is and always has been a composite culture. This was evident in the popular response to the May 2003 terrorist attacks in Casablanca, which targeted Jewish social clubs and restaurants among other places associated (in the minds of the bombers, at least) with "Western" influence. A week later, tens of thousands marched through the city's streets, chanting "Jews and Muslims united—the only solution."

In response to Israel's 2006 assault on Lebanon, three prominent Moroccan Jews, among them the veteran leftist Avram Sefarty, brought an action before a Moroccan court to charge Amir Peretz, Israel's defense minister and leader of the Labor Party, with war crimes. Peretz was born in Morocco, and like many Israeli-Moroccans retains dual citizenship. The three Jews argued that he was therefore subject to Moroccan law and that a warrant should be issued for his arrest and extradition.

Under the blue skies of Tamnougault, boundaries melt as surely as the pisé walls of the ancient Draa villages: boundaries between Jew and Arab and Berber; between East and West, between Africa and Europe. The polarities of the war on terror, of Zionism, the paradigms that are the great lies of our time, dissolve. The borders of what we call "the Arab world" or even "Islam" appear porous, host to multiple identities, as do the borders surrounding "the Jews," who until relatively recently were widely perceived—inside and outside Europe—as a non-European people. That they have become arch-representatives of the West, proxies for American power, is a tragic distortion of a complex history, the upshot of the Israel–US alliance and Zionism's disastrously reductive impact on Jewish identity.

My two Jewish grandmothers were a study in contrasts. Olga was pale and round and soft and spoke in an identifiably Jewish, frequently plaintive accent that I otherwise heard mainly in movies. We called her Grandma. Edith, my father's mother, also spoke in an accent I mainly heard in movies, only it was a Katherine Hepburn–Myrna Loy accent: ironic, brittle, sophisticated. She was tall and elegant and we never, ever, called her Grandma. She was always simply Edith.

Edith never denied or doubted that she was Jewish, but she bore her Jewishness in a very different way from Olga. Her mother was one Hortense Josephy Brodek, whom I knew well, since she lived to the age of ninety-one, and died when I was eighteen. Hort was sometimes formidable—her manner was regal and had the punctiliousness of an age of formality long past—but also patient and reasonable. She instructed us how to eat soup: not clumsily inserting the whole spoon, narrow end first, into our gobs, but lifting and tilting the spoon so that the liquid poured gently over our lips. Every summer, she vacationed at Whiteface, a turn-of-the-century resort in the Adirondacks.

Hort's father was Hugo Josephy, who had been born in Mecklenburg in northeastern Germany in about 1845. Thanks to the fact that one of Hugo's sister's descendants is a genealogist, I know something about our common ancestors.[24] One strand of Hort's lineage can be traced back to Moorish Spain, and even beyond, to the tenth-century Exilarchs of Baghdad, including the unsavoury David Ben Zakkai, who schemed against the great Saadia Gaon, a scholar who encouraged Arabic–Jewish philosophical and linguistic interchange. In the 1050s, Ben Zakkai's descendants (or people who claimed to be) traveled the length of the Arab world to take refuge in Granada with Yusuf Naghrela, the son and successor of Shmu'el HaNagid, vizier to the royal family of Granada, general of their armies and one of the greatest Hebrew poets of any age. In "On Fleeing His City," written sometime between 1020 and 1065, HaNagid mingled the personal, the political, and the military:

> I'll climb cliffs
> and descend the innermost pit,
> and sew the edge of desert to desert,
> and split the sea
> and every gorge,
> and sail in mountainous ascent
>
> until the word "forever" makes sense to me,
> and my enemies fear me,
> and my friends in that fear
> find solace
>
> then free men will turn
> their faces towards mine,
> as I face theirs.[25]

Naghrela, Shmu'el's son, with whom my ancestor is said to have taken refuge, was apparently a freethinker and advocated an ecumenical approach to religious faith. In 1066 he was killed when a mob attacked both the palace and the Jewish community. Twenty years later, the Almoravids, a fundamentalist Berber regime from the High Atlas, conquered much of Moorish Spain. Their intolerant puritanism forced Jews, along with dissident Muslims, to flee. Many, including Maimonides, went to North Africa. Others made their way to Christian-controlled areas of the peninsula. Among them was one of Ben Zakkai's descendants, Hiyya al-Daudi ("Chaim of the line of David"), a poet, composer, rabbi and advisor to Alfonso I, founder of the Kingdom of

Portugal on territory "reconquered" from the Moors in 1139. In reward for military services, one of Hiyya's sons, Yahia ben Rabbi, was presented by Alfonso with a Moorish village and became known as "Lord Aldeia dos Negros" or "Dom Yahia o Negro." His son Yahia ibn Ya'isch was born in Cordoba in 1110 or 1115. He also served Alfonso and was designated by the king as the first Chief Rabbi of Portugal, with his headquarters in Lisbon.

Thirty years later, the fourth Lateran Council compelled Jews to don "the badge of shame." As clerical anti-semitism grew more aggressive, some of Yahia ibn Yai'sch's descendants converted, and some died at the hands of the Inquisition. One, Samuel Yachia, made his way north, bypassing Amsterdam, where so many other Portuguese Jews settled, and landing at the mouth of the Elbe in 1605. He was a coin maker and adopted the surname Henriques (after a relative, Henrique, who had been burned at the stake in Portugal at the age of eighty-one). Samuel's offspring moved eastwards, and Michel Henriques became Court Banker ("Court Jew") to the Duke of Mecklenburg-Schwerin in 1677—at which time he changed his name to Henrichsen. He was Hort's great-great-great-grandfather.

Mecklenburg was a backwater. Jewish emancipation followed in Napoleon's wake but was swiftly rescinded.[26] The feudal duchy entrenched itself, and in the 1860s Hort's father made his way to New York. Descendants of the Josephys and Henrichsens who remained in Germany (and had not converted in earlier generations) perished in the holocaust. The Yad Vashem database of Jews killed in the holocaust lists some thirty-eight Josephys from the Mecklenburg area.

Hort married Charles Brodek, whose father and mother, Samuel and Frederica Brodek, were born in Silesia, then part of Prussia (the name Brodek derives from a small village, now in the Czech Republic; the Yad Vashem database shows some seventeen Brodeks, mostly from nearby Breslau). Like so many, Jews and non-Jews, the young Brodeks left Prussia after the failed revolution of 1848 and arrived in New York around 1854. Samuel ran a clothing store in Manhattan. Charles, his youngest child, born in 1872, went through the New York public school system and graduated from City College in 1890. He established himself as a successful commercial lawyer with offices on Wall Street. Twice he represented corporate clients before the Supreme Court. Letters he published in the *New York Times* are precise, dispassionate elucidations of constitutional legalities, carefully apolitical. He and Hort were contributors to relief funds for eastern European Jewry, from as early as 1905, when they gave money to an appeal for the victims of the pogroms in Russia. Hort was an active member of the National Council for Jewish Women, which provided assistance to poor Jews in both America and Europe, campaigned for votes for women, and played an active role in the international feminist movement. Charles was a long-time supporter of the Jewish Publication Society and was said to have been a friend of Stephen Wise. He was scholarly, gentle, judicious and much adored by his children.

His eldest daughter, Edith, grew up among New York's German Jewish elite. She attended Vassar, was brainy, beautiful, and sociable. At the age of twenty-one she married Jack Marqusee. Jack's father Julius Marqusee had arrived in New York from eastern Poland in 1882, along with the curious surname.* Julius's wife Anna joined him four years later. Crisscrossing rural

---

* The name is a rarity and has been misspelled and mispronounced more ways than any of its bearers can remember. The family tradition is that it is pronounced "Mar-kuh-see." I can find no trace of it among Polish Jewish records. But there are innumerable variants—Markuze, Markaze, Markuse, Markuza—among the names of the victims of the Lodz and Bialystock ghettos. But what about that peculiar *q*? Polish rarely uses *q* except for loan words. And *k* more frequently than *q* might be used to transliterate the Hebrew letter *qoph*, which in Israel today is pronounced the same as the letter *kaph*, but which Oriental Jews have traditionally pronounced distinctively, making what is called the voiceless uvular plosive sound—a *k* articulated from the back of the palate, identical to the Arabic letter *qaf*, as in *Qu'ran* or *Al-Qaeda*. Both Hebrew and Arabic *q*s are descended from the Canaanite *qof*, the nineteenth letter in the Semitic *abjad*. Marcuse seems to be a German version of the same name, and like Markowitz, Marcus, Marcos, Markus, Marquez, etc. derives ultimately from the Latin name Marcus.

Connecticut as an itinerant peddler, Julius acquired shares in tobacco farms that he managed to parley into a fortune (he was wiped out in the crash of 1929 and died a few years after). Julius lived as an observant Jew; his wife wore a wig and spoke only Yiddish. But he wanted his first son, named Isidore at birth, to be an all-American boy. So Isidore became Jack and was educated at Lawrenceville, a prestigious, expensive and hitherto exclusively gentile boarding school. In World War I, Jack saw action as a cavalry courier and was decorated for bravery under fire. He was a proud and active member of the American Legion, a Republican, an investment broker and real estate developer (in Florida), a big spender who buried all those around him under an avalanche of charm. No wonder EVM hated him.

Jack and Edith were part of a lively social set, wealthy, urbane, and exclusively Jewish. As Jews they were not admitted to country clubs, so they set up their own, whose facilities were as good as any the gentiles had to offer, and whose membership was, in its own way, just as exclusive. They had no interest in religion, which they regarded as unsophisticated, at best "quaint" and at worst "vulgar." But they were intensely aware of the anti-semitism in the world around them and donated heavily to Jewish charities, Zionist and non-Zionist.

During the Depression, Edith went to work, initially as a saleswoman behind a counter in Bonwit Tellers, a chain of fashionable New York clothing stores. In 1947, she was appointed a branch manager and two years later a merchandise manager for the whole chain. For many years she was Bonwit's chief coat and suit buyer, a job in which, the *New York Times* reported in 1955, "she gambles many thousands of Bonwits dollars every season on the game of fashion, hoping that the styles she picks will sell." The *New York Times* journalist was impressed by Edith's knowledge of the industry, her taste, her hard nose for prices and the fact that examining hundreds of suits and coats from scores of manufacturers left her looking not the least "frazzled." "Know why I don't have ulcers?" she said. "I've got a happy home life. It keeps me going in this rat race."

Edith in fact did not enjoy a happy home life, but it remained important to her till the day she died—in 1982—to pretend that she did. Jack had a second home, a second life, and effectively if not legally a second wife in Florida. Her friends and her children knew this, but Edith never spoke of it and maintained the fiction that hers was a complete marriage. I was much closer to Edith than I ever was to EVM. She certainly knew me much better than he did. In some ways, she knew me better than my parents did. She took me to Broadway shows (*South Pacific* and *The Sound of Music*), foreign movies (Bunuel's *Exterminating Angel*) and restaurants, where she introduced me, at the age of sixteen, to scotch on the rocks. During summer months, I stayed with her in her Manhattan apartment for weeks on end, doing as I pleased. Wherever my intellect and interests wandered—from baseball to politics to movies to medieval literature or Jane Austen—she tried to follow. I sometimes confessed my more inchoate feelings to her, feelings about the weirdness of the passage of time, or of the loneliness of walking crowded streets, and she listened. Once she told me that she wouldn't want to be sixteen again, a wonderful way of expressing an unglib, unpatronizing sympathy with a serious-minded young man. Perhaps I somehow reminded her of the earnest, studious, high-minded father she so loved, and who was so different from her extrovert husband.

Edith was touchy about social status and social slights, though she dished them out to others freely. She regarded rabbis with ill-concealed disdain. She also regarded people who hid or denied their Jewishness as contemptible, and she herself never even considered the option. It was utterly beneath her dignity, and dignity was important to her. I remember her speaking of so-and-so being an anti-semite, or some club or society that did not welcome Jews, and doing so in a lowered voice, with a wary, sidelong glance and through gritted teeth. She was brisk and caustic and, selectively, affectionate. To some people, she seemed crusty and remote. A tough critic. But not of me, or my father. We could do no wrong.

Olga bitterly resented Edith. She resented the fact that her daughter preferred her mother-in-law's company and sought her mother-in-law's advice about the oscillating state of her marriage. She resented the fact that her grandchildren preferred to stay with their other grandmother, and she was certain it was "because she's richer."

I have two Olgas in my memory. The first has a smile, radiating out of light blue eyes. Plump arms that hold and hug, not too tight. She laughs at my father's jokes and blushes at his teasing. She makes luscious matzoh ball soup, gefilte fish, latkes, flanken. She's delighted with everything I say or do. I recite the Pledge of Allegiance. I quote Patrick Henry. I know the three branches of government. She listens, then turns to whomever's near and says, "He knows the whole Pledge of Allegiance! He says 'give me liberty or give me death.' Did you hear? Executive, legislative and judiciary!" She's ravished by my charms.

The second Olga is not so pleased—with me or anybody else. She's sad. She's resentful. The blue eyes are blocked, blank. The arms are crossed over the large bosom, as if to keep out any appeals to a tender heart. I sense that the world has become unrecognizable to her, and her grandson is part of that world. I am an alien. For my part, I have no patience with her. She's sour and prejudiced. I condescend to her. I avoid her. And she always comes with Aunt Gert, the know-it-all whose opinions never ceased. "Now you know I don't like Italians, but at least they're loyal to their own kind. They respect their families." With a sharp glance at myself. She vented her views on the state of the city's schools, the prejudice against Jews in a certain bank, the kind of people she saw at her bus stop. People who worked and people who were on welfare. Jews who passed for gentiles, colored people who passed for white. "Let me say this to you, Gert . . ."

my father would begin, trying to soothe her, while my exasp-
erated mother huffed, "Oh Gert, you really can't say that."

Olga and Gert dressed like extras in a thirties movie. They
were astonished and a trifle resentful at every new suburban
convenience. They thought we were all spoiled and overprivi-
leged. Had any children ever had it so easy? Looking back, I
wonder if my adventures in student politics stirred uneasy
memories of EVM.

Gert was all sharp edges, whereas Olga was round and soft. But
you never had one without the other. And Olga never, ever
challenged her sister, the younger sister who had somehow—in
her lofty miserableness—acquired total power over the elder.
Nonetheless, Olga retained something that Gert never had. I
heard it sometimes in her laugh, almost a girlish giggle, but deeper
and fuller. For all her bitter experience, there was a childishness in
that laugh. "I have memories of my mother laughing so hard she
peed in her pants," my mother wrote, "but my overall image is of
a very sad person."

After completing high school, Olga had studied at a commercial
college and become a proficient typist and qualified legal secretary.
Her command of grammar, spelling, punctuation, and an orderly
sentence were superior to EVM's. Over the years, she had earned
cash by typing legal documents, furtively, at home. After her
divorce, she took full-time work as a secretary for a firm of labor
lawyers. Long after her death, I began to feel ashamed of the way I
had treated her. I think of the hardness of her life, as a wife, as a
mother, and as a worker. I also call to mind the Olga I never knew,
the Olga who had married EVM when he was Eddie Moran. What a
remarkable decision to carry that name, the misleading brand that
made Ed so self-conscious. It must have been a heavier burden for
her than for EVM because her ethnicity had always been unambiguous. Marriage to Ed, becoming a Moran, must have introduced a
host of unfamiliar uncertainties. This grandmother whom I remembered as timid and defeated had once been extraordinarily

brave, maybe reckless. There must have been something in EVM exciting enough to get her to take such a leap into the unknown.

In the Peekskill riots of August and September 1949, anti-Communists attacked leftists attending a Paul Robeson concert in the Hudson valley town forty miles north of New York City. Shortly after the violence, the Jewish War Veterans ordered members and posts not to take part in any way in "public appearances of or utterance by Communists, Fascists and all other subversive elements." In EVM's eyes, the JWV leaders had "recklessly suggested that the Jewish War Veterans take themselves out of community activity" at the very time when democracy needed defending. "The mistake at Peekskill was that the Jewish War Veterans were sold a bill of goods and teamed up with the wrong crowd." During the first riot, JWV members in uniform were assaulted by red-baiters. Yet the local JWV post, along with Jewish store-owners and businessmen in the area, continued to contribute funds to the anti-Communist war chest. Despite that, EVM reports, "The Jewish residents had to stand on guard all night to protect their homes." Behind the anti-Communist mania, EVM warns, is a "rising tide of anti-semitism."

During the autumn of 1949 EVM, approaching his fiftieth birthday, made his second and last bid for public office, running for city council on a Fusion ticket—the type of fly-by-night do-gooder reform operation he'd long sneered at. He set up another Independent Citizens' Committee, whose members were the same as in 1946. On the ballot paper, EVM was listed on the same row as Newbold Morris, the one-time La Guardia ally running as a Republican-Liberal-Fusion candidate against both the Democratic incumbent, O'Dwyer, and the ALP candidate, Marcantonio. O'Dwyer won easily. Marcantonio came third but notched up 13 percent of the vote. Despite the red-baiting and quarantine by the major parties, the ALP still commanded hundreds of thousands of votes. But this time EVM was running without the ALP and was thoroughly drubbed. "Without a machine—it's really tough going," he reflected in a valedictory letter sent to supporters.

> No cause that is worthy is ever really lost. I have said so many times and I only hope that you will never tire of its repetition even when we can't have victory in addition to platitudes. I shall say nought about the future—but if you know me, I'll find a good fight to get into and you'll be hearing from me again.

But they would only hear from him, sporadically and with decreasing frequency, in the pages of Jewish publications. In the *Jewish Review*, he waxed indignant over a senate filibuster against another bill to admit European refugees and at "alleged liberals who were passive when action might have served to stop Hitler." However, one liberal with an unimpeachable record on fascism was singled out for an EVM diatribe. Dorothy Thompson was the most well-known and widely admired woman journalist in the USA during the thirties and forties. She had covered the rise of the Nazis in Germany and in 1934 became the first foreign journalist to be expelled by them. In print and on the air, she warned consistently for the next decade of the horrors of the Nazi regime and in particular of the persecution of the Jews. (She is said to be the model for the Katharine Hepburn role in *Woman of the Year*, made in 1942.) In the thirties, Thompson argued that emigration to Palestine was the only option for German Jews; she supported the Ha'avara.[27] In 1943, Thompson was an honored guest of the American Zionist Emergency Council. She met Weizmann and supported the call for a Jewish homeland in Palestine. But in 1948 her views began to change. "I am increasingly disturbed by what I see in Palestine," she told the anti-Zionist rabbi Elmer Berger, especially "the procrastination of Israel on the question of permitting repatriation of the refugees. I had to speak out about this for the same reasons I had to speak out about Hitler. But my Zionist friends do not seem to understand the universality of simple moral principles." Berger warned her that if she continued to raise awkward questions for the Zionists, "the propaganda goons" would bring their campaign against her "into every lecture agency, every editorial room, every publishing house where they could muscle their way through a door."[28]

That seems to have included the *Jewish Review*. EVM denounces Thompson as a "reactionary" and belittles "her latest love . . . the Arab cause." He's particularly indignant over the charge of "dual allegiance" which Thompson leveled against American Zionists. He quotes Whitman: "This is not a nation but a teeming nation of nations," and Brandeis: "Let no American imagine that Zionism is inconsistent with patriotism." He notes bitterly that "dual allegiance" was the very charge used by Hitler against German Jews. When Catholics support the Vatican, he argues, nobody questions their allegiance. In any case, EVM is confident that the government of Israel will seek "less influence on the American scene" than the Vatican (an incorrect prophecy).

What was it that Thompson had said that earned her such opprobrium? In an article entitled "Israeli Ties and US Citizenship: America Demands a Single Loyalty," published in *Commentary*, then a liberal magazine sponsored by the American Jewish Committee, she wrote:

> Sooner or later the Jewish nationalist, which today means the Israeli nationalist, will have to choose allegiances . . . There is no room in American nationality for two citizenships or two nationalities. To say it extremely brutally: no one can be a member of the American nation and of the Jewish nation—in Palestine or out of it—any more than he can be a member of the American nation and the British or German nation.

Thompson notes that Jewish nationalism arose in emulation of eastern and central European nationalisms but would have made no progress were it not for Hitler. After the war, "among millions of Jews the reaction to the German action was to release a counter-nationalism of unprecedented vehemence." The Zionist appeal is located in "the dark regions of the soul and the reactions of despair, in which the terrorized become terrorists, the victims of genomania become genomaniacal."[29]

Thompson argued that there was no place for Zionism in American national identity, and here she blundered, badly. Though she had observed the arc of Nazi anti-semitism at close quarters, she seems to have forgotten its depiction of the Jews as cosmopolitan, rootless, of mixed loyalties, and therefore alien to the nation-state.

In the same issue of *Commentary*, Oscar Handlin, pioneer multiculturalist, responded in a civilized tone unimaginable in the pages of the magazine today: "We never pretended that any group of Americans would lack special sympathy for the country of its antecedents, that emigration would dissolve the ties of home and kin and ancient aspirations." American Zionists' shared loyalty to Israel and the United States is "not a departure from the American pattern" and no different from political advocacy by Italian and Irish Americans. "In all these cases particular groups of Americans sustained and supported a country with which they had hereditary ties of some sort," Handlin argues, then adds a crucial caveat.

> But they did so in terms of standards that had universal currency among all their fellow citizens—the spread of democracy through the world, the self-determination of nations, international action for peace, the desirability of aiding small peoples against great oppressors. One did not have to be a Jew or an Irishman or an Italian to find justice in these arguments.[30]

Handlin seems to take it for granted that Zionism qualified for Americans' support on these universalist grounds. But it was precisely this assumption that Thompson questioned. She notes that Israel claims not only to be a Jewish state but to be the state of and for "World Jewry." Yet "the claim that every Jew in the world is, by his very existence, a member of the Jewish nation from which he cannot and may not extricate himself is a claim never made before by anybody except anti-semites." She charges the Zionists with fomenting anxiety among American Jews. As someone who'd actually witnessed the rise of fascism in Europe, she states categorically, "I find no analogy between the outbreak in Hitler's Germany and the danger in this country" and warns that "the continual beating of the drums of anti-anti-semitism can be and has been overdone." She regrets that the "dangerous tendency to equate anti-Zionism with anti-semitism" had led to "a highly strained and by no means healthy condition of the press." Finally she asks, "If all the Jews of the world are to have an actual or potential home in Israel, what extended encroachments on the Arab world are implied?"

It was the immediate plight of the Palestinian refugees that alarmed Thompson and to which she devoted more time and energy than any other journalist in the USA. EVM's verdict on messenger and message alike was dismissive: "We say to Dorothy Thompson that she should, like (her) Arabs, fold her tent and silently steal away."

UN resolution 194, passed on December 11, 1948, states that "refugees wishing to return to their homes and live at peace with their neighbours should be permitted to do so at the earliest practicable date, and . . . compensation should be paid for the property of those choosing not to return and for loss of or damage to property." Israel has consistently refused to abide by any of these stipulations. From the outset, Zionists disavowed all responsibility for the refugees—well before the notion emerged that they had been exchanged for the Oriental Jews. It was Dorothy Thompson, not EVM, whose voice in 1949 proved to be prophetic.

When the UN called for the internationalization of Jerusalem, as envisioned in the original partition resolution, EVM was outraged at what he regarded as a blatant "seizure of a part of Israel." In this instance the US and Britain supported the Israeli position, but to EVM's horror the USSR had "done an incredible flip-flop and is now ranged on the side of the Vatican and the Arabs." Israel rebuffed the UN by announcing that it would move its capital, unilaterally, to Jerusalem. EVM was delighted at the news: the Jewish state "has met the unfair challenge of the world and taken what it owns unto itself." During these days, Dorothy Thompson noted, the psalm of the Babylonian exile, "If I forget thee O Jerusalem" was being "invoked throughout this nation on behalf of a purely political solution of the status of that city." If Christians were to similarly "politicize" the same verse, she observed, it would signify "a revival of the Crusades."

In the winter of 1949–50, EVM's marriage to Olga finally broke apart. For some time, he'd been collecting the occasional fee from divorce work, in the course of which he represented and later conducted an affair with the woman who was to become his second wife. He had accompanied her to Arkansas—where divorce law was less stringent—and on the way back was in a car accident that badly shook him. On his return to the Amalgamated, he confessed the affair to Olga, who, my mother writes, "went berserk." Ed left and moved in with Mabel in Manhattan, bringing to an end a quarter-century of active residence in the Bronx. My uncle Marty was in Colorado and called my mother with the news; she hitch-hiked back from college in upstate Ithaca to find "not unexpect-edly, my mother in hysterics and Gertie goading her on." She phoned EVM, with Olga and Gert hovering above her, and agreed to meet him, at a safe remove. "He was so frightened of Olga and Gert that he was afraid to drive into our neighborhood." When they met, she cried, and her father told her, tersely, "We'll have none of these tears." "But," she protested, "you still love mom!" To which EVM replied, "Hell no!"

Two years later, he filed a suit for divorce in Florida—another refuge from New York's Catholic-restricted divorce laws. In the Bill of Complaint, EVM states that his wife "for many years prior to the separation and without reason, cause or provocation, continuously nagged, harassed and belittled" and "persistently found fault with plaintiff." Olga was accused of "cold and aloof indifference" and being forever "irritated with plaintiff over fancied grievances." During their marriage, EVM swore, he "did everything within his power to make their home comfortable and happy."

On November 15, 1949, the Bronx lodge of the Free Sons of Israel held a gala "Ed Morand Night," a tribute to EVM for sixteen years' service to fraternal life, perhaps a morale booster and farewell for a brother who was saying goodbye to the Bronx in awkward circumstances. The roster of speakers must have fulfilled at least some of EVM's long-cherished fantasies. Lodge brothers, many of whom confessed to never having agreed with a word he said, showered him with praise, as did city councilman Jeremiah Bloom, state senator Arthur Wachtel, Jim Watson, recently appointed president of New York's civil service commission, James Sheldon, the director of the Non-Sectarian Anti-Nazi League, and councilman Charles A. Keegan of the Bronx—the same Charles Keegan who, as US military governor of Bavaria in 1946, had been attacked by Mike Quill as a fascist and anti-semite. At the conclusion of the speeches, a lodge brother reported, EVM was for once "at a loss for words."

An era was closing. *PM* had ceased publication, proportional representation for council elections had been repealed. The ALP was finished. In 1950, Marcantonio finally lost his congressional seat to a candidate backed by the Democrats, Republicans and Liberals. As the Korean conflict intensified, Henry Wallace recanted his association with Communists and subscribed to the anti-Soviet crusade. The Popular Front, even in its last American stronghold, New York, was dead, and EVM was politically homeless. His community, his family, and his political reference points were all disappearing.

He replayed the battles of the past, insisting that they were the battles of the future. In January 1951, he published an article in the national magazine *The Free Sons of Israel* entitled "Is There an Easy Road to Freedom?"—a line from a Carl Sandburg poem.

> Being an alarmist has its drawbacks. You don't get to meet the right people—the ones who should be warned. Your Lodge brothers grimace a bit when you get up on the floor. As soon as they hear the words "anti-semitism" they take a look at the nearest exit.

EVM detects "Hitler's ghost flitting around the Halls of Congress . . . and right on the block where you live." He cites indications of German resentment over the Nuremberg verdicts, US officials cosying up to Franco, and the availability of Nazi propaganda in Yorkville, a German neighborhood in New York. "Under the cloak of fighting Communism, plain unadulterated anti-semitic fascism is creeping back . . . Next time Dachau may be on Manhattan island."

The post-war years did indeed witness a brief re-emergence of American anti-semitism, which certainly tinged the anti-Communist persecution. But it proved the prelude to a significant transformation for American Jews. Anti-semitism was discredited by Nazism and the holocaust in both official and popular realms; it was no longer possible for a Father Coughlin to preach and reach millions via the airwaves. As restrictive quotas and informal bars were dismantled, Jews flooded into the professions and, thanks to the long economic boom, enjoyed rising incomes. By the 1960s, when I was growing up, the Jewish working class that had done so much to shape US labor politics had all but vanished. Jews had been "assimilated": they had become an integral part of America's white majority.

Jim Watson died in 1952. His funeral at St Mark's church in Harlem was packed and spilled out into the street. EVM was there. "I had been his confidant for nearly two decades—knew of his innermost thoughts and aspirations—for himself, and yet at all times for his people." He acknowledges that Jim suffered from "a strange fault—he was too decent and for all his years in public life still a bit naïve He lacked the capacity to hate." EVM recalls "many hours" spent "trying to make him fight—and, we must confess, forget the rules." Eyeing the dignitaries paying tribute to his old friend in death, he comments that "there were some whose consciences might have been a bit uneasy. They had not risen up to be counted on causes and issues which would have heartened Jim." Still, he "never bore anyone malice when they let him down. We did and frankly still do."

EVM enjoyed a final fling as a columnist for the *American Hebrew*, a Brooklyn-based weekly in which "It's on the Tip of My Tongue" appeared, sporadically, in 1951 and 1952. He savages the "loyalty" tests being applied to federal, state and municipal employees as a violation of all known norms of due process, but at the same time he feels compelled to explain himself:

> We have never been a member of the Communist Party. Having a particular phobia about party regularity per se and an intense distaste for bosses either right or left—it just wasn't in the cards for us spiritually or psychologically to sign up . . . We joined the American Labor Party. It was sponsored by *Sidney Hillman*, politically conceived as a good idea by Roosevelt and Farley—and we know of no reason why any American should not have thought it entirely proper to join.

He defiantly catalogs his affiliations: "it was our privilege to be active in Spanish War Relief," "We worked like a devil for Russian War Relief. So what? . . . If anyone wants to know why we have never been appointed an ambassador just read the above dossier."

On April 25, 1952, in a column printed adjacent to a picture of the then Golda Myerson, Israeli Minister of Labor, at a New York fundraiser, EVM surveys the recent rash of left-wing apostates celebrated for their revelations of Communist perfidy. He confesses to a special interest in the "psychological aspects" of "radicals who change their mind and tune and wind up as arch-enemies of the very people and causes" they once espoused. He speculates that the reasons motivating the "modern Judases" are "more personal than doctrinaire. Somewhere along the line there has been a slight. One's ego has been wounded and all the frustrations and doubts suddenly become real and the drama starts to unfold." And here he seems to be reflecting on his own experience on the left, and perhaps congratulating himself for not taking the Mike Quill route.

The last ever "It's on the Tip of My Tongue" appeared on the back page of the *American Hebrew* on May 9, 1952. Headed "The ADL and Joe McCarthy," it is an irate response to news that Anti-Defamation League representatives had had a private meeting with the Wisconsin witch-hunter. "The only way I would consider walking in and having a chat with McCarthy is by express stipulation that I did *not* have to shake hands with him and that he was present *only to surrender*." EVM is appalled, as so often in the past, at the blindness of the Jewish leadership. "All liberals must be on the alert lest McCarthy sell himself as 'kosher' to a national Jewish organization." Leaning for the last time on his favorite post-war analogy, he writes: "The idea that the democratic world could not do business with Hitler was not easy to sell—remember? Let us hope it will not be as difficult to sell the idea that we cannot do business with McCarthy."

But the turning of the political axis that would render EVM's worldview redundant was clearly visible on the front page of the same paper, where a banner headline declared: "Israel Anti-Red,

Senators Assert; Hail State as US Ally and Bulwark Against Communism in Middle East." In the year that followed, Soviet policy shifted against Israel and Stalin unleashed an anti-semitic purge under the pretext of crushing the so-called Doctors' Plot. In 1956, the Anglo-French-Israeli invasion of Egypt made a final nonsense of the conceit of Zionist anti-imperialism. After 1953, the year I was born, the year my father named names, EVM falls silent. There are no further clippings. No carbon copies of letters, personal or public. No unfinished short stories. No speeches. And, as far I can tell, no further political activity. Except for one significant incident. In 1965, at the age of sixty-five, EVM took himself down to Selma to join the King-led March on Montgomery. He called his son Marty, who was then working for the ILGWU—for David Dubinsky, Sidney Hillman's long-time rival, sometime ally and latterday enemy—in Atlanta. Marty asked, "Dad, what are you doing in Selma?" The response, quick as a flash, and on the tip of his tongue for decades, was, "*Son, what are you doing elsewhere?*"

I was sipping tea in a darkened room in a dusty village somewhere off the Lahore–Multan road in Pakistan. My host was a rental car driver. We'd been chatting as we made our way across the flat plains of southern Punjab, beginning with cricket, and eventually, in a transition common across South Asia, leading to politics. We soon found ourselves agreeing on the barbarism and insanity of the invasion of Iraq and of US foreign policy in general, and I had been invited to his house to meet his family and continue our talk. Now, with a palpable heaviness, he said, "But why do they act like this? I think it must be the Jews."

I wasn't surprised by the remark. Across Pakistan, and in many other Muslim (and indeed non-Muslim) countries, there is a casual assumption that the Jews are behind the West's assault on Muslim populations. It's a safe bet that many millions around the world believe some form of the 9/11 mythology: that the Jews working in the Twin Towers were warned in advance, that Mossad or Israel or the Jews organized the whole thing.

My host mentioned that he'd heard these stories, but readily agreed when I described them as conspiracy theories. What he raised next, however, required more discussion. "Maybe it's all because the Jews run America."

This thesis, or a variant on it, is even more widely believed than the Twin Towers legends (and, obviously, not only in the developing world). The US's atrocious behavior in Iraq and its support for Israel are explained by Jewish influence—often specifically the influence of "Jewish money."

I asked my host how many Jews he thought there were in the US.

He pondered for a moment, then answered: "Maybe about 50 percent?"

He was struck when I told him it was under 3 percent, and more than happy to abandon the Jewish power thesis when I explained its improbability, and offered him an alternative. This has been my experience in all the conversations on this topic I've had with people in Pakistan, ranging from NGO workers to mullahs to young male cricket fans in replica Nike trainers.

What's common to all these encounters is the absence of any personal hostility to Jews. Certainly as soon as I have identified myself as a Jew, I have felt nothing but the warmest welcome, coupled with intense, entirely friendly curiosity. There is also a widespread awareness that Muslims and Jews were once friends and neighbors, and a puzzled sadness that this is no longer so.

The anti-semitism I encountered in Pakistan was driven not by hate, but by confusion. People are looking for an explanation for the horrors of US and Israeli aggression. Israel identifies itself with the Jews and with the West, while the West identifies itself with Israel, as do many Jews. These facts, as glossed in the rhetoric of the fundamentalist right, are what lead people towards blaming the Jews for the nightmares of the twenty-first century. In the absence of left and anti-imperialist analyses (the Pakistani left has never recovered from the Zia era), they grasp at an ethnic conspiracy theory. In this, of course, they are not alone.

In all the discussions I've had in Pakistan, people have always been quick to accept that oil, money, greed for power, colonialism, racism, etcetera are much more likely to explain US policy than "the Jews." After all, these are the same factors they see shaping their own society. So the good news is that this form of anti-semitism is not deep-rooted and is easily challenged. The problem is that there are so few people around challenging it.

Some years earlier—before General Musharraf's coup of 1999 and before 9/11 guaranteed US support for his regime—I found myself in Quetta, the dusty, escarpment-fringed capital of sparsely inhabited Baluchistan, a few hours' drive from the Afghan border. My hosts were community activists engaged in running youth clubs in slum areas, agricultural cooperatives, literacy schemes, environmental projects, reproductive control centers for women, as well as human rights monitoring. They were Pashtun, proud inheritors of the Gandhian tradition of Khan Abdul Gaffer Khan; they were also devout Sunnis, though rigorously non-sectarian and anti-fundamentalist. They had been teasing me about my US passport as we drove by the modern marble madrassas, built with CIA funds, from which some years previously the Taliban had surged. That night, in keeping with local traditions of hospitality, I was treated to a lavish (male-only) feast of lamb chops, spicy kebabs, salads, rice, yoghurt, almonds and dried fruits. Amidst the conviviality, I happened to mention that I was Jewish—and was immediately embraced as a brother. The Pashtun have an origin myth that they are descended from one of the Ten Lost Tribes of Israel. And that proud belief was not in the least in contradiction, for them, to their Muslim, Pashtun or Pakistani identities.

Across the border in India, a very different set of views about Israel and the Jews is current. Back in the days of the freedom struggle, Gandhi and the Indian National Congress opposed the creation of a "Jewish National Home" in Palestine. Nehru insightfully analyzed the triangular relationship between Zionism, Arab nationalism and British imperialism. Newly independent India voted against the UN Palestine partition plan in 1947 and the admission of Israel to the UN in 1949. As a leading force in the Non-Aligned Movement in the 1950s and 1960s, India backed anti-colonial movements in the Middle East and cultivated friendly relations with Nasser's Egypt.

Over the years, however, a clandestine relationship with Israel developed, thanks in part to Mossad, which acted as an unofficial—and deniable—diplomatic courier. Israel supplied arms to India in 1971, and intelligence collaboration was established, especially with regard to Pakistan, which was then building alliances with Arab regimes. In the late 1980s, Prime Minister Rajiv Gandhi, keen on improving relations with the US, began the process of upgrading ties with Israel. As the Indian press put it at the time, "The road to Washington passes through Tel Aviv."

Since full diplomatic relations were established in 1992, military and commercial links have grown exponentially. The process escalated under the right-wing BJP-led government of 1998–2004. The Bharatiya Janata Party is the political wing of the Sangh Parivar, the family of organizations dedicated to the ideology of Hindutva ("Hinduness"): an authoritarian, Hindu-supremacist, virulently anti-Muslim movement. Its founders were admirers of Hitler and Mussolini, but it also has a long history of support for Israel and Zionism.

In many respects, Hindutva and Zionism are natural bedfellows. Both depict the entities they claim to represent as simultaneously national and religious, territorial and transcendent. Both claim to be the sole authentic spokespersons for these entities (Hindu and Jewish). Both share an ambivalent historic relationship with British colonialism. Both appeal to an affluent diaspora. And, most important at the moment, both share a designated enemy ("Muslim terrorism").

During the Kargil War of 1999 (in which Indian and Pakistani troops clashed in Kashmir), Israel supplied India, at twenty-four hours' notice, with high-altitude surveillance vehicles and laser-guided targeting systems. In the wake of 9/11, the alliance was deepened, with Hindutva and Zionist worldviews dovetailing snugly with the US war on terror. In May 2003, India's then National Security Advisor Brajesh Misra spelled out the strategy in an address to the American Jewish Congress, in which he pleaded for a "Tel Aviv–New Delhi–Washington" axis. A few months later, Ariel Sharon arrived in India as an honored guest.

Much to the chagrin of its left supporters, the Congress-led coalition government that replaced the BJP after the 2004 elections tightened the embrace of both Israel and the USA. In the course of 2005, India's ministers of Science and Technology, Commerce and Industry, and Agriculture and Food all visited Israel, holding high-level meetings with political and business leaders.

Israel is now the second-largest supplier of arms to India (after Russia), providing missile radar, border-monitoring equipment, night vision devices, and the new Falcon reconnaissance aircraft, among other items. India, in turn, is the biggest purchaser of high-tech Israeli weapons and accounts for almost half of Israel's arms exports. In addition, several thousand Indian soldiers have received "anti-insurgency training" in Israel.

Though the Indian presence in the USA is highly diverse (many are Muslims), there is an affluent, suburban constituency within it that identifies with the Indian right and more broadly with Indian elite aspirations for economic and military status. Many see American Jews as the "model minority" and seek to emulate their political clout. A number have openly declared their intention of constructing a lobby similar to the Israel lobby. The attraction has been reciprocal. In 2003, the American Israel Political Action Committee and the American Jewish Committee met in a "joint forum" with the newly formed US Indian Political

Action Committee on Capitol Hill. The meeting was opened by congressman Gary Ackerman, who stressed the two countries' common concerns: Israel, he said, was "surrounded by 120 million Muslims" while "India has 120 million Muslims" within.

In a speech at Tel Aviv University in 2006, the Indian ambassador described India and Israel as "heirs to great and ancient civilizations" which "emerged from foreign domination as independent nations around the middle of the last century" and whose "historical interaction . . . is vividly embodied in the presence of Judaism in India for over 1,600 years."[31] These have become familiar themes in India–Israel colloquies (many held in the USA), where there is much emphasis on shared Indian and Jewish "values." It's a rag-bag of inconsistent analogies. A unitary set of values is attached to a unitary culture or religion which is attached to a state (and its diaspora). Then the whole package is tied up with the help of the "war on terror."

It's ironic that Indian Jews should find themselves used as a lynchpin in this marriage of convenience. Of course, India's population is so various, its diaspora so far-flung, that it can claim some kind of relationship with almost anyone anywhere. India's small Jewish population was itself dispersed in communities diverse in language, ritual, historic origin. During the 1950s and 1960s, most Indian Jews emigrated to Israel (many also went to the US), primarily for economic motives. Today, perhaps only 6,000 remain in India (out of a population of one billion).

That has not deterred Zionists from seeking recruits there. In November 2006, 218 members of the Bnei Menashe, a people from Mizoram in northeast India, arrived in Israel. They were promptly settled in northern Galilee as part of a drive to strengthen the Jewish presence in the area after the war against Lebanon.

The Bnei Menashe, who speak a Tibeto-Burmese language, claim to be descendants of one of the Ten Lost Tribes of ancient Israel (they are "Sons of Manasseh"), but their link with Judaism is in fact of recent origin. Like other tribal peoples in northeastern

India, they had been converted from indigenous religious practices to Protestant Christianity in the late nineteenth century. In 1951, a local Pentacostalist leader named Challianthanga announced that God had ordered his people to return to their pre-Christian religion, which he claimed was Judaism, and to their original homeland, which he claimed was Israel. He attracted a band of followers who adopted some Jewish customs while retaining faith in Jesus as the Messiah.

In 1979, an Israeli organization learned about the group and made contact with them. Over the following decades many were converted to Orthodox Judaism and some began settling in Israel and the Occupied Territories, principally Gaza. Significantly, much of the funding for this operation came from the International Fellowship of Christians and Jews, an evangelical body that solicits Christian support for Israel.

In Israel, champions of the Bnei Menashe openly describe their immigration as part of the solution to "the demographic problem," that is, the numerical preponderance of non-Jews in Palestine. For the Bnei Menashe to be eligible to immigrate under Israel's Law of Return, they must be accepted by the Rabbinate as Jewish, which means they must undergo formal conversion in India. Here the Zionists faced an unexpected problem: thanks to communal and caste histories, the issue of mass religious conversion is an inflammatory one in India. In Mizoram, churches complained about Jewish proselytizers. Under Indian pressure, the Israeli government halted conversions of the Bnei Menashe, while agreeing to admit those who had already undergone conversion; hence the arrival of the 218 immigrants in 2006.

During a visit to Delhi in February 2007, the Ashkenazi Chief Rabbi of Israel, Yona Metzger, met with Hindutva notables at the home of L. K. Advani, former deputy prime minister. In the 1980s, Advani gained notoriety when he launched and led the "Rath Yatra," a provocative nationwide tour aimed at mobilizing support for replacing the 500-year-old Babri mosque in Ayodhya, north India, with a Ram temple. The upshot was the violent demolition of the mosque in December 1992 by Hindutva fanatics, an act of communal aggression that led to riots across the country. Advani had visited the besieged mosque on the very day of its demolition, and was charged by police with making "inflammatory speeches to spread communal hatred." In 2002, as Home Minister in the BJP-led government, Advani was grossly culpable in the Hindutva-inspired pogrom in Gujarat, which took the lives of 2,500 Muslims and left some 150,000 homeless.

"It is seldom that I go to somebody's residence to participate in a reception," Rabbi Metzger told his hosts that evening. "Our custom does not allow this. But, here, I came to Shri L. K. Advani's residence as if I were going to my own home. It is a debt that we owe to the leader." Metzger and his hosts issued a "Hindu–Jewish" declaration against terrorism and religious violence. "Several Hindu leaders expressed their dismay at Muslim violence," the rabbi told the *Jerusalem Post*. "They told me that both Judaism and Hinduism were the mothers from which all other religions suckled. But sometimes the offspring bite the breast that feeds them."[32]

11

Confessions of a "Self-Hating Jew"

After that dinner-table confrontation with my father in 1967, I remained nervous for many years about broaching the subject of Israel with almost anyone. I was uncertain about the arguments and the facts, and intimidated by the reaction my single transgression had elicited. Nonetheless, I find that in an essay I wrote in 1969, at the age of sixteen, the following passage appears as part of a lengthy indictment of the hypocrisy of suburban liberals:

> What does brotherhood mean to us when we hear the sickening, racist comments our oh-so-proud, oh-so-Jewish elders make about Arabs and those "ungrateful," "anti-semitic" black militants? What can religious values mean when they include the unquestioning dogmatic support of the militaristic, racist state of Israel simply because its populace is primarily Jewish?

In context, my blast at Israel is merely one in a litany of indignities, given less weight than such outrages as hall passes, mandatory attendance at classes, and the scramble for grades. I must have picked up the phraseology from the Black Panthers, whose newspapers I devoured at the time, and who gave voice in the USA to the wave of Third World anti-imperialism that had, post-1967, embraced the Palestinian cause. I was also thinking of the recent controversy in the Ocean Hill–Brownsville section of Brooklyn, now seen as a watershed in black–Jewish relations in the USA, a key moment in the bitter breakdown of the old alliance.

Panicked about black discontent and ghetto insurgencies, the City Board of Education had initiated an experiment in "community control," in which management of schools devolved to locally elected boards. In the mid-1960s, despite a minority student enrollment of more than 50 percent, only 8 percent of the City's teachers and 3 percent of administrators were black; the teachers' union was 90 percent white, and more than 50 percent Jewish. In Ocean Hill–Brownsville, the newly elected, black-dominated local school board, determined to redress the imbalance, fired a number of teachers—all white, all union members, some Jewish. In the ensuing clash, teachers' union leader Albert Shanker (a "democratic socialist" and late product of the garment worker-dominated Jewish labor milieu descended from the Bund) emerged not only as a populist champion of meritocracy over alleged racial favoritism, but as a tough-talking scourge of anti-semitism, a charge he and his supporters leveled with regularity at their opponents in the black community.

The city-wide teachers' strikes in the autumn of 1968 (seeking reinstatement of the fired teachers and an end to the "community control" experiment) were conducted amidst a loudly amplified barrage of ethnic antagonism. Much of the media took Shanker's cue and focused on anecdotal evidence of "black anti-semitism." However, studies by the Anti-Defamation League and the American Jewish Committee showed that at this time militant blacks were less likely to be anti-semitic than non-Jewish whites. Other polls showed that white Catholics backed Shanker and the teachers' union in even higher proportions than Jews. A writer for the *Nation*, covering a teachers' picket line in Brooklyn, remarked on the unexpected affinity between the Jewish teachers and the Irish Catholic policemen. The Jewish–Irish alliance of which EVM had dreamed came to pass, though founded in a

politics—shared white resentment in the face of black demands—
far removed from his Popular Front imaginings.

His second wife Mabel was a long-serving teacher and a
supporter of Shanker and the strike—as she made clear, at length
and with much anger, in the course of a visit she and EVM made
to us during this period. I was, of course, firmly on the other side.
I identified with black nationalism and all that passed for black
militancy; I could see no argument against community-based
grassroots democracy. To me, Shanker, the teachers' union and
their allies were typical Cold War liberals of the older generation,
people who made heroic statements when the battleground was in
the distant South but changed their tune when it shifted to the
northern cities.

Mabel moved without pause from the strike to the behavior of
her black students, who had in recent years become disrespectful,
rude, and used bad language. At which point, I couldn't help
myself. I guffawed. She had fulfilled all my own stereotypes.

"Now, he's laughing!" she said with umbrage. It seems I had
also fulfilled a stereotype.

What did EVM make of it? I don't remember him saying
anything. He had always been a labor man, a supporter of the
teachers' unions, a battler for academic freedom. Whenever in the
past Jews had been fired *en masse*—in even smaller numbers—he
had been quick to charge anti-semitism. He had also believed that
Jews and blacks were allies, must be allies, and cursed Jewish
racism. In response to the discriminatory quotas in elite education
institutes he'd argued for a two-pronged strategy: fighting the
quotas on civil liberties grounds while building Jewish counterparts to the institutions from which Jews were excluded (medical
colleges in particular). He had argued that Jews needed their own
organizations, their own voices, and that without these Jews
would not be empowered as citizens in the larger democracy. He
had argued that the Jews needed a whole state—and here blacks
were getting just a school district. What analogies was he

wrestling with? No wonder he was silent. A few months after I came to Britain in the autumn of 1971 (initially as a student), I received a letter from him. It was handwritten and he didn't keep a carbon, but as I remember he told me that he and Mabel would be coming to England and would visit me. He added that in his experience the English were all anti-semites, and English women were flat-chested. Soon after, we met up in London. We went to a bad movie ("Stinker!" EVM pronounced) and had a bad Chinese meal. When, later, my parents followed me and set up a new home in Britain, he and Mabel visited again, twice. Somehow the two of us, Ed and I, managed to get away and spend time together on our own. I chattered to him about my literary ambitions and he made wisecracks about the English. In a delicatessen he spied some creamy chicken liver pâté and demanded, in a voice designed to be heard across the street, "a pound of that chopped liver." At the time I had grown a scruffy beard. EVM didn't like it and kept riding me about it. "Leave him alone!" my mother pleaded. EVM replied: "I'm trying to make him a mensch!" He never really bothered me. What drove my mother crazy amused me. He was my cantankerous grandfather, and I enjoyed him.

On a brief visit to New York, I arranged to meet EVM outside the Bronx County Courthouse. He wanted me to see him in action. He was seventy-three or seventy-four years old but still working, occasionally, as a public defender. I spotted him pacing the top rung of the courthouse steps. He seemed to have shrunk since I'd seen him in London. He was squat, but energetic. His thin, silky white hair was combed straight back from his wide forehead. He wore a gray suit and tie (I was in jeans and sweatshirt). He looked worried but when he caught sight of me advancing toward him, he smiled— a smile he quickly buried. After a perfunctory hug he was talking straightaway. This morning he was appearing in a committal hearing—his client was on a murder charge—and after he'd dealt with that we'd have softshell crabs for lunch. First, however, there were some people he wanted me to meet.

He whisked me into the courthouse, introducing me to the security guards, the cloakroom attendants, stenographers, clerks and fellow attorneys. Men named Ed Flannery and Mike O'Leary and Frank Kinsella. Large-waisted men who seemed to have been sitting on chairs for decades. When EVM presented his grandson—"he lives in London, wants to be a writer like his grandfather"—their broad faces creased with smiles and they stuck out meaty hands with a firm grip. EVM was clearly proud of the fact that he knew everyone and everyone knew him. I'd never seen him in this mode before—swaggering, bantering. It was EVM the politician, not EVM the grumpy husband-father-grandfather. He was positively chirpy.

We entered the courtroom, where he introduced me to the judge at his bench. "Your grandfather's a great character," the judge told me, and I said yes, I knew that. I took a seat in the public gallery directly behind the defense table. The defendant was brought in by the uniformed guards. He was a young black man with a large Afro. As soon as he was in sight of the judge, he started talking.

"Your Honor, I don't want this old fool to be my lawyer. He won't listen to a word I tell him. I got a right to a representative of my choice . . ."

The judge banged his gavel and ordered the defendant to be silent, then told him to approach the bench. He looked at EVM: "Counsel?" EVM rose and joined his client before the wooden dais.

The disaffected defendant continued, "This old man thinks he knows everything but he's just an old fool."

He towered over my grandfather, who looked up at him with a sneer, showing his famous nose in handsome profile, and spitting back, "Listen, sonny, you ain't no day at the beach either."

Before the defendant could reply, the judge intervened. Calm and patient. I thought: he's seen this before. He said that he would order new counsel for the defendant, in accordance with his rights, and he thanked EVM for his time and his efforts on behalf of his client.

"Thank *you*, Your Honor," EVM said with a little bow, then swiveled around and strode back to his table, hitching up his trousers. Positively cock of the walk. He felt he'd scored a point: he'd got in the last word. I smiled at his pugnacity. I pitied his pugnacity.

We took the subway downtown and picked up softshell crabs and ice tea from a deli—where he also seemed to know and be known by everyone—then went to his apartment for the feast. He was living on the Upper West Side, a few blocks from where he'd grown up, ending where he began. As we ate, he told me what he thought about people. Nixon. Rockefeller. Aunt Gert, "that certified virgin" who'd made his life "a living hell."

"And that other grandfather of yours, what a snob, a show-off with money. And how about that great-grandmother of yours, the Jewish Betsy Ross?"

As I recall he gave me only one piece of political advice. "Never trust a social democrat." I obviously failed to get the point, because a few years later I joined the British Labour Party, and spent a couple of decades immersed in it.

Something else he said that I did not take seriously enough at the time was his repeated suggestion that I write his biography. It was, he said, a great story; he had all the papers. He talked about it in a flippant tone that let me know he wasn't entirely serious; it was an idea he liked to play with. I don't remember what I said but I do remember laughing inwardly at the very idea of it. What an absurd thought! What an illusion! That his life merited such a memorial and that I would want to spend time writing it. What did his story have to do with mine? What could it possibly mean, what relevance could it have?

Mabel arrived home carrying groceries and a look of reproach. We'd made a mess of the table, littering it with bits of oily crab and potato chips. "It's not enough I clean up after you once a day . . ." she complained.

"I'm shmoosing with my grandson, for god's sake!"

She stormed into the kitchen and loudly unpacked the groceries, giving the refrigerator door a hearty slam.

He shook his head. "Women, you can't live with 'em, you can't live without 'em."

That was the last time I saw him.

Despite EVM's warnings, in my new life in Britain I was never in the least self-conscious about being a Jew. Of course I knew that nearly everyone I met would not be Jewish. Whenever the subject was relevant, I was always happy to say I was a Jew, and I can't remember any difficulties about that. The Jews I met at university were from South Africa, Holland, and Egypt. In the left-wing groups that proliferated on campus, and which I stayed away from at the time, there seemed a disproportionate number of Jews, who as far as I could tell lacked no confidence at all. But gradually I learned that being a British Jew wasn't the same as being an American Jew, or at least a New York Jew. There were fewer of them and more uncertainties about their acceptance.

In the early 1970s I felt ambivalence about the whole subject of Israel and Palestine, part of a general ambivalence I felt at the time about political commitment. Palestinian terrorism confused and horrified me. It seemed part of the ultra-left, Baader-Meinhof-style cult of violence, which I considered a wrong turn. But listening to and meeting Arabs and Palestinians, reading Said's *The Question of Palestine*, becoming aware of the existence of Israeli dissidents, including the anti-Zionist Matzpen, deepened my understanding.

Mainly, what turned me into an anti-Zionist was just following events, and finding the pro-Israel narrative and its underlying Zionist claims unsustainable in the face of the evidence. This wasn't a truth forced on me from outside. In the end, after some hesitation, I sought it out, in the same way and for the same

reasons I sought out alternative understandings of the world role
of the United States and Britain or any number of other political
questions. What made it possible for me to do that was the
context: the re-emergence of Palestinian nationalism associated
with the growth and development of the PLO. Here was a
Palestinian voice independent of the Arab regimes, a movement
building a nation on the ground, reaching across a diaspora,
reaching out to the victims of colonialism everywhere. It was a
stunning achievement, and should not be obliterated by the
dissipation, division and corruption that beset the movement
later. Whatever theoretical disagreements I might have had with
Zionism, as a Jew or as a democrat, would have never acquired
any significance were it not for the visibility and the persistence of
the Palestinian struggle on the ground.

For some years, the subject of Israel continued to be a vexed
one between me and my father, whom I remember ranting against
the militant Palestinian leader George Habash, sneering at him as
"that murdering fuck." But in the end, the Zionists tested his
humanity beyond endurance. After the news broke about the
Sabra and Shatila massacre in 1982, he phoned me from New
York. "OK," he said, "you were right. They're bastards." He
started to make contributions to Palestinian causes and to raise the
issue among his friends.

No one out there has to be a Jewish son to imagine the sense of
vindication, the lightness of heart, the elation, I derived from this
paternal admission.

There are (at least) two points to this story. First, the Zionist
dominance of the diaspora, and especially the diaspora in America, is a mutable, historical phenomenon—not the inevitable
expression of "Jewish self-interest"—and the continuation of
that dominance is by no means guaranteed. Second, though we
could now add Israel to the list of things we agreed on, this did
not signal the end of the tensions, resentments and edgy differences between my father and myself. In fact, these grew as the

years passed. They had other sources, more intangible, more intractable than politics.

I was working as a media officer for the Stop the War Coalition in the buildup to the demonstration of September 28, 2002. A journalist phoned and asked me to respond to charges made by the Union of Jewish Students that groups supporting the march were "usually quite anti-semitic on campus" and that the demonstration itself could "incite people against Israelis, Zionists and ultimately Jews."

I condemned the allegations as "outrageous," and was quoted correctly. I was angry but not surprised. From its inception in the weeks after 9/11, there had been attempts to stick the anti-semite label on the anti-war movement. To those who saw the world in the wake of that atrocity as polarized into two camps, we, the anti-war movement, were in the wrong one—with the terrorists, the jihadis, the anti-American, anti-Israel, and therefore anti-semitic camp. After all, it was not just America that had been attacked; it was New York, a great Jewish city, and it had been attacked by Muslims. Protest against the US military response—against the attack on Afghanistan and the war on terror—was seen as expressing a latent hostility to Israel and to Jews. For many Zionists, resistance to the US's will had become tantamount to resistance to Israel.

On the other side, there were conspiracy theories, some of which smacked of anti-semitism: that Mossad had been involved in the attack, that Jews working in the Twin Towers had been forewarned. However, these were not credited by the vast majority attending anti-war events. Here, amidst confusion, fear, and the usual barrage of contending theories, there emerged an analysis focusing on politics and economics, an awareness of where jihadism had come from, how the US was linked to it, and how the US and British allies intended to use the moment to advance their long-term interests.

One of the most striking features of the early anti-war events in Britain was the Muslim presence, which for me was a hopeful sign in bleak times. An aggrieved and angry section of the population was entering a political, secular arena—and I didn't see why they should have to abandon their Muslim identity in doing so. While asserting their Muslimness in various ways, they were at the same time articulating the concerns, anger and understanding common to the movement as a whole, often in a more well-informed vein. Above all, the Muslim presence and the welcome it received from most of us was a standing defiance of the divisions being imposed on the population by media and politicians.

I was aware that there was a complex spectrum of opinion and experience among both Muslims and Muslim activists, that they were grappling with difficult questions of representation, leadership, alliances, with the whole extremely tricky enterprise of taking full part in the shared democratic arena without conceding your distinctiveness, especially at a time when you are being attacked for that distinctiveness. I couldn't help but observe this process through two analogies: the African-American and the Jewish struggles for equality. And as I've studied EVM's wayward journey, I've often been thrown from the past into the present as EVM's dilemmas echo those faced by Muslim activists today.

Since what has come to be called the "left–Muslim alliance" in Britain has been misrepresented and caricatured—by both its detractors and its advocates—it's worth noting that it was initially a product of circumstances. In the worst leftist tradition, theory was later adapted to suit practice.

What happened was that the date chosen by the Stop the War Coalition for its major national "Don't Attack Iraq" demonstration coincided with the second anniversary of the second Intifada, and the Muslim Association of Britain had earmarked the same date for their own "Freedom for Palestine" demonstration. The MAB had been one of the key forces in organizing a large and successful demonstration earlier in the year during the Israeli assault on the West Bank and Gaza. Neither organization was in a position to change the date of its demonstration, and the alternative was either to combine them somehow, or have them compete.

I thought then and still think it was right to reach out to Muslims, that expressions of Muslim identity on demonstrations are an appropriate and inevitable response to the shrill Islamophobia of our day. I also believed profoundly that the point of all this was to enable us to build a movement in which the whole would be greater than the sum of the parts, in which sections of the population with diverse backgrounds and common concerns would meet, interact and make something new. There was an argument within the Stop the War movement about the wisdom of widening the demands of the demonstration to include Palestine. Clearly, it was important that the primary message on Iraq—where our aim was to deter an act of imminent aggression by our own government—not be diluted. There was the worry that people who supported or felt ambivalent about Israel would be alienated. However, none of us thought the political linkage between Iraq and Palestine was in any way arbitrary or in fact anything other than obvious. For me what was most important was that we didn't end up with two demonstrations—betokening two separate movements, one "Muslim" and the other "white."

I'm sure some people were kept away, but overall my feeling is that the complaints about the addition of the Palestine issue emanated mainly from people who were looking for grounds on which to attack or distance themselves from the demonstration. "I don't see how the two issues come together," the Union of Jewish Students spokesperson commented. "They're either not serious about the war on Iraq, or they're using the Palestinian issue to score cheap political points." Just what would those cheap political points have been? Why is raising the issue of Palestine

"cheap"? The implication here was that we were being oppor-
tunists, even that we were cashing in on anti-semitism.

As it turned out, the September 28 demonstration—estimated
at 350,000 to 400,000—was at that time the biggest anywhere since
9/11, and presaged the extraordinary global manifestation of
February 15, 2003. For those of us lucky enough to have taken
part, it was a bracing display of unity in diversity. This was the
Britain I lived in and knew and was part of, and it had made itself
politically visible. The crowd were remarkably patient (it was a
long slow trek if you were anywhere near the back of the column),
proud of themselves and of their interjoined communities. None
of which stopped it being described in some US media as "an orgy
of anti-Americanism."

There was also, among some supporters of the march, an
uneasiness about anti-semitism. I learned later that there had
indeed been a tiny group chanting "Death to the Jews" in Arabic.
They were quickly halted by Arabic speakers who objected to the
slogan. More significant were the home-made placards which
linked the Star of David to the swastika by an equals sign. This
was spontaneous and reflected neither the emphasis nor the
influence of any of the sponsors of the demonstration. Of course
people are right to object to this equation. The Star of David is a
symbol of Jewishness, not merely of Israel, just as the crescent is a
symbol of Islam, not of Pakistan or Turkey or Malaysia, in whose
flags it appears.

Of course, the crude equation of the Jews with their greatest
persecutors is precisely the attraction of this populist analogy. It is
meant to shock and offend. It is meant to turn against the Zionists
their own exploitation of the holocaust, their own definitions of
legitimate victimhood. But it does so in terms borrowed from the
Zionists; it compounds Jews and the state of Israel, and then links
both with an emblem of absolute reaction. It's not a controlled and
revealing analogy, just an emotive blast, and it can legitimize anti-
semitism. Of course, when it comes to the casual, thoughtless

abuse of the Nazi analogy the home-made sign-makers are amateurs compared to the Zionists, who from the mid-1930s have branded every expression of Palestinian resistance to Jewish colonialism as "Nazi."

There is anti-semitism in British society and the left is not immune to it, just as it is not immune to other forms of racism and bigotry. And just as Jewish appeals not to wash dirty linen in public have to be resisted, so do similar appeals from the left. Edward Said feared that a "nasty, creeping wave of anti-semitism" was insinuating itself into Palestinian politics, and it helps no one to deny it.

Nonetheless, in attending hundreds of anti-war and left-wing events, in Britain, the USA, and elsewhere, I've encountered only a handful of remarks that might be construed as anti-semitic. Once, in a discussion of the foibles of the US media, the talk came round to the *New York Times*. A woman who had previously said nothing interjected, "Well, look who owns it!" Apparently the fact that the paper is owned by Jews was enough to explain everything. A more complicated example occurred in the spring of 2002, while Israeli troops were hammering towns and camps on the West Bank. A speaker at a protest said that, this Easter, it was the Palestinians who "were being crucified." When I heard this my heart sank, and looking around I knew I wasn't the only one dismayed. The speaker's intention was unimpeachable: she was looking for a word to encapsulate the injustice being done, at this moment, as we sat in safety, to the Palestinians. It had never crossed her mind that this phrase might be anti-semitic and she would have hotly denied any such intention. But she should have known better, and it is a failure of the movement that she did not, that despite her accurate and detailed knowledge of the current plight of the Palestinians, she was unaware that for 2,000 years Jews had been persecuted as the crucifiers of Christ, or that her words might be taken as evidence that to be pro-Palestinian was to be anti-Jewish.

On a few occasions, disputes have arisen about Jewish speakers on anti-war platforms. Now the fact is that there have been Jews on anti-war and pro-Palestine platforms from one end of the country to the other and it has not been any kind of issue. It should be noted that early efforts by the anti-war movement, including the Stop the War Coalition, to make contact with rabbis and Jewish community organizations met with a negative response. But that had nothing to do, or should have had nothing to do, with the issue that arose in relation to the national anti-war demonstration held in London in September 2003—six months into the occupation of Iraq. It was called for a Saturday on the eve of Labour Party conference (a long-established tactic) which also this year happened to be Rosh Hashanah. In the past, major demonstrations had been held at Easter and during Ramadan, so the clash with Rosh Hashanah should not in itself have been an issue, though the Board of Deputies of British Jews tried to make it one, suggesting that Jews who took part in the march would be "desecrating" the High Holiday.[1] But given the background of smears and allegations, once the coincidence of dates had been noted, steps could and should have been taken to ensure it was not misconstrued, and that Jews would be made welcome and visible on the demonstration. Practical suggestions about how to do this were made by Jewish anti-war activists, but were rebuffed. One Jewish activist was informed briskly that the whole Rosh Hashanah issue was being trumped up by the Zionists. A sore point was the failure to include a Jewish speaker (as opposed to a speaker who may have happened to be a Jew) on the platform. Given the significance of Rosh Hashanah and the accusations of anti-semitism, you would have thought the organizers would have made it a priority to avail themselves of any one of the number of possible speakers representing Jewish groups or combinations of groups. Instead, they left it to the obscurantist misogynists of Neturei Karta to stand in, mutely, for Jewish opposition to the war on terror.

The reasons given for the omission varied. We were asked, quite reasonably, to recognize the inevitable difficulties in getting a practicable speakers' list agreed for a major national demonstration, though with some twenty speakers on the day, there should have been room for at least one from a Jewish organization. What was unacceptable, however, was the non-sequitur, repeated in private and in public, that "the Chief Rabbi was the only major faith leader in Britain not to oppose the Iraq War." Apart from letting a number of other religious denominations off the hook, since when did the left recognize the Chief Rabbi as representative of all Jews, and why should his idiocy be a reason not to mark Rosh Hashanah in an appropriate manner, not to have a Jewish speaker?

For those working to build support for the anti-war movement in their synagogues and community organizations (I was not one of them) this was a blow, as it was for anti-war Jews in general, including anti-Zionists. Though knowledge of this discussion never traveled far, for some of those who did learn about it, it was an "Ah ha!" moment; for others, an "I told you so" moment. "*You see, they are anti-semitic. There is a different attitude towards Jews.*" For some this is a moment of vindication, of personal triumph. For others, of disappointment and despair.

But really it's neither. The failure to have a Jewish speaker on Rosh Hashanah in 2003 was a serious disservice to the movement and specifically to the cause of Palestine. What it reflected was not necessarily anti-semitism but the resistance of some leaders of the movement to any input from below, coupled with a crass approach to ethnic diversity in general. Beyond the leaders, a larger group were ill at ease or perplexed by the specific issues raised. The incessant abuse of the charge of anti-semitism over the years has offended and wearied people, and inevitably coarsened their response to criticism. It's been suggested that this affair reflected a fear of alienating or posing awkward questions to Muslim activists. If that was the case, the leaders seriously underestimated their target audience. Muslim participants in the coalition that built the large anti-war demonstrations have in my experience always been eager to have Jewish speakers on anti-war and Palestinian platforms. In fact, the frustrations felt by Jewish activists mirror those experienced by many young Muslim activists. They too find themselves amalgamated into a demographic, denied the right to their divisions.

The very existence of a public discussion about the "Israel lobby" has roused cries of "Jewish conspiracy theories." It is entirely legitimate to examine the political clout, tactics, resources, social composition and system of alliances of the pro-Israel forces in the USA, a conglomeration that includes but reaches beyond the "Israel lobby." It is entirely legitimate to debate the degree to which US (or British) policy on Israel is driven by domestic political considerations (so long as one also asks what shapes the relevant domestic constituencies and where their power derives from), to argue about who's wagging whom, the tail or the dog (Israeli and US elites), to identify the facts regarding the wealth of some Jews or the influence of some Jewish social groups and how it is used on behalf of Israel—all of these political realities can and should be specified and analyzed.

But it is not possible to engage in this discussion realistically and usefully in the absence of an understanding of the history and role of Jewish stereotypes. It has to be conducted with a vigilant care for precise discriminations: between a Jew, some Jews, many Jews, most Jews, and the Jews; between Judaism, Jewishness, and Zionism; between conspiracies and convergent interests; between degrees and types and contexts of "power." Failure to make these discriminations concedes vital ground to the Zionists and disarms the Palestine solidarity movement.

In May 2003, Tam Dalyell, the then Labour MP and Father (that is, longest continuously serving member) of the House, was reported to have blamed the Iraq war, and specifically British involvement in it, on a "Jewish" or "Zionist" "cabal." Dalyell's record as a parliamentary maverick and forensic critic of British military adventures was and is an honorable one. And he had not, in fact, used the wretched phrase "cabal." Nonetheless, the remarks he made in press interviews were redolent with hoary anti-semitic mythology. He roped together a variety of leading government figures on both sides of the Atlantic and declared not only that they were all "Jewish" (though some had never identified themselves as such), but that it was this shared Jew-ishness that accounted for their hawkish politics. There was an implied warning: a religious minority was exercising an undue, malign influence on British and US foreign policies.

What was disturbing was that someone could lead a public career distinguished by the exercise of logic and still succumb unthinkingly to an "it's in the blood" pseudo-logic that linked genealogy to religion to politics to national loyalty without pausing for breath. Dalyell insisted he was merely "being candid." But this was no more than a polished specimen of the "people are afraid to say it, but we all know what they're like" school of racist apologetics. You can find it in tabloids and phone-ins any day of the week. However, to his credit, Dalyell regretted his remarks and acknowledged his error.

When I published an article criticizing what Dalyell had said, I was told by a liberal Zionist that it didn't really count, didn't really get the anti-war movement off the hook, because I was a Jew. In fact, non-Jewish anti-war activists, including the leaders of the STWC, also unequivocally rejected Dalyell's mythologiz-ing. However, when along with other Jews I signed a statement condemning Israeli behavior in Gaza, the same liberal Zionist told me (told all of us) that this time we didn't count because we were really signing as leftists, not as Jews.

"Jewish power." Years ago, Rabbi Elmer Berger, a long-time victim of Zionist defamation, said he flinched whenever he heard the phrase, and that what was necessary was to distinguish between Jewish influence, the influence of particular Jews, and

"Jewish power," which was a metaphysical notion.[2] Today, the "Jewish power" school of thought has made a return. It's a tragedy, and not only for Jews. Its entire thrust is, of course, an ideological and tactical gift to the Zionists. If we in the anti-war and pro-Palestine movements misidentify our enemies, we will not defeat them.

The term "Jewish lobby" is not only unscientific; it strengthens and legitimizes the entity it seeks to expose and weaken. First, both Jews and non-Jews are active in the Zionist movement. Second, though many Jews do take part in pro-Israel activities, the majority do not, and a small but growing minority actively oppose them. Third, the phrase draws a categorical and unqualified equation between being Jewish and being pro-Israeli. The Israeli media routinely refer to the pro-Israel forces in the US as "the Jewish lobby": they endow a political constituency with an ethnic legitimacy, and thereby hope to place it beyond criticism. Surely the left needs to dispute this sleight-of-hand, not fall for it.

As precise and frank as we have to be about the weight and deleterious influence of "the Israel lobby," we also have to be equally frank and precise about what are referred to as American or British "interests." And it is here, not in their legitimate anatomizing of "the Israel lobby," that John Mearsheimer and Stephen Walt fail. In keeping with the "realist school" of international relations to which they belong, they posit a self-evident, coherent US national interest, note that this interest has been ill served by the US's pro-Israel policies, and then seek to explain the "discrepancy" by reference to the power of the Israel lobby.

Traditionally, the left has rejected the idea of coherent "national interests," seeing them as a mask for conflicting class interests. In the anti-globalization movement, the national interests, not to mention humanitarian pretensions, proclaimed by Western powers are commonly recognized as expressions of corporate priorities. Amazingly, otherwise well-informed people vex themselves over the apparent contradiction between the US's friendship with Israel and its friendship with Saudi Arabia, accepting at face value that what the Middle East conflict is about is competing Arab and Jewish interests, and that the US error is merely to keep choosing the wrong side. In the same vein, James Petras, a well-regarded leftist analyst of US power in Latin America, argues that in relation to the Middle East, the US government has been hijacked by "Zioncons." US policy in the region is, in effect, controlled by "agents of a foreign power."

The most disturbing part of Petras's analysis is the appeal to the American public to "take back" US foreign policy from the "foreign agents," to make it a servant once again of the American people. As EVM knew, as surely Petras knows, it has never been any such thing. What would a "re-Americanization" of US foreign policy in the Middle East amount to? Would an American regime freed of the influence of Jews or Zionists, but otherwise unchanged, look with favor on a genuinely independent Palestine? Or tolerate militantly nationalist forces in Iraq, Iran or Egypt? Five years after opposing partition in 1948, and earning EVM's ire as a result, Kermit Roosevelt—who spent a lifetime serving both US diplomatic and corporate interests—played a central role in the CIA overthrow of the nationalist government in Iran and the installation in its stead of the Shah's pro-Israel dictatorship.

Petras's revival of the "dual allegiance" charge betrays an ignorance of the enemy he purports to be fighting. It's the old error of Dorothy Thompson and the American Council for Judaism, who wrongly asked Jews to choose between their Jewishness and their Americanism, failing to see that Zionism could be made all too compatible with Americanism. It's also a repetition of the Wallace misreading of pro-Arab US oil interests, with the political evaluations reversed. If you see Zionists as alien infiltrators who have distorted what would otherwise have been a benign US policy (in a region of the world whose oil reserves made it, long before the birth of the state of Israel, a central strategic concern of US policy makers), then you have substituted a kind of hermetic meta-history for the real thing.

Petras, like Dalyell, seems unaware of the way postulates about the secret power of a pro-Israel Jewish network echo older themes—of world Jewish conspiracy, of Jewish "clannishness," of an overriding masonic-style allegiance among Jews to fellow Jews. That's a serious gap in these two men's understanding not only of anti-semitism, but of the global politics of racism in general. Marx's strictures on Jews in his early writings are vile and stupid, but even at his most purblind he would have dismissed ferociously and without hesitation the categories out of which the Petras analysis is fashioned.

In response to Norman Finkelstein's critique of his thesis, Petras observed sadly, "I am afraid that when it comes to dealing with the predominantly Jewish lobby, he has a certain blind spot, which is understandable." Petras has made the same charge against Chomsky, whose "analytical virtues are totally absent when it comes to discussing the formulation of US foreign policy in the Middle East, particularly the role of his own ethnic group, or the Jewish pro-Israel lobby and their Zionist supporters in the government." For Petras, Finkelstein and Chomsky are examples of "the tragic myopia or perverse refusal of Leftist Jews to face up to the prejudicial role of the major Jewish groups promoting the Israel First policy."

In effect, Petras accuses Finkelstein and Chomsky of letting the Jews off the hook, or dissolving their particular responsibility in a more diffuse anti-imperialist indictment. But Petras commits an opposite error—of letting Americans off the hook. The real ethno-nationalist myopia here lies with Petras and his fantasy of a US foreign policy purged of "foreign" influence. Neither Finkelstein nor Chomsky need any lectures about the power and ruthlessness of the pro-Israel forces in the USA. Speaking for myself, I have no doubts that Zionism has coursed through the diaspora like a poison. It has twisted Jewry, Judaism, Jewishness, Jewish culture and the minds of many Jews. The blindness of the majority of American and British Jews to the criminality of Israeli behavior toward the Palestinians beggars belief and is an index of moral, spiritual and intellectual decadence. The money that Jews (and others) give to groups that undermine free speech, defame dissidents, deny them jobs in academia, sink political careers, is obscene. As Elmer Berger discovered to his shock back in the mid-1940s, this is the Zionist *modus operandi*: character assassination, disinformation, denial, bullying, intimidation. These have for many years become the standard practices of many Jewish organizations and Jewish leaders, in both the USA and Britain, and no one on the left—certainly not Finkelstein or Chomsky—would deny its reality or shamefulness. Nor should anyone be scared off from making that indictment by charges of anti-semitism.

What then are we being asked to concede by Petras et al.? Not that the Israel lobby exists and is a perfidious force, but that it is the *sole determinant force* in US policy on the Middle East. Our reluctance to accept that misleading assertion is then attributed to vestigial ethnic loyalty. Our attachment to Jewishness allegedly results in our denial of an actually existing collective Jewish guilt. In other words, Jewish ethnicity really is the story here—just as the Zionists always said it was. And when individual Jews disagree, and do so by offering substantive arguments (as do Chomsky and Finkelstein), they are answered not with arguments of like substance, but with the assertion that they are only saying what they're saying because they're Jewish. It's a circular, inherently racist argument, and the fact that it is taken seriously anywhere on the left is a depressing indication of the renewed acceptance across Western societies of an intellectually unexamined ethnocentrism that has become common ground, post-Cold War and post-9/11, among liberals and conservatives—and against which the internationalist left should be standing its ground.

According to Petras, it's time to "move ahead and decolonize our country, our minds and politics as a first step in reconstituting a democratic republic, free of entangling colonial and neo-imperial alliances." This is the same evasive, shortcutting, "take back America" rhetoric that inverts the global pyramid by seeing the US as the "colonized" country. The alternative to Zionism is not Americanism, but an internationalist humanism. In US popular culture, the real obstacles to Palestinian solidarity remain white and Western supremacism, the mantle Zionism wraps itself in. One reason Zionism enjoys such success in this arena is that it goes with that flow.

The Jewish vote is relatively insignificant in Britain, but British policy has been strongly pro-Israel (sales of arms coupled with support for anti-Hamas sanctions). Other EU governments (including countries where support for Israel is a definite vote-loser) have pursued similar courses, as has the EU as a whole. What's decisive here is not Jewish power but Western power.

The more a movement grows, the more disparate is the consciousness of its participants, and the more likely it is that simplistic or delusional or conspiratorial analyses will make themselves felt. In the face of mounting frustration at Israeli aggressiveness, and mounting disbelief at the willingness of Jews to justify it, there will be individuals who find sense in this nonsense. Conspiracies and stereotypes are easier to assimilate intellectually than the complex, long-accumulated realities of an economic, geopolitical, and cultural struggle. Nonetheless, by and large the movement responds negatively to the Dalyell and Petras theories. At their best, such ideas are tactical gifts to the enemies of the Palestinian people. They make it harder to break Jews from Israel and easier to delegitimize the movement as a whole with the British and US public. And they are, at root, perniciously illogical. Like the Zionists, the self-styled exposers of "Jewish power" insist that the racial category of Jewishness is real and politically determinant.

In January 2006, the Chief Rabbi of Britain, Jonathan Sacks, warned that the Jews were threatened with "a tsunami of anti-semitism." Sacks complained that Israel was being blamed for all the world's problems, and that the Jews were being blamed for Israel. It was rich coming from someone who takes umbrage at "inappropriate metaphors" and "exaggerated criticisms" of Israel, while regularly trumpeting the unbreachable bond between Israel and the Jews of Britain.

Reading the US press you'd be forgiven for thinking that Britain was awash with anti-semitism, not as dire as in France, but boding ill. So just how bad is it for Jews in Britain today? The most concrete, though certainly not the only measurement is given by the Community Security Trust (the main body concerned with the safety and security of Britain's Jews), which reports that in 2006, there were 595 anti-semitic incidents in the UK, the highest since the CST began keeping records in 1984. Of these, 112 were violent incidents, of which four involved intention to do grievous bodily harm or worse. Some 20 per cent—134—took place during the 34 days of Israel's war against Lebanon. During the whole year, 54 incidents included specific reference to Lebanon.[3]

As with all racist incidents, the perpetrators should be brought to account, the victims supported and the causes analyzed. To get to grips with what these figures do and do not indicate, you have to ask questions about proportion and context. Nationally, the police recorded 50,000 racially or religiously aggravated offences in 2006. According to the British Crime Survey these were only a fraction of the 260,000 hate crimes perpetrated during that year. This implies that whereas a Jew had, in 2006, a roughly one in 500 chance of being the victim of a hate crime, a member of an ethnic minority with roots in Asia, Africa or the Caribbean had a more than fourteen to one chance, and it was far more likely that the crime would involve physical assault or injury. Significantly, these ethnic minorities also experience racism at the hands of immigration authorities, police, and the criminal justice system, as well as in housing and employment, to which Jews are not exposed. Nor is there any discernible threat of Jews being subject to such treatment. Finally, nothing about Jews in the British media remotely compares to the racist treatment—sensationalist, stereotyped, hostile—dished out to Muslims or young blacks.

But in a sense all this is irrelevant. What the Chief Rabbi and the Board of Deputies and other pro-Israel voices are really preoccupied with is what they call "left-wing anti-semitism," something unmeasured and unmeasurable by any of the CST's current methods. According to the Chief Rabbi, "Modern anti-semitism is coming simultaneously from three different directions": its traditional home on the far right, "a radicalized Islamic youth inflamed by extremist rhetoric," and "a left-wing anti-American cognitive elite with strong representation in the European media."[4] Now just what stereotype does that last category smack of?

The thesis of a specifically "left-wing anti-semitism" relies on a politics of insinuation, the attribution of hidden or unconscious agendas. The hallmark of the anti-semitic left is said to be not its criticism of Israel, but the severity of its criticism, and in particular its anti-Zionism, "its refusal to recognize Israel" and concomitant denial to Jews of the rights allegedly granted to others. In other words, left opposition to Israel is deemed anti-semitic to the extent that it diverges from what the pro-Israel camp defines as proportionate or acceptable criticism.

That in some quarters anti-semitism functions as the anti-imperialism of fools, especially in the Arab world, is undeniable. But conversely, there is a putative anti-anti-semitism in the West that functions as a camouflage for Israel.

In 2006 a so-called British All-Party Parliamentary Inquiry into Anti-semitism reported that "contemporary anti-semitism in

Britain is now more commonly found on the left of the political spectrum than on the right." Its chairman, the pro-war MP Denis McShane, referred in a radio interview to what he called "a witch's brew of anti-semitism including the far left and ultra-Islamist extremists," who use criticism of Israel as a "pretext" for "spreading hatred against British Jews." Historian David Cesarani explained to the Inquiry that anti-semitism "no longer has any resemblance to classical Nazi-style Jew hatred, because it is masked by or blended inadvertently into anti-Zionism, and because it is often articulated in the language of human rights." In other words, regardless of context or caveats, anti-Zionist ideas and concerns about human rights must be seen as telltale signs of latent anti-semitism.[5]

The All-Party Parliamentary Inquiry set out to prove a thesis about "left-wing anti-semitism" and was not in the least deterred from publicizing that predetermined "finding" by the scanty, anecdotal, and uncorroborated nature of the testimony on which it was based. "We received no evidence of the accusation of anti-semitism being misused by mainstream British Jewish community organisations," the MPs stated—a statement that seems to originate from a parallel universe, easily contradicted by large numbers of individuals with direct experience of that misuse. When it came to nailing down the specific transgressions of alleged left-wing anti-semitism, the report could offer nothing more than this: "Some witnesses spoke of a specific 'left wing anti-semitism' which arises when the language used to criticize Israel exceeds the boundaries of genuine political debate . . . the boundaries between anti-semitism and legitimate expressions of support for the Palestinians have become blurred in some quarters." But blurred how, when, by whom, in what way, is not specified.

One arm of the EUMC (European Union Monitoring Committee on Racism and Xenophobia) working definition of anti-semitism is "Holding Jews collectively responsible for actions of the State of Israel." Here for once we ought to be able to share the solid ground of a recognized common feature of racism. Yet it is also precisely here that the Zionists are the most guilty and disingenuous party. One undisputed common finding in all recent studies of anti-semitism in Europe is that the number of incidents rises and falls in line with the conflict in the Middle East and especially reports of Israeli atrocities. But the All-Party Inquiry, the Board of Deputies and other bodies committed to the Israeli cause simply refuse to address what that coincidence means, or what can be done about it, and that is because they themselves have invested so heavily in blurring the very lines they accuse others of transgressing.

Everyone agrees that it is deplorable to blame an individual Jew, and abjectly criminal to subject Jews to harassment or attack, because of Israeli policies. But none of the reports asks who is responsible for the popular linkage between the State of Israel and those Jews who live in Britain. Who makes it their business, their overriding and persistent business, to reinforce this particular analogy?

According to a poster issued by the United Synagogue, the largest Jewish denomination in Britain, the sixth of its six core "values" is "the centrality of Israel in Jewish life." This, among other things, makes a nonsense of the first core "value": "the welcoming of every Jew." And it gets worse. A few years ago a new sabbath prayer was added to the United Synagogue's standard siddur. "Heavenly Father: Remember the Israel Defense Forces, the guardians of our Holy Land. Protect them from all distress and anguish, and send blessing and prosperity upon all the work of their hands."[6]

Or take the Association of Jewish Ex-Servicemen and Women, an organization of Jews who served in the British armed forces. On June 27, 2006, in an event described by AJEX as "unique in its annals," a ceremony was held outside the Ministry of Defence, on the Thames Embankment, to honor Orde Wingate, whose stone memorial is erected there. Wingate was an Indian-born British officer, a committed evangelical Christian who believed the creation of a Jewish state was the literal fulfillment of New Testament prophecy. In 1936, he was transferred from Sudan to Palestine to assist in the intelligence effort against the Arab revolt. Wingate's great service to the Jews was his creation of the Special Night Squads, armed groups of Jewish settlers led by British officers. Although their ostensible priority was to stop Arab sabotage of the Iraq–Haifa pipeline, they functioned as death squads, entering Arab villages by night to intimidate, terrorize, torture, and execute. Wingate made no secret of the fact that the entire tactic was premised on collective punishment. In this respect, he was indeed a major contributor to Zionist theory and practice. In honoring him, however, AJEX dishonors the contribution of British Jews in the war against fascism, and reinforces the link in the popular mind between British Jews and violent Zionism.

The Board of Deputies of British Jews has for more than a century enjoyed an unrivaled status as a representative of Jews in Britain (its US counterparts compete among themselves). During that time it has opposed Jewish participation in every broad anti-racist movement, from Cable Street in the thirties through the Anti-Nazi League of the mid-1970s to the GLC's anti-racist programs in the 1980s and the campaign for immigrants' rights today. In 2005, the Board joined the Chief Rabbi in condemning the democratic, lengthily debated decision of the Synod of the Church of England to withdraw its £2.5 million investment in Caterpillar, the US-based corporation that manufactures bulldozers used by Israeli forces to demolish Palestinian homes and farms. "The timing could not have been more inappropriate," the Chief Rabbi complained, just when Israel found itself "facing two enemies, Iran and Hamas." The Caterpillar disinvestment, Sacks threatened, would have "the most adverse repercussions on . . . Jewish–Christian relations in Britain." The Church panicked and rescinded the decision.

For the most part the British media treat the Chief Rabbi and the Board of Deputies as the authentic (and exclusive) representatives of Jews in Britain, despite the fact that neither is elected by or accountable to the Jewish community as a whole. The Chief Rabbi heads the Orthodox Synagogues, to which a minority of Jews are affiliated. He can make no claims on behalf of Reform, Masorti, Chasidic, Sephardic, Liberal, independent Orthodox or non-synagogue-affiliated Jews. Similarly, the Board of Deputies consists of representatives of a variety of Jewish bodies (synagogues, youth groups, charities, etcetera). It's not inclusive nor is it accountable to the wider community in whose name it speaks.

The blame for the misidentification of Jews as a whole with Israel lies principally with the Jewish establishment, with the Zionists, with the Israeli spokespersons who justify every lawless, brutal act as a necessary part of the battle for Jewish survival. And with all those who've installed the cult of Israel at the centre of Judaism and Jewishness.

Popular disgust against Israel reached a new high point with the assault on Lebanon in the summer of 2006, during which the Jewish state mounted what Human Rights Watch described as "an indiscriminate bombing campaign" tantamount to a "war crime." The horror was epitomized in the massacre at Qana, where an Israeli air attack left at least 28 dead, 13 of whom were children.

In New York, *Forward* reported that "few if any of the most influential Jewish organizations are raising any moral objections to Israel's military tactics. None of the major Jewish groups released statements of condolences, sympathy or regret before or after the Qana incident." During a meeting with the then Israeli Vice Premier Shimon Peres, not one member of the Conference of Presidents of Major American Jewish Organizations asked the Israeli politician about the carnage in Lebanon. "I see 100 percent support and not an iota of decrease in support in the Jewish community for Israel's conduct in Lebanon," said Martin Raffel, associate executive director of the Jewish Council for Public Affairs.

Rabbi Irving Greenberg, former Chairman of the United States Holocaust Memorial Council, founding President of the National Jewish Center for Learning and Leadership, and a Professor in the Department of Jewish Studies at City College, said he could find no flaws at all in Israel's conduct. "If I have any criticism of Israel," he said, "it is that there was an underestimation of the risk" from Hezbollah, which justified "a need to inflict punishment on the host [Lebanese] population." Although people in the Jewish community "feel anguish that Jews are killing civilians, they honestly don't think that there is any serious alternative right now." The Jewish War Veterans, EVM's old group, announced that they would be sending IDF "Convenience Kits" to "those brave Israeli soldiers who are fighting the terrorists who threaten their borders and their very existence."[7]

The president of the Union for Reform Judaism, Rabbi Eric Yoffie, said that although questions regarding the "appropriate policies to protect civilians" are warranted, "people are overwhelmingly supportive of this war, across the board." Speaking later at an event called to show solidarity with Israel, Yoffie went further: "Could the rights and wrongs of this conflict be any clearer? If Israel's cause is not just in this war, then no cause can ever be just." Yoffie was particularly affronted by those who accused Israel of failing to exercise "proportionality." Citing a string of dubious analogies, he said: "We know what President Roosevelt did when the Japanese attacked Pearl Harbor. We know what President Kennedy did when the Russians put missiles in Cuba. And we know what President Bush did in Afghanistan, when it gave refuge to those who attacked us on September 11."[8]

Of all the justifications of the unjustifiable that poured from the lips of the transatlantic Jewish establishment during the war on

Lebanon, none was quite as shocking as Jonathan Sacks's speech to a pro-Israel rally mounted in London by the Board of Deputies of British Jews:

> Today I want a message to go forth from us to Israel to say: Israel, you make us proud . . . You have taken a land with no natural resources and turned it into one of the great economies of the modern world. You have created a democracy in a part of the world where no one thought it possible. You have taken a desolate land and made it blossom and bear fruit.

Sacks then asked why it should be that "a people who have consistently said Yes to peace and No to terror, find itself today fighting in Lebanon and Gaza?" The answer, he insisted, was "so simple, yet so unbelievable":

> Israel is fighting today in Lebanon because six years ago it withdrew from Lebanon. Israel is fighting today in Gaza because one year ago it withdrew from Gaza. And Israel discovered the terrible truth spoken by the late Mother Teresa, that no good deed goes unpunished. Every gesture of goodwill undertaken by Israel has been seized on by its enemies as a sign of weakness. Every Israeli effort towards peace has led without exception to an increase in violence against Israel.[9]

Never had Jewish leadership so isolated itself from global opinion, and never had it so misrepresented the spectrum of actual Jewish opinion in the diaspora. For at the same time as the rabbis were vindicating, some positively celebrating, the indiscriminate murder of civilians, more Jews than ever before were making known their dissent. The escalating Zionist stridency at the top of the community is in fact an indicator of the weakening of Jewish support for Israel at the base. Of course, there is still a long way to go. But in the summer of 2006 there were more visible signs of

Jewish opposition to Israeli policy than had been seen in the USA and Britain since the birth of the state in 1948.

Given the low to which Jewish leadership sank in the summer of 2006, I was not shocked when a young Jewish leftist told me that she was sometimes seized by an urge to turn up outside her local synagogue on a Saturday morning with a full-page color photo of the victims of Qana and push it in the faces of the worshippers. I understood how she felt, but I also knew (as did she) that she was wrong. People have a right to worship without being molested; Jews have a right to worship—or not—without being molested by other Jews. The suggestion that those who attend synagogue are complicit with the crimes of Qana is in the end merely a recapitulation of the bogus Zionist claim on Jewishness. So the young woman was wrong tactically and wrong in principle. But not, I think, wrong in feeling. The denial by the majority of the Jewish population of what is being done in their name is frustrating, unconscionable, perverse; the sheer monumentality of it defies comprehension or explanation—almost! It is a political priority for the Palestine solidarity movement to encourage Jews to break with Israel. And a good way to insure that happens more slowly than it needs to is to impute or be seen to be imputing a collective Jewish guilt for Israel. It's not a question (merely) of being sensitive to the feelings of Jews, but of being serious about effective Palestinian solidarity.

Let's compare, for a moment, the presence of anti-semitism within the Palestinian or anti-war movements to the presence of other forms of racism (anti-Arab, anti-Muslim) within the opposing camp. In both the US and Britain, support for Israel (not to mention the Iraq and Afghanistan wars) is frequently accompanied by open ethnic hostility. Nor is this confined to an extremist fringe. In fact, it is a racism more legitimized by, more prominent within, more typical of their politics than the stupidities mentioned above are of ours. Racism arises from the premises of Zionism, whereas rejection of racism is at the heart of anti-

Zionism. Compared to the deformations of anti-Zionism or Palestinian solidarity by anti-semitism, the essential formation of Zionism by racism (anti-Arab, anti-Muslim, white-supremacist) is commonplace and frequently undisguised. Where anti-semitism can be and is being challenged within the framework of anti-Zionism and of the democratic anti-racist left, anti-Arab racism is entirely compatible with and largely unchallenged within the Zionist milieu. The same Jewish leaders who are quick to spot and denounce any hint of anti-semitism among critics of Israel have nothing critical to say about Israeli politicians who compare Palestinians to insects or rodents or dub all Israeli Arabs "fifth columnists." They say nothing about the calls for ethnic cleansing of the Holy Land (transfer) that are visible on posters from one end of the Jewish state to the other. This institutional, state-empowered, life-destroying racism is ignored, while the wrong-headed but essentially impotent anti-semitism of Palestinians who express their outrage at the "yehudi" is wrenched out of context and offered up as an excuse for Israeli violence.

Given the wanton, persistent and cynical abuse of the anti-semitism charge—something nearly everyone active in Palestinian solidarity experiences at one time or another—it's not surprising that people are wary of the boy crying wolf. But remember the story. Because the boy falsely and repeatedly cried wolf, when a real wolf actually turned up one grisly night, no one believed him. And the boy was eaten by the wolf.

As I've pored over EVM's literary remains, it's hit me again and again: the analogy between the struggles of the Jewish diaspora in the USA and those of the contemporary Muslim diaspora in Britain and Europe. I think even EVM would have recognized that Islamophobia is drawn from the template of anti-semitism. Like the Jews, the Muslims are accused of a dual allegiance, or an incomplete allegiance to their adopted land. Their cosmopolitanism, their very indeterminateness as a category, makes them a threat. An international Muslim conspiracy every bit as implausible as its Jewish counterpart has been posited, and Muslims are asked (as others are not) to clarify where they stand in relationship to this larger, global identity. Muslims today, like Jews in the past, are offered "good" and "bad" role models (defined by the media and the state), and expected to pick one or the other. Like Jews in the past, Muslims are suspect for their alleged two-facedness, their ingrained habit of dissembling in order to gain acceptance or advantage. Crucially, both Islamophobia and anti-semitism have unfolded, historically, against a broader background of restrictions and attacks on immigrants and refugees.

After 9/11, I found people who'd never described themselves as Muslims, or whom I had never particularly perceived as Muslims, defiantly declaring their Muslim identity. (There were of course others who preferred to bury this identity.) There were Muslims who prayed and Muslims who didn't, drinkers and non-drinkers, atheists and humanists, Marxist Muslims and Muslim Marxists, doctrinaire salafis and intuitive sufis, and a much larger group seeking to find their own way through Muslimness. What was overriding was a refusal to apologize for Islam or for being a Muslim. Like the Jews in the past, the Muslims were being scapegoated for a global crisis, and in that situation the first duty was to refuse to lie down at the sacrificial altar.

In the years that have followed, I've watched Muslims in Britain wrestle with many of the dilemmas that preoccupied EVM. Is there, should there be, a Muslim vote, and on what basis should it be cast? Who speaks for Muslims, and to whom are these spokespersons accountable? Which Muslim voices are authentic, which suborned, which are treacherous? What are the lines of division within the Muslim population, and where and how should these be acknowledged? Radical separatism and one-sided assimilation are both widely rejected, but where does the balance lie, and what is the role of the state and of the community's own organizations in determining it? What is the relation between the fight for equality as Muslims (against Islamophobia) and the fight for equality within Muslim communities (against the religious right)? How does one defend the right to adhere to traditions that are under racist attack but are at the same time desperately in need of democratic reform? What is the role of symbols of recognition, of inclusion, when measured against the realities of inequality?

In seeking a path through these thickets of related questions, Muslims and their allies have been handicapped by a popular debate on multiculturalism sensationalized by the media and exploited by politicians seeking domestic scapegoats for their own failures. "Self-separation"—allegedly practised by the Muslim community and endorsed by the state—was blamed for the London outrage of July 7, 2005. Erstwhile liberals worry that Britain is "sleepwalking into apartheid."

In reality, the options being proffered here are entirely unreal. We live neither as discrete, homogeneous segments of a rainbow nor as indistinguishable members of a monochrome uniformity. No culture, not even the prevailing culture of the white majority, is a single entity without internal tensions and divisions. Those within the Muslim population who try to answer the climate of Islamophobia by retreating into that illusion will in the end strengthen their enemies. That's one of several sad lessons the history of Jews and Zionism has to teach the modern Muslim diaspora.

As posed by Labour ministers, the onus to integrate falls on the minority community. Muslims must demonstrate their commitment to British values; like the Jews, they are being asked to show themselves worthy of "the rights of man and the citizen," something not required of others. In other words, their rights, their acceptance, are conditional. It should not be difficult to imagine what either Zalkind Hourwitz or EVM would have made of this. And I suspect the latter could not have resisted mentioning that some of those lecturing Muslims about "divisiveness" and "separation" spend their lives sheltered in lavish gated communities with twenty-four-hour high-tech security.

Recent years in Britain have resuscitated another conundrum all too familiar to EVM. How do ethnic minorities build alliances with the left? How do they reconcile autonomy with broader democratic participation? Can the left be trusted not to abuse the grievances of ethnic minorities? I've watched in dismay as Muslim friends have made what seemed to me errors in trying to answer these questions. Errors they might have been spared had they been more alert to the perils of reinventing the wheel. But then reinventing the wheel is an inevitable and necessary part of what radical politics must be about. EVM spent much of a lifetime doing it.

What's been most admirable about the Muslim struggle in Britain since 9/11 has been the refusal to compromise on the right of British Muslims to criticize British foreign policy (a right which EVM as an American Jew had to scramble for in the 1930s). While this right is acknowledged in theory, its actual exercise is regarded by some as symptomatic of a Muslim "narrative of victimhood" that sits ill with the new totems of "national cohesion" and "integration." In fact, it's part of an internationalism that is now a growing common ground between Muslims and non-Muslims in Britain.

A local Muslim community radio station in Hendon was looking for a Jew for their Friday-night topical discussion programme and, thanks to the Jewish Socialist Group, I was lucky enough to fill the spot. The topic was "Are we [i.e British Muslims] in danger of hating Jews because of Israel's actions?" Since a Zionist group had declined to participate, I found myself the sole studio guest. Listeners submitted questions by email and TXT, and the presenter expanded on these. The questions ranged from the naïve to the sophisticated, but the premise of all of them, and of the entire discussion, was that *it would be wrong for Muslims to hate Jews because of Israel*, and that this was a tendency Muslims had to resist.

Some listeners were puzzled that I described myself as a Jew even though I did not support Israel. Some believed support for Israel was a scriptural commandment for Jews. Others cited various unsavory goy-bashing passages from the Talmud and asked if it was because of beliefs of this kind that Israeli soldiers behaved as they did in the West Bank and Gaza. Why could Muslims eat kosher food but Jews could not eat halal? Was it true that Jews had massacred Muslims in the fifteenth century? Was it true that Jews controlled the media in the twenty-first century? The hardest questions to answer were those that asked, bluntly, whether there was any hope for the Palestinians, whether attitudes in Israel would soften, whether the Jewish diaspora would join with Muslims in protesting Israel's cruel behavior. There was no holocaust denial, but there was anger that other crimes against humanity were not acknowledged in the same way (Iraq, Chechnya, Kashmir).

In my attempts to respond, I was listened to with courtesy and eager attention. There was a hunger for hard facts and logical analysis. What made it possible to pursue the discussion, however, was that I fully shared the listeners' anger over Iraq and Palestine, and specifically that I acknowledged the Nakba and the historic dispossession of the Palestinian people.

After nearly two hours of Q and A, I was completely exhausted. The presenter decided to bowl me a last googly: wasn't I just what they called a "self-hating Jew"? Having run out of sober logic, all that popped into my mind was a Larry David joke. When accused of being a self-hating Jew (because he's whistling a tune from Wagner), Larry replies: "I do hate myself—but not because I'm Jewish!"

The presenter cracked up, as did the producer and the technicians gathered in the little studio. So if nothing else, I've had the satisfaction of telling a bona fide Jewish joke on a Muslim radio station.

"If I am not for myself, who will be for me? If I am for myself alone, what am I? If not now, when?" I can't remember when I first came across Hillel's marvellously succinct ethical-existential catechism, but I know it grabbed me at once. Strangely (or not, some will say), it was the first item in the list that baffled me. The other two seemed comparatively self-evident. But I grew up in a world where selfishness didn't seem to need any special rabbinical license, where there seemed to be many powers exercising themselves on my behalf, where there were many people who were "for me."

But I was wrong. "If am not for myself . . .", then others will claim to be "for me." In the current climate, Zionists and Jewish leaders will claim to be for me, and in so doing will thwart and destroy what is precious to me.

Hillel's saying is found in the Pirkei Avot (Chapters of the Fathers, a tractate of the Mishna), where it appears among a mixed bag of rabbinical wisdom. "Do not engage in excessive conversation with a woman. This is said even regarding one's own wife—how much more so regarding the wife of another." That Talibanism appears not far from this true gem: "Love work, loathe mastery over others, and avoid intimacy with the government." At the moment, it's hard to imagine finding that sentiment displayed anywhere in a Jewish building.

The historical Hillel came from Babylon to live and teach in Jerusalem some time in the first century BC. He was, approximately, a contemporary of Augustus and Jesus and Philo Judaeus. Though his oral teachings were not compiled until several hundred years after his death, in the sayings attributed to him a distinctive personality emerges:

- Be of the disciples of Aaron—a lover of peace, a pursuer of peace, one who loves the creatures and draws them close to Torah . . .
- Do not separate yourself from the community. Do not believe in yourself until the day you die. Do not judge your fellow until you have stood in his place . . .
- A boor cannot be sin-fearing, an ignoramus cannot be pious, a bashful one cannot learn, a short-tempered person

cannot teach, nor does anyone who does much business grow wise.

- In a place where there are no men, strive to be a man.

Sometimes for me Hillel veers close to Kabir, the fifteenth-century lower-caste north Indian humanist mystic who seized his listeners by the throats: "Man attains a human birth, why does he waste and destroy it?" Or Ghalib, the refined nineteenth-century Urdu poet (a celebrated wine drinker and mango connoisseur), who wrote, "Difficult enough a common task often proves to be / Not every man manages to achieve humanity." Or Thoreau, for whom self-enrichment was intimately tied to exploration of the world and responsibility for one's fellow beings. Here he is explaining exactly why he spent that night in jail as a result of his anti-Mexican War protest:

> When a sixth of the population of a nation which has undertaken to be the refuge of liberty are slaves, and a whole country is unjustly overrun and conquered by a foreign army, and subjected to military law, I think that it is not too soon for honest men to rebel and revolutionise. What makes this duty the more urgent is the fact that the country so overrun is not our own, but ours is the invading army.

For Thoreau, as for Hillel, social injustice had to be met with a challenge from the whole self: "Cast your whole vote, not a strip of paper merely, but your whole influence."

Hillel believed that the Jews would no longer be a territorial entity and that the Mosaic law had to be interpreted in that light. He spoke to Jews as individuals dispersed across far-flung empires. In his tantalizingly compact formula, the subject is "I," not "we." Hillel refuses to posit a contradiction between the first and the second clause, between the duty to the self and to humanity; one cannot be fulfilled in the absence of the other. The final clause compresses the ever-present urgency of human choice in the context of the first two.

So in taking part in the political movements to which I subscribe, in writing this book, in defining myself as an anti-Zionist Jew, *I am for myself*, and at the same time and without contradiction for others. And I'm trying, if often not succeeding, to do it now, to put it into practice. I find in anti-Zionism emancipation both as a Jew and as a human being, and any consequent diminution in my Jewishness is strictly in the eye of the beholder.

DuBois, Fanon, Malcolm X, Amedkar and many others have analyzed the self-loathing of oppressed people as an internalization of the oppressors' view of the self. It's a denial of selfhood that futilely seeks validation, protection, reward, from power—a mental adaptation common among oppressed peoples, and certainly, in the past, as EVM often noted, among Jews. An antidote is necessary, and part of it is a reappropriation of one's own history. In a small way, this book constitutes my own attempt at such a reappropriation.

But do let me say a brief word for self-loathing. Anyone who entirely lacks this trait is not to be trusted. And it is generally acknowledged as an ethical principle that correction of the self comes before chastisement of others. For the privileged self, a form of self-rejection—not personal, but political—may be necessary to reach out to others, to know oneself and become fully human. Even for the internalizer of racism, self-rejection may serve a purpose, may play a part in a necessary journey toward a sustainable self. Albert Memmi, a Tunisian Jew whose view of assimilation was bleakly pessimistic and who scoffed at all efforts to shake off the "tragedy" of being a Jew, nonetheless defended the efforts he'd made in his youth to find in the international left an escape from Jewishness. "I sought not so much to reject myself as to conquer the world," he wrote, looking back from the 1960s on those optimistic popular front days:

> Self-rejection can be a shabby trick, a final surrender, a plea for
> acceptance completely lacking in nobility. But it can also be a first
> step towards revolt, the first awakening gesture of the oppressed,
> the furious rejection of that which he has been in servitude.[10]

Some Jewish friends have told me they feel shame over Israel. I
feel anger, disgust, frustration but not, I think, shame—except in
so far as I don't do enough to put a stop to the horrors. The anger
I feel is indeed more intimate, the compulsion to protest acquires a
more personal character, than it would if I were not a Jew, if these
things weren't being done in my name, spun out of a history I
share. Still, it's not shame over being a Jew. It's anger at what
other Jews are doing.

In the late nineteenth century, self-hatred was an attribute
assigned to Jews mainly by anti-semites, in particular those
affronted by alleged Jewish efforts to "pass" as gentiles. More
sympathetic analysts saw assimilated Jews as prone to hysteria and
"neurasthenia," modern disabilities to which their uncertain
standing in the world (neither one thing nor the other) made
them especially susceptible. Like the anti-semites and the psy-
chologists, the Zionists linked the Jewish malaise to rootless
cosmopolitanism. And they purported to offer a political cure. For
Max Nordau and other early Zionist ideologues that meant the
creation of "muscle Jews"; for the Labor Zionists, of "worker
Jews"; for Martin Buber a "renewed rootedness."

In 1898, Karl Kraus, the German satirist and critic whose
mission was to expose and analyze the political abuse of language,
mounted a fierce attack on Zionism. He noted the Zionist
rejection of the pluralistic nature of world Jewry, indeed their
rejection and dislike of Jews as they actually were. He warned that
Zionism was an attempt to break the Jews from their home in the
West and from modern scientific culture, and thus to re-immerse
them in obscurantism. He accused the Zionists of "Jewish anti-
semitism," observing that their "cry of 'out with Jews!' " is shared

with Aryan anti-semites."[11] Kraus himself was berated as a self-hating Jew: for several years he was a practising Catholic. But to the Nazis he remained an "arch-Jew," the embodiment of that spirit of acid mockery, that Jewish virus of critical reflection, that they believed had undermined European civilization.

In 1923 Josef Prager published *Repression and Breakthrough in the Jewish Soul* in which he argued that Western Jews suffered because they must repress their "Jewish" attributes. He contrasted their broken selfhood with the whole and healthy eastern European Jews who, however poor, illiterate or brutalized, at least knew who they were. But it was with Theodor Lessing's *Jewish Self-Hatred*, published in 1930, that the malady entered the popular jargon. Lessing was another ex-assimilationist and one-time convert to Christianity, who came to equate Zionism with Jewish "self-esteem."[12]

By implication, the self-hating Jew is contrasted to the non-self-hating Jew, but this latter category remains almost completely unexamined. It's there, perpetually, as a reference point, a putative state of psychic and political health. What is the self that's supposed to be hated here? Who defines it and how? What is its center? Where are its peripheries? The Jewish self is a compound, and in the end it's impossible to demarcate clearly its Jewish from its non-Jewish sources, and attempts to do so are reductive, self-repressive, and (dare I say?) smack somewhat of selective self-hatred.

Behind the construction of Jewish self-hatred is the idea that the blurring of boundaries between Jew and non-Jew, the impact of modernity and emancipation, was somehow a spiritual tragedy for the Jew, or at least for numerous individual Jews. Yet it is precisely this blurring that enabled Jews to make contributions to science, literature, politics, critical thinking.

The self we are told we hate is identified (at others' insistence) with Israel, with Zionism, and with a narrow and chauvinist construction of Jewishness. We are told that for a Jew to deny the

Jewish state is to deny his or her selfhood. But for us the real act of self-hatred, of traumatic self-betrayal, would be to repudiate the various strands of our own being and beliefs—democratic, humanist, anti-racist—in favor of a narrow political definition of "Jewish interests." No one else can live my life for me. I cannot subcontract my ethics, my relationship with the human race, to a state or a religion—or indeed a political party. For me, being an anti-Zionist is inextricable from being a democrat, a socialist, a humanist, and a rationalist. Anti-Zionism is not in the end merely a negative category. Within it is a necessary affirmation: an affirmation of internationalism, of humanity—and therefore of one's own humanity, one's own self. It's an anti-label. It's up to each of us to fill in the blanks. Listen to Hillel.

Any democratic impulse on the part of a relatively privileged person can be seen as neurotic because it is not self-interested; it may even involve, disturbingly, self-denial or what appears to be self-abasement. And yes, a predisposition to side with the underdog, to resist power and authority, to embrace embattled minority positions, may well be fueled by a host of inner demons, as EVM's life demonstrates. But what demons fuel the predisposition to side with power, to exercise power, to mitigate the atrocities of power? The neuroses of Zionism dehumanize real human beings, and politically they constitute a major mass Jewish delusional condition. Whatever neuroses we anti-Zionist Jews may be driven by, we're not in the same pathological league.

What's hardest to absorb is the sheer monumentality of denial: the refusal to accept anything as fact that does not conform to race–tribe pride. I suppose it's just a matter of seeing what you want to see. But what extraordinary willpower is exercised in order not to see so much that lies in plain sight! The pleas of the world are kept out by an armor of self-righteousness. It's not just the messenger who gets shot; reality itself becomes the enemy, and any compromise in that war is seen as fatal.

I used to enjoy the old joke: "Jews are like everyone else, only more so." Now it strikes me as self-aggrandizement disguised as self-effacement. The truth is that we are like everyone else, only at the moment, too many of us have made ourselves less so, less human. "They hate us not for what we do but for who we are." No, they hate us for the way we use who we are to justify what we do. What is done in our name.

I'm not a subscriber to postmodernism's dissolution of the self. While the self is multiple and mutable and multilayered, it is also—mysteriously but palpably—real and one. Only the self (if not now, when?) steps forward into the future, only the self is purposive, though it never knows fully its own purposes. Zionism is and has been for many years one of those forces determined to stop us stepping forward as true selves. Why is the attraction of the other counterposed to the preservation of the self? Why is an attraction to the Enlightenment, to Marxism, to African-American music, to non-Jewish cultural traditions (or foods), indeed to Palestinian traditions, a denial rather than an expression of the self, indeed an expansion of the self that is not (unlike the Zionist self) necessarily at the expense of others?

I've been asked: why not simply reject Jewish identity, repudiate the category? I hope that this book has at least made clear why for me this road would be a preposterous self-misrepresentation, a denial of history, and a concession I am unwilling to make to Zionists or to anti-semites. Jews today can no more escape the question of Zionism than they could the question of anti-semitism in earlier eras. The problem today isn't that Jews are in denial of their Jewishness or of the threat of anti-semitism, but that Jews are in denial about Israel, Zionism, the Nakba, the occupation, the wall.

Over the years I've collected responses to the self-hatred charge. Israel Shahak noted long ago that this was "a Nazi expression. The Nazis called Germans who defended Jewish rights self-hating Germans." On a comic note, I've heard the veteran anti-Zionist Lenni Brenner tell audiences that any number of his ex-wives and ex-girlfriends would be happy to testify that "self-hatred" was not his particular problem. There's an episode of *The Simpsons* in which Krusty the Klown is denied a place in Springfield's Jewish Walk of Fame ("where the chosen get chosen") when it turns out that he has not been bar mitzvahed and therefore does not qualify as a Jew. "All these years I thought I was a self-hating Jew," Krusty moans, "now I find out I'm just an ordinary anti-semite!" And there's the Larry David joke, one of my favorites.

But recently I heard of a more robust response to the old canard. A young left-wing Jewish activist, the nephew of a friend, found himself engaged in argument about Israel with a Zionist fellow student, who duly accused him of being a "self-hating Jew." My friend's nephew replied: "I don't hate myself, I hate you, you fucking bastard!" Now while this might not constitute the final word in sophisticated political repartee, it does seem to me to embody a healthy undefensiveness, the combative spirit of the Hillel aphorism.

As for my dad, I don't think he really thought I hated being a Jew, not even at the acme of his annoyance with me. But the "self-hatred" accusation was the only political response he had to hand when he heard his son, a Jew, saying such things. As I've studied EVM's papers, I've come to understand more clearly the chain of events that meant that in 1967 this paradigm sprang to my dad's mind.

But what would EVM have made of me—the me I've become since he knew me? Would he have hated me? Have I turned into one of the Jewish quislings he despised? Would he damn me with those other Jews who refused to learn the lessons of history, in particular the lesson that Jew-hatred never dies? Have I lived too long in England, that land of toffee-nosed colonialists and anti-semites?

But the EVM who confronted the fascists on the streets of the Bronx, who bristled under imposed uniformity, who couldn't stop raging against bullies and hypocrites, surely he would have understood? The man who got into a fight in a bar the night they fried Sacco and Vanzetti, wouldn't he have been with the internationals protesting at the apartheid wall? Wouldn't he have spotted how Muslims were now being treated as Jews had once been treated, charged with dual loyalties, with being party to a global conspiracy, with being an alien threat to a homogeneous society? That powerlessness against which my grandfather railed all his life, that he'd tried to outwit, camouflage, convert into its opposite . . . wouldn't he have recognized it today among the Palestinians? Wouldn't his whole being have alerted him to these analogies, these dangers, and made him shout from any platform he could find that it was all despicable—and that Jews, more than anyone, should recognize it when they saw it? In studying EVM's life and writings, I've felt many echoes of my own concerns and dilemmas, as well as some of my own compulsions, errors and bad habits. Maybe it is genetic? But on inspection it turns out to be history, not chromosomes. Not a tradition consciously handed down but one lived through and therefore changing from generation to generation.

So EVM, forgive me, but I think my anti-Zionist politics are actually an evolution of your legacy, working its way through another half-century of history.

Yes, we stand on the shoulders of giants but even more, I think, on the squat, hunched, burdened shoulders of forgotten people like EVM. His leather case turned out to be an heirloom beyond price, a treasury of aspiration and frustration, the paper residue of his incomplete, error-strewn struggles to be a Jew, a leftist, a leader, a man, a husband, a father, his incomplete (often self-defeating) struggles against the labels applied to him. These form some of the foundations on which I stand. And from which I've had the good fortune to have stumbled my way out of Zionism. I wouldn't have wanted to spend my life in that prison. The people who call us self-haters want to steal our selves from us—appropriate *our* selves for *their* cause—and speaking as a self, I'm damned if I'm going to let them get away with it.

Acknowledgments

Thanks to the following for reading the manuscript at one stage or another and supplying invaluable critical comment and vital encouragement: Liz Davies, Steve Faulkner, Mick Gosling, Pat Harper, Megan Hiatt, Brian Klug, Michael Letwin, Jeff Marqusee, Randy Ostrow, Colin Robinson, Aditya Sarkar, Mark Steel, Achin Vanaik. Tom Penn at Verso provided insightful guidance and solidarity throughout. Special thanks to my uncle Martin J. Morand, inveterate asker of hard questions, for allowing me to plunder his memories and for his advice and support over the years.

Notes

Preface

1 Peter Cole, trans. and ed., *The Dream of the Poem: Hebrew Poetry from Muslim and Christian Spain 950–1492* (Princeton: Princeton University Press, 2007), p. 60.

1 Names and Faces

1 Martin Gilbert, "Introduction" to Avraham Tory, *Surviving the Holocaust: The Kovno Ghetto Diary* (London: Pimlico, 1991), p. ix.

2 Steven Fraser, *Labour Will Rule: Sidney Hillman and the Rise of American Labor* (London: Cornell University Press, 1991), pp. 8–9.

3 Michael Stanislawski, *For Whom Do I Toil? Judah Leib Gordon and the Crisis of Russian Jewry* (Oxford: Oxford University Press, 1988), pp. 49–51.

4 Ibid., p. 184.

5 Henry J. Tobias, *The Jewish Bund in Russia: From Its Origins to 1905* (Stanford: Stanford University Press, 1977), pp. 160–65.

6 Ibid., pp. 221–2.

7 Ibid., p. 248.

8 Ibid., p. 229.

9 Ibid., pp. 210–11.

10 Isaac Deutscher, *The Prophet Armed: Trotsky, 1879–1921* (London: Verso, 2003), pp. 62–3.

11 Leonard Shapiro, "The Role of Jews in the Russian Revolutionary Movement," in Ezra Mendelsohn, ed., *Essential Papers on Jews and the Left* (New York: New York University Press, 1997), p. 313.

12 Fraser, pp. 12–20.

13 Alfred W, Crosby, *America's Forgotten Pandemic: The Influenza of 1918* (Cambridge: Cambridge University Press, 2003), pp. 4–11; "A Letter from

Camp Devens," September 1918. http://www.pbs.org/wgbh/amex/influenza/sfeature/devens.html

2 *The War Against Analogy*

1 http://www.adl.org/israel/carter_book_review.asp
2 http://ccarnet.org/kd/Items/actions.cfm?action=Show&itemid=887 &destination=ShowItem
3 The European Union Monitoring Centre on Racism and Xenophobia (EUMC), "Working Definition of Antisemitism." http://fra.europa.eu/ fra/material/pub/AS/AS-WorkingDefinition-draft.pdf

4 *The Emancipation of the Jews*

1 Ritchie Robertson, *Heine* (London: Halband, 1988), p. 13.
2 Baruch Spinoza, "A Theologico-Political Treatise." http://www. philosophyarchive.com/text.php?era=1600–1699&author=Spinoza&text =A%20Theologico-Political%20Treatise
3 Sander L. Gilman, *Jewish Self-Hatred: Anti-Semitism and the Hidden Language of the Jews* (Baltimore: Johns Hopkins University Press, 1986), p. 103. See also Ilan Halevi, *A History of the Jews, Ancient and Modern* (London: Zed, 1987), p. 140.
4 Gilman, p. 91.
5 Ibid., p. 94.
6 Moses Mendelssohn, *Jerusalem, or On Religious Power and Judaism* (London: Brandeis University Press, 1983), trans. Allan Arkush, p. 123.
7 Ibid., p. 33.
8 Ibid., p. 73.
9 Ibid., p. 81.
10 Ibid., pp. 130–31.
11 Frances Malino, *A Jew in the French Revolution: The Life of Zalkind Hourwitz* (Oxford: Blackwell, 1996), p. 12.
12 Ibid., p. 31.
13 Ibid., p. 19.
14 Ibid., p. 49.
15 Ibid., p. 13.
16 Ibid., pp. 47–8.
17 Ibid., pp. 72–3.
18 Ibid., p. 68.
19 Ibid., p. 75.
20 Ibid., pp. 80–81, 90.
21 Ibid., p. 108.

22 Ibid., p. 103.

23 Lionel Kochan, *The Making of Western Jewry, 1600–1819* (London: Palgrave Macmillan, 2004), pp. 275–88.

24 "The Americanization of Reform Judaism," American Jewish Historical Society (website). http://www.ajhs.org/publications/chapters/chapter. cfm?documentID=218

25 Pittsburgh Platform, 1885. Jewish Virtual Library. http://www.jewishvirtuallibrary.org/jsource/Judaism/pittsburgh_program.html

26 Columbus Platform, 1937. Jewish Virtual Library. http://www.jewishvirtuallibrary.org/jsource/Judaism/Columbus_platform.html

27 Pittsburgh Platform, 1999. Jewish Virtual Library. http://www.jewishvirtuallibrary.org/jsource/Judaism/refprin99.html

5 *The Prophet Armed*

1 Lenni Brenner, *Zionism in the Age of the Dictators: A Reappraisal* (London: Croom Helm, 1983), p. 57.

2 Ibid., pp. 58–9.

3 Ibid., pp. 64–5.

4 Ibid., pp. 71–6.

5 Ibid., pp. 72–3.

6 *New York Times*, October 29, 1937.

7 *New York Times*, October 25, 1939.

8 *New York Times*, November 2, 1939.

6 *A Militant Jew*

1 John Newsinger, *The Blood Never Dried: A People's History of the British Empire* (London: Bookmarks, 2006), p. 135. For the Revolt of 1936–39, see also Baruch Kimmerling and Joel S. Migdal, *The Palestinian People: A History* (Cambridge, Mass.: Harvard University Press, 2003), pp. 102–33.

2 Newsinger, p. 135.

3 Ibid., p. 139.

4 George Antonius, *The Arab Awakening* (Safety Harbor, Florida: Simon, 2001), p. 411.

5 Brenner, pp. 38–44.

6 Rafael Medoff, *Militant Zionism in America: The Rise and Impact of the Jabotinsky Movement in the United States, 1926–1948* (Tuscaloosa: University of Alabama Press, 2002), p. 161.

7 "The Struggle for Free Speech at CCNY." http://www.virtualny.cuny. edu/gutter/panels/panel15.html

7 *In Ancient Palestine*

1 Robert Alter, *The Five Books of Moses: A Translation with Commentary* (London: W. W. Norton, 2004), pp. 739–40.

2 Halevi, p. 41.

3 Israel Finkelstein and Neil Asher Silberman, *The Bible Unearthed: Archaeology's New Vision of Ancient Israel* (London: Simon and Schuster, 2002), pp. 240–43.

4 Herbert Marks, "The Twelve Prophets," in Robert Alter and Frank Kermode, eds., *The Literary Guide to the Bible*, (Cambridge, Mass.: Harvard University Press, 1987), p. 210.

5 Spinoza.

6 Thomas Paine, *The Age of Reason*, in his *Collected Writings*, ed. Eric Foner (New York: Library of America, 1995), pp. 677–80.

7 William Blake, *Complete Writings*, ed. Geoffrey Keynes (London: Oxford University Press, 1972), p. 391.

8 *The War in the Bronx*

1 Fraser, p. 519.

2 Ibid., pp. 17–22.

3 Ibid., p. 493.

4 Gilbert in Tory, pp. xvii–xxiv.

5 *New York Times*, January 17, 1943.

6 *New York Times*, January 4, 1945.

7 *New York Times*, February 19, 1945.

8 Herbert Morrison to Parliament, July 31, 1946. http://www.palestine-encyclopedia.com/EPP/Chapter05_10f3.htm

9 Tony Cliff, "A New British Provocation in Palestine," *Fourth International*, Vol. 7, No. 9, September 1946. http://www.marxists.org/archive/cliff/works/1946/07/provocation.htm

10 "A Flag is Born." American Jewish Historical Society website. http://www.ajhs.org/publications/chapters/chapter.cfm?documentID=268

9 *Nakba*

1 Elias Khoury, *Gate of the Sun*, trans. Humphrey Davies (London: Vintage, 2006), p. 146.

2 Ilan Pappe, *The Ethnic Cleansing of Palestine* (Oxford: Oneworld, 2006), p. 46.

3 Ibid., pp. 44–5; Avi Shlaim, *The Iron Wall: Israel and the Arab World* (London: Penguin, 2000), p. 35; Ilan Pappe, *The Making of the Arab–Israeli Conflict: 1947–1951* (London: IB Tauris, 2006), pp. 108–13; Avi Shlaim,

"Israel and the Arab Coalition in 1948," in Eugene L. Rogan and Avi Shlaim, eds, *The War for Palestine: Rewriting the History of 1948* (Cambridge: Cambridge University Press, 2001), pp. 79–101.

4 Norman G. Finkelstein, *Image and Reality in the Israel Palestine Conflict* (London: Verso, 1995), p. 71.

5 Pappe, *Ethnic Cleansing*, pp. 92–6; Baruch Kimmerling and Joel S. Migdal, *The Palestinian People: A History* (Cambridge, Mass.: Harvard University Press, 2003), pp. 158–61.

6 *New York Times*, May 26, 1948.

7 Pappe, *Making of the Arab–Israeli Conflict*, pp. 34–6, 99–101; Kimmerling and Migdal, pp. 146–7.

8 Chaim Simons, "A Historical Survey of Proposals to Transfer Arabs from Palestine," 1998. http://www.vho.org/aaargh/fran/livres4/simons.pdf

9 John Rose, *The Myths of Zionism* (London: Pluto Press, 2004), pp. 120–24.

10 Pappe, *Ethnic Cleansing*, pp. 166–70.

11 Shlaim, pp. 29–30, 32, 38; Pappe, *Making of the Arab-Israeli Conflict*, pp. 113–21; Kimmerling and Migdal, pp. 152–4.

12 Bert Cochran, *Labor and Communism: The Conflict that Shaped American Unions* (Princeton: Princeton University Press, 1977), p. 301.

13 *New York Times*, November 4, 1948.

14 Virginia Gildersleeve, quoted in Paul Charles Merkley, "Christian Attitudes towards the State of Israel." http://mqup.mcgill.ca/extra.php?id=12

15 Elmer Berger, *Memoirs of an Anti-Zionist Jew* (Beirut: Institute for Palestine Studies, 1978), *passim*. For the history of the ACJ, see Thomas A. Kolsky, *Jews against Zionism: The American Council for Judaism, 1942–1948* (Philadelphia: Temple University Press, 1990).

16 Berger, p. 26.

17 Ibid., p. 3.

10 Diasporic Dimensions

1 Abbas Shiblak, *Iraqi Jews: A History of Mass Exodus* (London: Saqi, 2005), p. 142.

2 Ibid., pp. 82–3.

3 Ibid., p. 84.

4 Elie Kedourie, "The Break Between Muslims and Jews in Iraq," in Mark R. Cohen and Abraham L. Udovitch, eds, *Jews Among Arabs: Contacts and Boundaries* (Princeton: Darwin Press, 1989), pp. 21–64.

5 Ibid., p. 47.

6 Shiblak, p. 94.

7 Ibid., pp. 100–103.

8 Ibid., pp. 146–51.

9 Ibid., pp. 151–66.

10 Rose, p. 185.

11 Joel Beinin, *The Dispersion of Egyptian Jewry: Culture, Politics and the Formation of a Modern Diaspora* (Cairo: American University in Cairo Press, 2005), pp. 2–7.

12 Ibid., p. 46.

13 Ibid., pp. 68–9.

14 Ibid., p. 93.

15 Ibid., p. 86.

16 Ibid., p. 87.

17 Ibid., p. 87.

18 Haim Zafrani, *Two Thousand Years of Jewish Life in Morocco* (New York: Sephardic House, 2005), pp. 1–9, 12–14, 33.

19 Ibid., pp. 112–13.

20 Ibid., pp. 294–6.

21 Ibid., p. 292.

22 Ibid., p. 301.

23 C.R. Pennell, *Morocco Since 1830* (London: Hurst and Company, 2000), pp. 344–5.

24 Peter Clemens, "Family Henriques-Josephy: An Example of German-Jewish Genealogy." http://mfp.math.uni-rostock.de/forschung/erf_jose.htm

25 Schmu'el HaNagid, "On Fleeing His City," in Cole, pp. 39–40.

26 Kochan, p. 296.

27 Jacqueline Rose, *The Last Resistance* (London: Verso, 2007), pp. 45–7.

28 Berger, p. 67.

29 Dorothy Thompson, "America Demands a Single Loyalty," *Commentary*, March 1950. http://www.commentarymagazine.com/cm/main/viewArticle.html?article=com.commentarymagazine.content.Article//978&search=1

30 Oscar Handlin, "America Recognizes Diverse Loyalties," *Commentary*, March 1950. http://.www.commentarymagazine.com/cm/main/viewArticle.html?id=979

31 "Israel and India in the Era of Globalisation," speech by Indian ambassador at the International Forum, Tel Aviv University, March 8, 2006. http://www.indembassy.co.il/amb_speech_telavivuniv_march8-final.htm

32 *Jerusalem Post*, 7 February 2007. http://pqasbpqarchiver.com/jpost/access/1214249611.html?dids=1214249611:1214249611&FMT=ABS&FMTS=ABS:FT&date=Feb+7%2C+2007&author=MATTHEW+WAGNER&pub=Jerusalem+Post&edition=&startpage=06&desc=Metzger+signs+anti-terror+pact+in+India+with+Hindus+worried+about+Muslim+-violence

11 Confessions of a "Self-Hating Jew"

1 Neville Nagler, letter to the *Guardian*, September 26, 2003. http://www.guardian.co.uk/letters/story/0,,1049887,00.html

2 Berger, p. 60.

3 "Antisemitic Incidents Report 2006," Community Security Trust, London, 2007. http://www.thecst.org.uk/docs/Incidents%5FReport%5F06.pdf

4 Jonathan Sacks, *Ha'aretz*, September 6, 2002. http://israel.icca.org/articles.htm?y=620051118152416

5 "Report of the all-party parliamentary inquiry into antisemitism," September 7, 2006. http://www.thepcaa.org/report.html

6 Brian Klug, "A Time to Speak Out: Rethinking Jewish Identity and Solidarity with Israel," *Jewish Quarterly* (UK), Winter 2002/3 (Number 188). http://www.chicagopeacenow.org/rr-36.html

7 *Jewish Daily Forward*, August 4, 2006. http://www.forward.com/articles/575/

8 Remarks by Rabbi Eric Yoffie delivered at temple Emanuel in Westfield, NJ, on August 1, 2006. http://blogs.rj.org/israel/2006/08/an_evening_of_solidarity_with.html

9 Speech given by Rabbi Jonathan Sacks, July 23, 2006. http://www.chiefrabbi.org/sp-index.html

10 Albert Memmi, *The Liberation of the Jew*, trans. Judy Hyun (New York: Orion Press, 1966), p. 21.

11 Gilman, pp. 234–43.

12 Ibid., pp. 300–302.